IN SEARCH OF GOODNESS

In Search of Goodness

EDITED BY RUTH W. GRANT

The University of Chicago Press :: CHICAGO AND LONDON

RUTH W. GRANT is professor of political science and philosophy and a
senior fellow at the Kenan Institute for Ethics at Duke University.

The University of Chicago Press, Chicago 60637
The University of Chicago Press, Ltd., London
© 2011 by The University of Chicago
All rights reserved. Published 2011
Printed in the United States of America

20 19 18 17 16 15 14 13 12 11   1 2 3 4 5

ISBN-13: 978-0-226-30683-4 (cloth)
ISBN-10: 0-226-30683-6 (cloth)

Library of Congress Cataloging-in-Publication Data

In search of goodness / edited by Ruth W. Grant.
   p. cm.
Includes bibliographical references and index.
ISBN-13: 978-0-226-30683-4 (cloth: alk. paper)
ISBN-10: 0-226-30683-6 (cloth: alk. paper)
1. Good and evil. 2. Ethics. I. Grant, Ruth Weissbourd, 1951–
BJ1401.I49 2011
170—dc22   2010024345

CONTENTS

This project was inspired by the film *The Lives of Others*, which depicts the moral transformation of two men under the Communist regime in East Germany. The first is a Stasi agent, a dedicated servant of the regime, expert at extracting confessions, who ends up protecting the man he is investigating. At the beginning of the film this second man too is dedicated to the regime, an apologist who becomes a daring critic as the film progresses. The film evokes an overwhelming atmosphere of oppression in that its characters are trapped in a world where it is almost impossible to lead a life of ordinary goodness. In a world this evil, goodness seems to require heroism. And since none of us live in a world without evil, the question is raised for all of us, "How good is good enough?"

I walked out of the film knowing that I wanted to undertake a "sequel" to the project on evil that I had organized a few years earlier. That project resulted in the publication of *Naming Evil, Judging Evil* (University of Chicago Press, 2006). I contacted some members of the "evil group," as well as new participants, and convened a group of colleagues to begin a collaborative investigation of goodness. The result is the book you now hold. The process was the same for both projects. We met for conversation over lunch throughout the academic year 2008–9, reading and discussing a wide range of materials relevant to goodness. We then held a working conference in February 2009 where invited guests provided comments on drafts of our chapters for the book. Our guest commentators were Sin Yee Chan (philosophy, University of Vermont), Susan Collins (political science, University of Houston), Laurence Cooper (political science, Carleton College), Andrew Delbanco (American Studies, Columbia University), Geoffrey Harpham (director, National Humanities Center), Daniel Hart (Center for Children and Childhood Studies, Rutgers University), James Wetzel (philosophy, Villanova University), and Susan Wolf (philosophy, University of North Carolina, Chapel Hill). Other participants were Jeffrey Church (political science, University of Houston), Douglas Maclean (philosophy, University of North Carolina, Chapel Hill), Noah Pickus (director, Kenan Institute for Ethics,

Duke University), Suzanne Shanahan (associate director, Kenan Institute for Ethics, Duke University), and Thomas Spragens Jr. (political science, Duke University). The commentators' presentations and the conversations throughout the conference were truly first-rate. I am very grateful to all who engaged in this project with us.

While the process for both projects was the same, the conversations were quite different. I think we all found it easier to talk about evil than to talk about goodness, and we began to wonder why. Why is goodness so elusive? Is moral goodness *the* good for human beings, or only one kind of good among many? Is there such a thing as an independent moral domain at all? Needless to say, we did not reach agreement on the answers to these questions. But the essays that follow offer a rich and varied treatment of our subject. I am indebted to the authors in more ways than they can imagine: for their insight, for their intellectual generosity, for their willingness to see the project through to the end, and most of all for their friendship.

I would also like to thank the Kenan Institute for Ethics for its generous support of this project and for the many ways it supports ethical inquiry at Duke University. Last, thanks are due to Duke University's Arts and Sciences Council, which provided additional funding.

Ruth W. Grant

How do people become good? And what does a good life look like? There are many reasons to raise these questions now. There is the general sense that, in the drive for success and personal fulfillment, modern Western culture has paid too little attention to cultivating, educating, or cherishing goodness. Some take the financial crisis as evidence of that failure. Calls for national service for the nation's youth, professional ethics programs, corporate social responsibility, and the growing number of university ethics centers all testify to this concern. At the same time, new research in neuroscience and evolutionary biology is challenging long-standing assumptions about the moral person. Researchers have found that making moral "decisions" is more a matter of "gut reactions" that take place in the emotional centers of the brain than of reflective rational judgment. Evolutionary biologists are arguing that altruistic behavior is "hardwired" because aiding others in the group serves the preservation of the species and thus provides an evolutionary advantage. Both streams of research are taken to suggest that "goodness" is a natural attribute of the mind, which raises as many provocative questions about the moral life as it answers.[1] Last, we are torn between conflicting contemporary narratives, one of moral progress and the other of moral decline. This alone might stimulate us to search for greater clarity about goodness. On one hand, in the contemporary West we seem to have an almost unshakable faith that development will bring with it the conditions for a more humane world. Moral progress is bound to follow material progress. On the other hand, "What's the matter with kids today?" is a refrain that has been sung since Aristophanes accused Socrates of corrupting the young. Each generation seems to see the next as morally lacking compared with its own. Is it possible that both the narrative of moral progress and the narrative of moral decline have some truth to them?

While any one of these contemporary discussions would be a sufficient reason to undertake an investigation of this sort now, none of them is really the motivating force behind this project. Instead, I believe the search for goodness is perennially interesting because it responds to a permanent psychological reality. Human beings need their own moral approval, and this is a psychological fact with profound implications. We all want to think of ourselves as good. In the absence of that approval, we experience very painful feelings: shame, guilt, remorse, and regret among them. Happiness requires a quiet conscience. Of course this does not mean that everyone always strives to do good; instead, it often means that people will make the judgment that whatever it is they do is good. Rationalization of wrongdoing is as much a testimony to the power of the need for moral approval as is a guilty conscience. In either case, we are justifying and judging, evaluating ourselves on some sort of moral scale.

And so one thing we want to know is, What is the standard of judgment? If the standard is set too low, "goodness" becomes complacency. If it is set too high, it may simply be out of reach. Is not being bad sufficient to consider oneself good? Socrates defined justice as "minding your own business" and said he sought only to avoid doing injustice. Yet he also serves as an exemplar of a very demanding standard of goodness. There is an ordinary goodness, expected of everyone, and also more difficult forms we might aspire to. How good is good enough? Ordinary goodness might do in ordinary times, but the question takes on a different aspect when political circumstances are included in the consideration. Awareness of the evils of the world can raise the question starkly. In an evil regime (And is any regime pure?), what does it mean to be a good person and a good citizen? Where innocence is not possible, heroism or saintliness might be the only alternatives—alternatives that are out of reach for most of us. Yet what explains the sense of responsibility that leads some people to reach?

Questions like these about goodness could be multiplied many times over. But two central ones, which I mentioned at the outset, are addressed by the essays collected here. The first is, *How do people become good?* This question includes not only how children develop morally but also how adults can become better and, most generally, whether and how moral progress is possible. The second, *What does a good life look like?* also immediately raises additional questions. Are there multiple, competing possibilities for what counts as a "good life," all equally worthy? Or is there a unified and transcendent conception of the good that should guide our judgment of the possibilities? What does a good life look like when it is guided by God? And, finally, how is a good life involved with the lives of others?

In pursuing these issues, the contributing authors have avoided certain other questions that invoke standard and familiar conceptual dichotomies: Are people generally altruistic or egoistic? Is morality driven by reason or emotion? Is moral behavior a matter of good choices or good character?

These binary categories—either/or—tend to focus discussions of goodness in ways that do not do justice to the complexities of the subject. The essays here seek to expand the terms of the discussion, reach outside disciplinary boundaries, and combine psychological, philosophical, and political considerations in their analyses and interpretations. They also share an approach that emphasizes retaining the complexity and exploring the particulars of moral phenomena. Almost every essay employs examples and illustrations from life, literature, or film as the matter requiring interpretation to enrich our understanding of goodness. You will find Achilles, Billy Budd, Oskar Schindler, and the people of Flagstaff, Arizona, in these pages. It is not accidental that I framed the question, What does a good life look like? to replace the more standard formulation, What is the good life? It is exceptionally difficult to define goodness or the good life, but it may nonetheless be possible to recognize it when we see it.

The difficulty of defining goodness, its elusiveness, is one of the more interesting things about it. Consider the multiple uses of "good." "I had a good day." "That was good, but not great." "She's a good horse." "What a good pie!" Used in these ways, the term seems to be a vague positive evaluation and nothing more. (And of course we could say the same about "bad" as a negative evaluation.) Would we want to claim that the good day and the good horse share the same quality called "goodness?"[2] Moreover, it has been argued that nothing is ever simply good, but is good only "in a way," relative to its kind, context, and situation. When we say that something is "good," we might mean that it tastes good, if it is the kind of thing people eat, or that it is good for something or someone in particular depending on the situation, or any number of other things.[3]

These problems are no less prominent when considering the moral good for human beings. Consider altruism as an example. We generally view altruism as a good thing and sometimes even speak as if it is the defining form of goodness for human beings. But it is not difficult to argue that altruism is not always good. Psychologically, altruism can be an expression of neurosis in some people who can give to others but not to themselves. In politics, some altruistic social programs are subjected to criticism from both the left and the right as doing more harm than good. None of the things we call "good" are good always or in every respect: not the pursuit of justice, courage, patience, or any other characteristic classified as "good." Oddly enough, it does make sense to say, "It is not always good to be good." And this raises the very interesting question, What is the standard of goodness we employ when making the judgment that something that we ordinarily call "good" is not? In other words, by specifying the characteristics of goodness, we have not really specified what goodness is, because we then find ourselves needing to reach for some other standard of goodness by which we can judge those characteristics. But it remains an open and contested question whether we can ever find what we are reaching for: whether there *is* "goodness" apart from the various things we call "good" in the circumstances or whether there is any measure by which to evaluate competing moral goods. If there is not and we want to know what a good person is, for example, we need to understand not what goodness is, but what a person is.[4] From this point of view, any consideration of goodness requires contextualization and flexible, practical judgment. And maybe that in itself is a good thing.

Alternatively, we might consider "goodness" or "good" as the antonym of "evil" rather than of "bad," and in this sense the concept seems to have greater clarity and definition. In thinking about "good" and "bad," we immediately confront the problems raised by the multiplicity of uses of the terms. But the pair "good" and "evil" is less ambiguous. It refers to the extreme poles on a moral scale. "Evil" might be something like sinfulness, wickedness, or cruelty, whereas "goodness" might be something like purity or innocence. But here we confront a paradox. It is a commonplace that a great deal of evil is done in the name of the good. This is so particularly when the two are conceived as mutually exclusive opposite extremes — this is the Manichean trap.[5] Once something or someone is labeled as evil, opposition to that "evil," of whatever sort, seems beyond reproach. The "good," in their righteousness, justify their own evil deeds. When goodness is conceived as purity or innocence, it seems inextricably linked to evil. Are there conceptions of goodness that are less susceptible to the abuses of righteousness? Goodness, the real thing, must be something it is not so easy to do evil in the name of. So this approach does not give us an adequate conception after all. Goodness remains elusive.

And so we embark in search of goodness in hopes of deepening and enriching discussion of our two central questions: *How do people become good?* and *What does a good life look like?* Each of the essays in this volume addresses one or both of these questions, and each could stand on its own. But perhaps because they are the product of a long conversation, some threads weave through them and give a greater coherence than is often found in edited volumes. Sometimes the connecting threads are obvious and bold; in other cases the links are more subtle. I have arranged the chapters as much as possible so that each connects both to the preceding essay and to the one that follows. For example, like chapter 1, chapter 2 raises the question whether morality depends on maturity. Chapter 3 follows chapter 2 in exploring, psychologically, people's willingness to take risks and to make sacrifices for others. Chapters 3, 4, and 5 all deal with extraordinary forms of goodness: the people we see as heroes, innocents, or saints. Chapters 5 and 6 describe how people become better in different sorts of communal relations with others. Chapters 7 and 8 both begin with reflections on the multiple uses of the word "good" and the question whether there is anything transcendent or universal that explains the multiplicity. Because the chapters are organized in this way, the effort of reading them from the beginning to the end, rather than in random order, will be repaid.

The collection begins with an essay by Philip Costanzo on the psychological origins of goodness in childhood. He argues that the two dominant explanations of moral development in children, what we might call the "socialization model" and the "cognitive maturation model," both give short shrift to the role of emotions as one of the multiple natural prerequisites for nurturing morality. Strong emotions attach to behaviors that are considered morally important. And so, ironically, it is only when the moral stakes are low that we are likely to guide our behavior by reasoned moral judgment. Emotion, social needs, and knowledge-seeking are all "hardwired," natural components of the human situation that enable the nurture of morality.

Ruth Grant's essay challenges the identification of altruism with goodness and the presumption that altruism and egoism are mutually exclusive. Using Shel Silverstein's *The Giving Tree*, she argues that there are forms of altruism that are not good because they are destructive of psychic health and human flourishing. She goes on to explore the relation between goodness and psychic health by examining the alternatives presented by Plato and Freud. In contrast to an "ethic of altruism" that relies on the dichotomy between altruism and egoism, an "ethic of psychic health" allows us to recognize forms of giving that are not "zero-sum" (contrast, for example, parental love with philanthropy as the model of giving); distinguish between healthy and unhealthy forms of altruism; encourage people to take personal satisfaction in giving, rather than measuring the goodness of their actions by the degree of sacrifice involved; and focus on cruelty, rather than egoism or selfishness, as a primary obstacle to goodness.

David Wong asks, How are moral conversions possible? He examines in detail three exemplary cases: the fictional Stasi agent who is the protagonist of the film *The Lives of Others*; Oskar Schindler, who helped many Polish Jews escape the Nazis; and a Ku Klux Klansman who left the Klan and became friends with a militant black activist during school desegregation conflicts in Durham, North Carolina. According to Wong, conversion involves much more than overcoming selfishness and attaining a clear vision of right and wrong. He interweaves his interpretation of the three exemplary cases with discussions of pertinent controversies in moral psychology and philosophy. He finds that in every case there is a crucial interaction between situation and character. And while each of these men does alter his beliefs, it is the way primal emotions are engaged that is critical for moral motivation. Wong also emphasizes the significant role played by others in bringing about moral conversion. None of these people are "heroes" in the usual meaning of the term. Their moral conversions are humanly explicable, not mysterious, and that is reason for hope.

Innocence, like heroism, appears to be a special and rare form of goodness. But we are ambivalent about it: at once nostalgic for lost innocence and contemptuous of those too innocent to navigate the ways of the world. Peter Euben recognizes this ambivalence and complicates the understanding of innocence through his analysis of Euripedes' *Bacchae* and Melville's *Billy Budd*. Both texts reveal a disturbing dialectical relationship between innocence on the one hand and violence, sacrifice, and evil on the other. Euben focuses on *Billy Budd*. His discussion is a provocative challenge to any simple understanding of innocence and particularly to the progressivist narrative whereby innocence is overcome as a rite of passage on the way to adulthood. Innocence, with both its hopeful, positive side and its darker side, remains part of who we are throughout life.

Stanley Hauerwas explores the relation between God and goodness beginning with Jesus' puzzling response to a young man who asks what good deed he must do to gain eternal life (Matthew 19:16–22). Hauerwas argues that goodness requires not good deeds as such, but a capacity for noncondescending love and friendship with the afflicted, a capacity most of us do not possess. This capacity requires, in turn, never regarding any person, no matter how severe his suffering, as one who would have been better off not being born. It requires regarding every life as precious. Hauerwas shows us what a good life looks like in the life of Jean Vanier, who built a home and friendships living with people who are mentally handicapped and founded a movement, "L'Arche," devoted to creating such homes for others. Jean Vanier's life helps us to make sense of Jesus' advice to the young man. In his life, goodness and God are indistinguishable.

The starting point for Romand Coles's reflections is the recognition that alternative visions of goodness are needed in a world where the dominant vision of "goodness" is deeply implicated in evil. He turns to Iris Murdoch's writings to show how we might begin to envision goodness differently by attending to beauty and its connections to excellence, contingency, and tragedy. The mountains of Flagstaff, Arizona, illustrate the combination of transformative and awe-inspiring beauty with tragic death from environmental degradation. And the collective efforts of the people of Flagstaff to tend to this place as a community (in particular, to protect the night sky from light pollution) indicate the alternative forms of goodness that might emerge out of an altered aesthetic sensibility.

Michael Gillespie begins with Nietzsche to diagnose the modern problem with respect to goodness. In a post-Christian world, without a unitary conception of the good, there is only a multiplicity of competing goods. Modern liberalism construes these goods as subjective preferences that can be regulated by liberal institutions. Alternatively, Nietzsche urges us to hark back to the Greeks to unleash a noble competition for dominance among the multiple goods. But Gillespie argues that Nietzsche is wrong to construe our choices as limited to either a banal liberalism or a return to heroic tragedy. He examines the problem as it appears in the *Iliad* and suggests that Nietzsche's interpretation of the tragic age of the Greeks is essentially correct. He argues, however, through an interpretation of Aristotle, that there is another alternative to the problem of the multiplicity of goods that does not end in tragedy. In Aristotle's view, our appetites for the various goods can be moderated and harmonized by a system of education and training that transforms the passions into virtues. Gillespie thus concludes that building on Aristotle might elevate, and even ennoble, liberal aspirations.

The book concludes with an essay in which Amelie Rorty argues that there is no such thing as goodness per se, a single property that belongs to all things we designate "good." She makes her case by canvassing Plato's multiple arguments for the primacy of the Idea of the Good and exposing the problems raised by his discussion, problems that set the agenda for later philosophers. She then turns to three post-Platonic philosophers — Aristotle, Epicurus, and Epictetus — who reject the Platonic account of the Good in favor of the view that goodness is to be found in the particulars and the details. Nonetheless, they retain the view that inquiry into what is desirable remains central to a well-lived life. Amelie Rorty's essay is thus a fitting conclusion to this volume.

She leaves us with this thought: One of the things a good life looks like is a life that includes the search for goodness.

NOTES

1. For a summary of recent findings see Jonah Lehrer, *How We Decide* (Boston: Houghton Mifflin Harcourt, 2009), chap. 6. For examples of how the significance of these findings is being portrayed in the popular press, see David Brooks, "The End of

Philosophy," *New York Times*, April 6, 2009, and Sharon Begley, "Adventures in Good and Evil," *Newsweek*, May 4, 2009. Both Brooks and Begley raise some of the unresolved questions.

2. Philippa Foot, *Natural Goodness* (Oxford: Oxford University Press, 2001), 2–3.
3. Judith Jarvis Thomson, *Goodness and Advice* (Princeton, NJ: Princeton University Press, 2001), 17–18.
4. I am indebted to Amelie Rorty for this observation.
5. Ruth W. Grant, ed., *Naming Evil, Judging Evil* (Chicago: University of Chicago Press, 2006).

ONE

The Nature and Nurture of Morality

Philip Costanzo

Wisdom has its root in goodness, not goodness its root in wisdom.
RALPH WALDO EMERSON

In this chapter, I intend to examine the developmental origins of human morality and goodness. There is an enormous body of research and certainly much debate about the developmental course of moral behavior and thought in the field of developmental psychology. However, a number of competing implicit assumptions in this body of work create controversy concerning the origins of goodness in human societies. In most developmental models of moral behavior and judgment, morality and moral perspective emerge in development—either through hierarchical socialization exchanges embodying rewards, punishments, and emotionally founded appraisals or through the maturation of reasoning capacities, abilities, and cognitive structures. While this might be an overly stark and minimalist portrayal of conceptual positions on moral development, it does represent a historical and sometimes harsh primary disagreement among behavioral scientists who ponder and research the dynamics of moral acquisition.

In both conceptual accounts, to be moral is to be "correct"—either intellectually or normatively correct depending on one's taste and one's reading of the empirical evidence. The underlying premise for both views is that correctness (including normative correctness) is the primary property associated with goodness. For adherents of the hierarchical socialization viewpoint, norms, values, and standards emerging from disciplinary and other social exchanges are internalized and act as guides to goodness as it is culturally defined. In the neo-Kantian psychological models such as those put forward by Kohlberg[1] and Turiel,[2] "correctness" is indexed not by the content of moral thought and action but by the principles and underlying cognitive models driving moral appraisal. Both of these are compelling approaches; yet each assumes that the states of instinct and affect, which are evident in humans from birth and as an endowment of evolutionary survival, are irrelevant to the expression and enactment of goodness.

By noting the assumptive bases of both socialization theories and social-cognitive approaches to morality, I do not intend to gainsay the very important contributions each has made to our understanding of life course transformations in moral appraisal; however, neither model grapples well with questions concerning the inherent moral status of humanity. This may be because each of these normative models is silent on the role of instinct and native emotionality as each bears on the emergence of moral goodness. Much of psychological scholarship on moral development is about the nurturing of morality in children. The focus of this work has been upon the proper conditions for fostering moral sensibility and moral reasoning. Considerably less attention has been paid to the "hardwiring" of morality. Are we inherently moral beings with biologically anchored predispositions to recognize good and evil? Are we prone by such hardwired and species-specific predispositions to engage in acts to benefit others? Are we inherently capable of experiencing the feelings of others? Does humankind have the inherent capacity for empathy? Such questions generally have been skirted by psychological inquiries into moral development. One can productively study the developmental acquisition of morality with only diffuse reference to the native state of human beings. In the case of the two visions of moral development discussed above, such diffuse references to essential states are evident. For the cognitivist, the essential state that drives moral development is embodied by the natural tendency of humans to seek and integrate information — to act as naive epistemologists, if you will. To the extent that knowledge is assimilated in ways that result in the emergence of intellectual principles in the course of development, so do morally relevant principles emerge. For the devotee of hierarchical socialization as the root of moral dispositions, the essential states driving the acquisition of morality are social dependence and sociability. To the extent that children are biologically predisposed to "need" others, they are likewise prone to acquire the norms of those who control their needs for nurturing affection and identity. In these latter accounts morality emerges from the social nature of humans.

In summary, the primary models of moral development in the field of developmental psychology view moral acquisition as a derived and "nurtured" consequence of inborn tendencies to either seek knowledge or gain social connection — and perhaps both.

MORALITY, GOODNESS, AND THE HARDWIRING OF EMOTION

It is curious that the psychological study of moral development has typically ignored the role of emotion as a hardwired and predisposing influence on the nurturance of morality and goodness. This is curious because in adults such phenomena as violations of moral principle and observing harm to others are frequently associated with visceral arousal. Primary emotions such as pride, disgust, sadness, and guilt—for example—can, like knowledge and sociability, serve as natural primes to the development of moral behavior and the appraisal of goodness and evil. Indeed, the natural and primal tendencies for humans to "feel" in the biological and psychological senses can be viewed as the most crucial hardwiring that moves moral development. Without the inherent capacity to feel the impact of human exchange, nurturance of either knowledge or norms would be rather ineffective. Socializers capitalize on their children's emotional readiness in order to convey standards of conduct or belief that are desirable and important from their own standpoints. Morality and moral codes emerge from the attachment of emotion to acts. Caretakers, both intentionally and subintentionally, use their children's natural emotional reactivity to instantiate codes of importance. Since codes of importance can vary from parent to parent and culture to culture, the very definitions of goodness and morality also vary. Thus one might argue that goodness and morality per se are not hardwired by nature. However, the emotional properties that are pivotal to nurturing morality are the hardwired antecedents. When one combines these evolutionarily endowed systems of feeling with both our natural sociability and our need for information, one can see that the natural prerequisites for developing and nurturing morality are multiple. As such, the tendency to become moral beings is rooted in the natural attributes that enable us to do so. We feel, we think, and we require the attachments of others. This tripartite natural endowment is at the heart of the acquisition of morality.

A VIEW ON THE EMERGENCE OF MORALITY

Based on the considerations above, I will define more completely my own particular long-term perspective on the emergence of moral appraisal and naive interpretations of goodness. The backdrop for this very speculative presentation is its contrast with neo-Kantian views of reason-guided moral appraisal. While it falls in the socialization camp, this view is considerably more bound to emotional origins than are traditional socialization perspectives. As you will see, I propose that the cognitive manifestation of moral inference is most prevalent in nonvalent circumstances. For the judgment of personally "important" transactions reflecting on moral status, I propose that our affective tendencies and our socialized, emotion-guided beliefs are far more accessible guides than our logic and principles of "correct" judgment.

In presenting this conception and its attendant speculations, I will first describe the history of my current propositions concerning the primacy of moral emotion, then briefly consider the question of domain distinctions in how we deploy our moral inference. My goal is to provide a viewpoint on moral acquisition that accounts for the interconnections between nature and nurture.

Approximately thirty years ago I attended a conference where I presented my research on parents' transmission of beliefs and values to their developing children. Our work had discovered that in value domains characterized by strong parental emotion, young children were precociously sophisticated in their moral judgments of negative behavior—they discriminated badly intentioned actors from well-intentioned ones. Oddly, however, latency-aged and young adolescents did not discriminate their goodness ratings based on actors' intentions. It was "as if" these older children had internalized an unbending standard in domains of high parental emotion. Surprisingly, this absolutist judgment tendency held whether these older children reported high or low levels of emotion in domains of high parental concern. The results in domains of low parental concern were as expected: older children were more "intention-relativist" in judging these domains than were younger children. It seems that strong parental emotion is a key factor in conveying to children absolute standards for the appraisal of goodness and evil. Apparently young children associate strong emotion with parents' mentoring them to carefully consider subjective cues in judging behaviors in those domains. As they get older, however, parents' expectations for children's "correctness" in these high-emotion areas preempt the prematurely sophisticated reasoning models conveyed earlier. The transmission of emotionally significant parental beliefs to children was viewed as predicated on the children's own system of emotional arousal—a kind of emotion-based contagion of morality.

The commentator for my presentation, a fine scholar in the Kohlbergian tradition, noted that children and their moral perspective are not molded by caretakers and socializers "like so much clay." He proposed that children negotiate moral perspectives through their own encounters with moral action and in concert with their cognitive development. Indeed, this commentator seemed offended by the idea that the constraints on young children are carried forward into later childhood and "undermine" the emerging moral perspective of developing individuals. That children are not fed their appraisal apparatus but grow it from within was this commentator's presumption. Thirty years ago this perspective was the dominant one in the study of moral development. Morality could not possibly emerge out of hierarchical socialization because such an emergence represents not moral reasoning but complicity—not moral independence but slavish conformity. This could not lie at the root of human morality.

Although the commentator also conveyed other opinions about the work (some of them quite positive), these are the ones that engaged me the most. As a young parent at that time, I found it hard to discriminate my disciplinary perspective from my naive parental viewpoint. Was it really true that my attempts to get my three-year-old to share or help would have no bearing on his later sense of right and wrong, good and evil, or "correct or incorrect"? Was I only minding my child until he became cognitively equipped to reason to his own beliefs, with little impact from hierarchical socialization? Would the major part of his moral growth come in the context of negotiations with peers? As a scholar, I was intrigued by the critique—it was an interesting counterpoint to my perspective at that time. As a parent, I must admit I was a bit distressed at the idea that I was rather irrelevant to my children's moral growth. I could try to be sure that evil would not befall them and that they had sufficient stimulation and experience to cognitively advance and be prepared to negotiate with peers, but would I be barking up the wrong tree of civilization if I exerted effort to teach my children (directly or by induction) the distinctions between good and evil that I felt so strongly? At this point I became a devotee of David Hume—his philosophical approach to ethics implied that parents are meaningful and that their strong affects and feelings are powerful influences on developing children. The capacity of even young children to naturally react to and process emotional communication fed the emergence of codes of moral importance. Moral appraisal and action must emerge at least in strong measure from our feelings and emotional inclinations toward people and events. Since I had been firmly trained in the "tabula rasa" tradition of behavioral, cognitive, and emotional origins, I reasoned that one's moral emotions must emerge from socialization experience. Here my theoretical preferences and my parental ideology converged: parents, in my mind, are many things to and for their children. However, in the world of morality, they serve as "importance markers." That is, they model, directly sanction, and indirectly convey attitudes and evaluative affect concerning acceptable or "good" behavior and unacceptable or "bad" behavior. I further assumed (with rather interesting data to support it) that these evaluative proclivities are transmitted to children and are encoded and internalized as both beliefs and emotion markers that drive the cognitive and affective processing of events and the people who populate, "cause," and are affected by those events. Of course, these socialization-based moral emotions are not manifested whole, unaffected by other experiences with peers or by changes in our reasoning models, but they constitute a set of guiding indexes that bias the way we process the moral relevance of information.

Many of the somewhat anomalous effects found by social psychologists can be linked to shared affective biases. It is not reasonable to blame victims for their suffering—but we often do so. It is not particularly a product of reason for individuals to implicitly assume that persons of a given race are more or less adequate than those of another race. Similarly, our in-group biases are not predicated on an intellectually guided sorting of information. If to these shared effects we add individual proclivities emerging from particularized socialization experiences, it is clear that affect often trumps reason. A further, somewhat anomalous turn in all this is that when we employ these biases, they often feel right, logical, and given by the "data." Indeed, if we consider the work of researchers such as John Bargh[3] and Dan Wegner,[4] these biases seem to occur "automatically" and without detailed reflection.

So for most of the past thirty years I became an unabashed supporter of the perspective that moral behavior and conceptions of good and evil were made up of subtle intergenerationally scaffolded and socializer-induced moral emotions—moral emotions that frequently trump or preempt our emerging cognitive sophistication. The impact of these morally conveyed emotions assumes prewired and naturally evident emotions in children. To some extent, applying information-guided principles is superfluous when we have strong a priori affect that indexes right and wrong or good and bad for each of us. It isn't that we do not "think" our way to "correct" inferences—the irony is that we are resplendent with human reason when the emotional stakes are low, but when the stakes are high, moral emotion is our typical intuitive guide. Systems of Western jurisprudence seem intuitively aware of this irony—juries must be instructed to employ a rational calculus in judging fault. The emotional significance of crimes (e.g., child molestation) renders balanced and principled reasoning difficult. In Jon Haidt's terms, these kinds of behaviors are "morally dumbfounding" even when mitigating circumstances should lessen judgments of fault.[5] More explicitly, Haidt observed that in morally intensified circumstances, particularly when powerful cultural taboos are violated, we experience a strong sense of wrongness, even while we feel at a loss for intellectually guided moral arguments to support that sense of wrongness. In short, we are dumbfounded.

In a chapter in the 1991 volume *Context and Development*,[6] I proposed this importance-marked distinction in social and moral judgment as one component of a dual-process model of moral "cognition." Emotion-governed moral inference and intuition (because of its early developmental roots) is dictated by the conservation of either individual or group identity (depending on cultural context). Familiar affects in response to current behavior are identity preservative. The second process in this pairing is devoted to accuracy and correctness—also an adaptive human need. In important transactions identity trumps correctness, and for this reason our emotions become our biased guide to the moral significance of actions.

I should note that while my initial view of the importance-marking process in moral acquisition was tilted in the direction of nurture, my current view is more balanced. As I noted earlier, some emotions—such as disgust, approach, panic, compassion, and dependence—are evolutionary legacies. These built-in reactive propensities are the emotional guides of the "innocent" and unsocialized. It is from this raw affective material that socialized emotions are conferred as we rear children. They render the child open to influence, under conditions that make the caretaker an important attachment figure who (to varying degrees) promotes the reduction in negative affect and the experience of comfort. To the extent that these emotional effects are connected to implicit or explicit moral tuition, they both transform instinctual approach/avoidance tendencies and are the starting point for creating socialized moral aversions and approach goals. In essence, socially constructed moral codes and feelings are derivative of natural emotional appraisal tendencies built on struggles for survival.

IS MORALITY A DOMAIN APART FROM OTHER SOCIALLY TRANSACTED DOMAINS?

This question is critical as we consider the notion presented above, that socialization of normativity is the primary origin of moral inference and the apprehension of goodness. Elliot Turiel, a superb developmental scientist who has been a major figure in the study of the development of moral reasoning, proposed that the moral domain has distinct properties that differentiate it from other social domains. These properties were proposed to transcend culture, gender, and other factors associated with the differential experience or social placement of individuals. Turiel distinguished moral domains from what he referred to as conventional domains. The moral domain of human action includes categories of action reflecting on justice, fairness, individual rights, and personal harm. The conventional domain consists of sets of socially constructed rules or customs outside the morally relevant ones that provide guides to appropriate behaviors. These might include such rule-regulated behaviors as eating with utensils, obedience to authority, and conformity to norms of dress and weight. In the original domain model, Turiel accorded the acquisition of hierarchical socialization to conventions, with moral acquisition being a product of peer negotiation in the context of cognitive development.[7]

Smetana[8] later revised this particular notion somewhat by proposing that hierarchical exchanges could indeed be components of moral domains if they involved the back-and-forth consistent with negotiation in a context of noncoercion. In essence, to the extent that parents behave like peers, they might have an impact on their children's moral development. While Smetana's revision of social domain theory provides an interesting advance over Turiel's notion, and while some interesting empirical exemplars are the product of this proposal, it still generates a conceptual quagmire when it comes to understanding the role of moral socialization. Parents and others blur this domain distinction by "moralizing" domains that would be considered conventional in the domain model. This is the cause of much human joy and accomplishment and probably more human misery. For example, eating with utensils may be a simple matter of learning manners. But in the instructional context socializers frequently link it to fairness to others, consideration of others' needs, and other moral categories. Body weight among girls and women is not simply a number, nor is it just a matter of conventional health practice. To many it is moralized. Indeed, the moralizing of the body has been cited as lying at the root of eating disorders including extreme and persistent dieting to achieve a version of moral "goodness." Most domains of behavior to which strong emotion is attached are moralized—frequently implying that the exemplifier is "good" in many ways while the "violator" is bad. It seems difficult to separate the moral from the conventional. To do so frequently discounts the effect of culture on interpretations of goodness. For Americans eating beef is conventional, whereas for Hindus in India it is an issue of moral import. For the first seven years of my life I believed I violated a moral stricture when I ate meat on Friday. I realize that such examples are commonplace; however, they do show why this domain distinction is a problem for those searching for the factors that give rise to moral appraisal and conceptions of goodness. Domains are made moral when strong, judgmentally relevant affect is attached to any of them. Indeed, a good deal of what gets referred to as "psychopathology" consists of chronic appraisal tendencies that moralize domains of action that are normatively unimportant to most people. Such emotionally distinct moralized proclivities are often referred to as "crazy." Yet each of us is "crazed" in those areas of human action in which we experience an intrinsic emotionally internalized need to exemplify a precept—and a sense of bereft "badness" when we violate it. Some of our moral preoccupations are shared, some unique. Each is socialized through emotional transactions in a hierarchical context and later revised and modified in peer relations. And like many of our early experiences, particularly those accompanied by moral induction, we implicitly conserve and retain the underlying criteria for goodness and self-worth across the life span. We are not yet close to understanding the bases for the durability of morally important beliefs and perspectives. But it may well be that at the heart of human goodness is the capacity to encapsulate and emotionally store moral reactions and then develop cues and indexes that trigger them.

In a 2002 chapter,[9] following an excellent treatise by Harman,[10] I argued that this capacity is akin to Noam Chomsky's[11] notion of the automaticity of the deployment of syntactic structures in language. This deployment of syntax in language inheres in the linkage between the surface structure of human language and its deep and inherent grammar. Many surface structures index or manifest the underlying grammar. The various surface structures are the products of the direct acquisition of conventional speech acts, idioms of language, and so forth. Nevertheless, despite this variety, they are naturally "matched" to and determined by constraints of linguistic deep structure.

In making the analogy of language syntax to morality, a key point is that "surface" or conventional actions index moral syntax in the same way surface language performance indexes inherent language competence. In this formulation, for example, eating with utensils or saying "thank you" might index kindness and caring for others. The more "important" the syntactical rule, the wider the range of conventional acts that will be employed to index or access it. In the case of morality, the critical process that defines the range of conventional behaviors is emotionally based importance marking. The level of felt emotion indexes how far actors have verged into the territory of syntactic deep structure. For example, if an underlying ethic of kindness is important to the perceiver or actor, it will be indexed by many acts ranging from smiles to polite actions to gift giving and such. These actions themselves are indeed conventional and likely are defined by socialization and acculturation.

However, the syntactic moral principle relating to the kind and caring treatment of others undergirds the emotional significance of these actions, as well as the emotional significance of failure to exemplify them. A corollary to this formulation that follows from the Chomsky-based analysis of linguistic structures is that whereas moral conventions or moral surface structures are acquired, the competence to index moral deep structure is "innate." Our emotional processing apparatus prepares us for moral analyses as well as for discerning good and evil in our own and others' behavior. Considering Turiel's analysis in the light of this formulation suggests that domains he defines as conventions are inextricably linked to those he refers to as moral. The linkage is enabled by emotionally driven processes of importance marking. As such, morality and convention are psychologically bound together, unified by the syntax of moral importance.

CONCLUDING COMMENTS

In this chapter I intended to explore the nature and nurture of morality from the perspective of a psychologist. As a related goal, I also meant to address the origins and development of "goodness"—the issue this volume addresses. I found the first intention considerably easier to enact than the second. Psychologists infrequently discuss, theorize about, or research goodness or evil. Such terms really do not fit into the psychologist's lexicon. In many ways I used morality as a proxy for goodness, and most probably I conflated the two concepts. Nevertheless, I believe a psychological understanding of the development of morality can help elucidate the trickier phenomenon of goodness. I hope I have conveyed four related points. (1) The hardwired components of morality are composed not of moral principles, but of psychobiological dimensions that enable the nurture of morality. Of these, the capacity for emotional discernment is a primary factor. However, secondary species-specific factors like attachment needs, reward seeking, and other built-in proclivities also are firm contributors to our inborn moral sense. (2) As a corollary point, the acquisition of morality and the acquisition of goodness are difficult to view as singular products or emergent properties of disembodied intellect and reason. As such, our primitive moral reactivity precedes the formation of our reason. (3) The natural emotional reactivity of humans can be viewed productively as a primary origin of the development of those importance markers that define durable moral codes and individual criteria for goodness. (4) Finally, domains of behavior aren't either inherently moral or inherently conventional; the relevance of any domain of human action to moral appraisal hinges on the attachment of strong emotion to behavior in that domain. The emotional transformation of socialized conventions into underlying moral competence can be likened to the transformation of everyday language performance into the innate syntactic structures indexing linguistic competence. This is quite appropriate, for like language, morality is a human system involved in making meaning of life. A primary process in making moral meaning is appraising and experiencing the "good" and "bad" of human action and intention. In this appraisal task, our feelings are the leading edge and guiding basics of our moral grammar.

NOTES

1. The scholarship of Lawrence Kohlberg on a stage model of the development of moral thought is voluminous. These are some exemplars of his work: Lawrence Kohlberg, "Stage and Sequence: The Cognitive-Developmental Approach to Socialization," in *Handbook of Socialization Theory and Research*, ed. David A. Goslin, 347-480 (Chicago: Rand McNally, 1969); Kohlberg, "From Is to Ought: How to Commit the Naturalistic Fallacy and Get Away with It: The Study of Moral Development," in *Psychology and Genetic Epistemology*, ed. Theodore Mischel, 151-235 (New York: Academic Press, 1971); Kohlberg, *Essays on Moral Development*, vol. 2, *The Psychology of Moral Development* (San Francisco: Harper and Row, 1984).

2. Elliot Turiel presented his domain theory of moral acquisition and his approach to moral development in numerous articles and chapters. These are a few of them: Elliot Turiel, "Distinct Conceptual and Developmental Domains: Social Convention and Morality," in *Nebraska Symposium on Motivation, 1977*, vol. 25, *Social Cognitive Development*, ed. C. B. Keasey, 77-115 (Lincoln: University of Nebraska Press, 1976); Turiel, "The Social Construction of Social Construction," in *Child Development Today and Tomorrow*, ed. William Damon, 86-106 (San Francisco: Jossey-Bass, 1989); Turiel, "Moral Development," in *Handbook of Child Psychology*, ed. William Damon, vol. 3, *Social Emotional, and Personality Development*, ed. N. Eisenberg (New York: John Wiley, 1998).

3. John A. Bargh, "The Automaticity of Everyday Life," in *Advances in Social Cognition*, ed. Robert S. Wyer Jr., 10:1-61 (Mahwah, NJ: Erlbaum, 1997).

4. Dan M. Wegner and J. A. Bargh, "Control and Automaticity in Social Life," in *Handbook of Social Psychology*, 4th ed., ed. D. Gilbert, S. Fiske, and G. Lindzey (Boston: McGraw-Hill, 1998).

5. John Haidt, "The Emotional Dog and Its Rational Tail: A Social Intuitionist's Approach to Moral Judgment." *Psychological Review* 108 (2001): 814-34.

6. Philip R. Costanzo, "Morals, Mothers, and Memories: The Social Context of Developing Social Cognition," in *Context and Development*, ed. Robert Cohen and Alexander W. Siegel (Mahwah, NJ: Erlbaum, 1991).

7. Turiel, "Social Construction of Social Construction."

8. J. G. Smetana, "Parenting and the Development of Social Knowledge Reconceptualized: A Social Domain Analysis," in *Parenting and the Internalization of Values*, ed. Joan E. Grusec and Leon Kuczynski (New York: Wiley, 1997).

9. Philip Costanzo, "Social Exchange and the Developing Syntax of Moral Orientation," in *Social Exchange in Development*, ed. William G. Graziano and Brett Laursen, 41-53, New Directions in Child and Adolescent Development, 95 (San Francisco: Jossey-Bass, 2002).

10. Gilbert Harman, "Moral Philosophy and Linguistics," in *Celebration: An Electronic Festschrift in Honor of Noam Chomsky*, ed. J. Fodor, J. Keyser, and A. Brand (Cambridge, MA: MIT Press, 1998).

11. Noam Chomsky, *Syntactic Structures* (The Hague: Mouton, 1957).

TWO

"Generous to a Fault"

MORAL GOODNESS AND PSYCHIC HEALTH

Ruth W. Grant

Is altruism good? In thinking about goodness we are so accustomed to equate it with altruism that the very question sounds odd. So much of our conversation about morality revolves around the twin concepts of egoism and altruism. To act egoistically, to benefit oneself, comes naturally, requires no particular education, and deserves no special praise. But seeking to benefit others seems to be the very essence of goodness, and those who sacrifice their own well-being or take personal risks for others are particularly honored for it. Indeed, the personal cost of an action is often taken to be sufficient testimony to its goodness.

Nevertheless, it is not difficult to argue that altruism is not always good. There are many examples of people who work tirelessly for the happiness of others but are unable to acknowledge and pursue their own wish for happiness. Cyrano de Bergerac's self-sacrifice is tragic, for example.[1] Some people devote themselves to the care of others to the point of ruining their own health. The attempt to be as morally good as it is possible to be can lead to a life that is out of balance, with no attention to other kinds of goods such as the development of one's own talents. Moreover, altruistic actions sometimes harm those they are intended to benefit. Once one begins to question the idea that altruism *is* goodness, other questions arise: What is the standard of goodness guiding the judgment that certain forms of altruism are *not* good? What is the idea of goodness that might lead one to conclude that it is not always good to be "good" (altruistic)?

Let me illustrate the problem through what appears to be a simple children's story, *The Giving Tree*.[2] In this story a tree loves a little boy. Every day when he is young, the boy climbs the tree, eats her apples, rests in her shade; and the boy loves the tree. As he grows older, he leaves the tree alone and comes back only when he wants something—apples to get money, branches to build a house, and finally the trunk itself to build a boat and sail far away. The tree is sad when the boy is away and happy each time she can give something of herself that will make him happy, though we are told that she is "not really" happy when he takes her trunk. Finally the boy comes back as an old man and needs only a place to rest, so the tree invites him to sit on her stump, and she is happy once again.

About a dozen people, primarily professors of religion and ethics, recorded their thoughts on this story in a published symposium.[3] The striking thing is that the story provoked reactions that were extremely strong and diametrically opposed. Some saw the tree as masochistic, the boy as narcissistic, and the story itself as "wicked," "vicious," or "evil." Others viewed the tree as the ideal of goodness and her relationship with the boy as the model of love, referring to the tree as an ideal mother or as the image of Christ. In their view it is precisely the tree's willingness to sacrifice her very substance, her trunk, that demonstrates the quality of her love and the depth of her goodness. In contrast, those in the first camp view this gift particularly as proof that the relationship is self-destructive and depleting for the tree. Moreover, the relationship is without any redeeming benefit to the boy's moral growth. He never learns gratitude, reciprocity, or self-sufficiency. One of the commentators put the question squarely, asking "whether we can commend in our everyday lives a love that seems so thoroughly to diminish the self, or that can reduce our prospects for flourishing as the creatures we were apparently meant or expected to be."[4]

Here is the answer to our question: psychic health or flourishing is the standpoint from which certain forms of altruism can be criticized. In thinking about altruism, we have uncovered an important and divisive conflict between two conceptions of goodness. Let me call the first the "ethic of altruism." According to this view, goodness is primarily a matter of concern for the well-being of others, which includes willingness to sacrifice out of love or out of duty. In its religious form, the concern for others is not primary but follows from love of or duty to God. The alternative view I will call the "ethic of psychic health." Here goodness is primarily a matter of care for the state of one's soul in light of what it means to thrive as a human being.

At first glance these alternatives appear to merely restate a familiar opposition between Greek and Christian approaches to ethics, and there is something to this. Consider, for example, Aristotle's view of generosity. For Aristotle, generosity is a mean between extravagance and stinginess, and the man who gives too much is criticized for neglecting himself.[5] An Aristotelian "giving tree" would give from leaves and branches but would never sacrifice her trunk. Contrast this with the following comment: "*The Giving Tree* presents an alternative ideal. It is that what appears to be self-loss may be in reality our deepest fulfillment, since service, not detachment, makes us into creatures with whom our fellows may in some way abide. . . . According to the Christian Gospel, this 'ideal' is set before us as a task to which we are called by the grace of God in Jesus Christ."[6]

According to this view, one cannot give too much. But for a number of reasons it would be a mistake to accept a simple identification of the "ethic of altruism" with Christianity and the "ethic of psychic health" with the Greek tradition.[7] First, a tension between these two ethical conceptions exists *within* Christianity. Christianity calls on believers to renounce the goal of flourishing in their own case in order to serve God. Yet, at the same time, God wills human flourishing. A scene in the film *Chariots of Fire* illustrates this tension nicely. A devout Scottish Presbyterian runner is challenged by his sister, who worries that his competitive racing is impious and distracts him from his missionary work. He replies, "God made me for a purpose, for China, but He also made me fast. And when I run, I feel His pleasure. To give it up would be to hold him in contempt. To win is to honor Him."[8] Second, what I am calling the "ethic of psychic health," far from belonging exclusively to the ancient world, has been said to characterize modern secular humanism: a society in which there are no goals or allegiances beyond human flourishing.[9] While this perspective may have begun with the Greeks, it has found its way into the modern world.

So we cannot avoid confronting the tension between these two rival ethics. The competition between them permeates our moral discourse. The polarization evident in the symposium discussed above is one indication of how far our moral reactions and commitments are informed by one or the other of these views. How can we come to terms with the competing claims of these two primary goods, altruism and psychic health? There are four distinct possibilities, the first two within the "ethic of altruism" and the second two within the "ethic of psychic health." First, we can recognize that there is a real and irreconcilable conflict between these two goods and put altruism first. We would admire the tree even though her altruism depletes her. Second, we could deny that there is a conflict: to be altruistic *is* truly to flourish. After all, the tree is happy. Many recent studies are motivated by a commitment to this point of view, trying to show that people who serve others are happier and even physically healthier and longer-lived than people who live more selfish lives.[10] Third, we can recognize that there is a real and irreconcilable conflict between these two goods and put psychic health and flourishing first. This is the point of view informing the judgment that it is possible to be too good. Susan Wolf makes this case by arguing that moral goods must be balanced with nonmoral human goods.[11] Sigmund Freud can be placed in this camp as well. He would want to know whether the tree's generosity to the boy comes at an excessive psychic cost. Last, one might argue that there is no real conflict because nothing can truly be morally good if it compromises psychic health and flourishing. In other words, the tree's generosity cannot be admired as good precisely because it compromises her psychic growth. She cannot relinquish the fantasy that the boy might remain a child forever; each time he returns she asks him to climb and play again, and she calls him "Boy" even when he is an old man. Jean Hampton develops this position, in explicit disagreement with Wolf, by arguing that "any 'altruistic' behavior is morally wrong when it prevents one from paying moral respect to oneself." Moral respect for oneself is then explained in terms of what is required for one to flourish and a recognition of one's value as a human being.[12]

I will devote the rest of this essay to exploring the third and fourth possibilities, those that accept psychic health as the primary standard. We are so accustomed to assuming the identity of goodness and altruism that I want to recover the perspective from which that position looks questionable. To do this I will look briefly at Plato and Freud. Freud, as I have already noted, represents the third alternative: that moral goodness can be costly in terms of psychic health. Plato denies the conflict and identifies true goodness with a truly healthy soul, my fourth alternative. Our question, then, is, What is the relation between goodness and the health of the soul?

Even a cursory consideration reveals the complexity of the problem. On one hand, certain psychic capacities that are components of a mature and healthy personality seem to be necessary conditions for goodness. Impulse control, empathy, and self-awareness are obvious candidates. For example, to function in a way that is beneficial to her child, a mother must be able to regulate her own feelings of anger, shame, or competitive envy. A father who is not aware of his own excessive need for love and approval from his child may be unable to say no when that is what his child needs to hear. As people develop into healthy, mature adults, they develop capacities essential for moral behavior. To the extent that their development is incomplete or damaged, they will have difficulty being good.

On the other hand, it is equally obvious that psychic health is not necessary for many kinds of goodness. On the contrary, much good behavior (like all behavior) is fueled by neurosis and psychic conflict. The expression "liberal guilt" carries this implication. Among other examples, Robert Coles describes vividly the complex psychological conflicts behind the generosity and self-sacrifice of a privileged white northerner who becomes an organizer in a small African American community in the South, and also of a Brazilian hairdresser and prostitute who regularly gives her earnings to destitute children.[13] Kierkegaard describes female nature as "devoted and selfless. In her self-abandonment she has lost herself, and is only happy when having done so, this being the only way she can be herself. A woman who is happy without self-abandonment, that is, without giving all of herself, no matter what she gives it to, is altogether unfeminine."[14]

Contra Kierkegaard, I would argue that the psychic costs of trying to live up to such an ideal are very great; yet, at the same time, women who try to do so might very well genuinely benefit others through their self-sacrifice. And if these examples show that unhealthy psychic states can be the motivators for good behavior, we might also consider the corollary: that increased psychic health might lead to decreased goodness. This is the charge sometimes leveled against Freud: that the search for honest, often painfully honest, self-awareness is ultimately nihilistic. "One need not be self-deceived in order to act maliciously. . . . Lucidity may render us exquisitely articulate and unapologetic about our aggressions."[15] So, I ask again, What is the relation between goodness and the health of the soul?

It seems that psychic health both is and is not a necessary condition for goodness. This paradox may be partially resolved by recognizing that it all depends on what counts as goodness and what counts as psychic health. For example, a person who overcomes her neurosis and gains new psychic freedom may become less dutiful than before but also may be more able to recognize and respond to the needs of others—less good in one respect, better in another. To explore these issues, I turn first to Plato and then to Freud. Each takes an extreme position on this question. For Plato, there can be no conflict between goodness and psychic health because the two are one and the same. For Freud, the demands of morality are the source of painful psychic conflicts.

PLATO

What does it mean to say that goodness *is* the health of the soul? Is the idea of psychic "health" anything more than an analogy? Socrates often uses it this way, claiming that medicine is to the body as justice is to the soul; that he is like a doctor administering painful but beneficial remedies through argument; that the health of the body is like lawfulness (justice and moderation) in the soul (*Gorgias* 464b, 475d, 504b–d). But he also speaks directly of a healthy condition of the soul (e.g., *Gorgias*, 526d). The soul has certain natural functions—living, "managing, ruling, deliberating, and all such things" (*Republic*, 353d–e)—and a healthy soul is one with the capacity to perform these functions well. It is through this conception of psychic health that Socrates explains to Glaucon what human goodness (virtue) really is.

> "To produce health is to establish the parts of the body in relation of mastering, and being mastered by, one another that is according to nature, while to produce sickness is to establish a relation of ruling and being ruled by, one another that is contrary to nature."
> "It is."
> "Then, in its turn," I said, "isn't to produce justice to establish the parts of the soul in a relation of mastering, and being mastered by, one another that is according to nature, while to produce injustice is to establish a relation of ruling, and being ruled by, one another that is contrary to nature?"
> "Entirely so," he said.
> "Virtue, then, as it seems would be a certain health, beauty and good condition of a soul, and vice a sickness, ugliness and weakness." (*Republic*, 444d)

A healthy thing is one so ordered as to perform its natural functions well. The virtues of a thing are those qualities that allow it to perform its natural functions well: for example, speed and stamina in a racehorse, justice in a human being. Hence, for human beings, virtue and psychic health are one and the same.

This is hardly satisfying. It seems to be true by definition, in an abstract sense. What does it mean to identify the right ordering of the soul with goodness or virtue more concretely? Socrates' argument in *The Republic* is that the familiar virtues—wisdom, courage, moderation, and justice—are all accomplished through the right ordering of the soul. A soul is well ordered when reason rules, enlisting the energy of the spirited part of the soul as an ally in governing the desires. A person with such a soul clearly would be moderate. Spiritedness directed by reason would yield courage rather than recklessness. To the extent that the rational faculties were well developed, this person would be wise. With envy, anger, ambition, greed, and lust under control, this person would be unlikely to commit injustices. But what about justice? Socrates identifies it with the right ordering of the soul itself, and it becomes difficult to distinguish it from moderation. He might have defined it as something like obedience to reason, but justice is defined as "minding one's own business and not being a busybody" (*me polupragmonein*, *Republic*, 433a). The discussion of the virtues yields a strikingly self-regarding, inward-looking conception of what it is to be a good human being. The crucial thing is to care for the health of your own soul.

It is precisely because the identification of goodness and psychic health makes goodness self-regarding that Socrates is able to meet the challenge posed by Glaucon and Adeimantus.[16] They had challenged Socrates to show that justice, like physical health, is the sort of thing that is good for itself as well as for its consequences (*Republic*, 367d). Throughout book 1 of *The Republic*, as various definitions of justice are being examined, Socrates never challenges the unstated premise of the conversation that whatever justice is, it must be good for the just man. And if justice is health of the soul, then justice is indeed good for the just man. Justice is not a matter of sacrificing your own benefit for the good of others; justice is good *for you*. Immediately after the long passage quoted above, Glaucon declares that he is convinced: "If life doesn't seem livable with the body's nature corrupted, not even with every sort of food and drink and every sort of wealth and every sort of rule, will it then be livable when the nature of that very thing by which we live is confused and corrupted, even if a man does whatever else he might want except that which will rid him of vice and injustice and will enable him to acquire justice and virtue?" (*Republic*, 445b). If virtue is health and vice is sickness, who would choose vice?

It seems that a vision of goodness as psychic health provides good grounds for avoiding injustice. It might even provide grounds for pursuing justice in the form of meeting one's legal obligations. Socrates, in the *Apology*, indicates that he has behaved in exactly this way. But is there a role here for justice in a more positive sense — for seeking to right wrongs or to benefit others? Is there room for altruism and sacrifice if justice is "minding one's own business"?

In the *Apology*, Socrates raises and answers the question of just what his business is (20c–23b). It is his "service to the god," which requires him to question his fellow Athenians as to the extent of their wisdom. He pays no attention to his private affairs or to the public business but instead functions as a "gadfly" (30e) and (take note) a "busybody" (*polupragmono*, 31c). He has become poor in this service; a "poor benefactor" and a "gift of the god to the city" (31b, 36d). His benevolence consists in persuading others to care for the right things: not wealth or power but virtue, truth, and the state of their souls (29e, 30a, 31b–c). Lest we dismiss this Socratic altruism as a singular phenomenon emanating from Socrates' special status as a philosopher or his special relationship with the Delphic oracle, we should note that he exhorts his supporters to treat his sons as he has treated them. They should see to it that his sons care for the right things (41e). Moreover, in the *Gorgias*, Socrates asserts that the best politics redirects the city's appetites and makes the citizens better: "That alone is the task of a good citizen" (517c). Socratic altruism benefits others through a particular kind of moral education, one that changes people's values so they come to a new understanding of what it means to benefit themselves.

If we were to approach Plato's works with the idea that egoism and altruism are mutually exclusive opposites and that altruism is goodness, we would find them simply baffling. Socrates' activities to benefit the city are perfectly consistent with his own benefit, as he repeatedly asserts (35d, 36c, 37d). To be sure, Socrates is a poor man, and he loses his life unjustly on account of his service to the god. But he makes it clear that poverty and death cannot harm him.[17] There is altruism here, but there is no self-sacrifice, no self-abnegation, no abandonment of his commitments, no loss of well-being. Crito pleads with Socrates to consider the effects of his death on his friends and family, and one might argue that responding to *those* pleas, putting friends and family first, would have been self-sacrificing. But Socrates does not make that sacrifice; he puts his own integrity first. He is concerned to keep his soul free of any unjust act (44c, 45d, 48d).

To the question I raised at the beginning of this essay, whether we can commend in our everyday lives a love that seems so thoroughly to diminish the self or that can reduce our prospects for flourishing as the creatures we were apparently meant or expected to be, Socrates would surely answer no. If Socrates were the model for the giving tree, we might imagine this: when the boy came to pick some apples, the tree would engage him in a long conversation; the apples would be forgotten; the boy would walk away a better human being; the tree would continue to thrive; and both would be happy.

FREUD

Plato's position lets us eat our cake and have it too. An egoistic concern for psychic health does not compromise goodness at all: quite the contrary. These two goods are entirely in harmony with one another, and goodness contributes to happiness.[18] Freud paints a darker picture. In his view, moral goodness is a source of suffering and a threat to happiness. This is because he understands moral goodness as obedience to those authoritative requirements and prohibitions that every society imposes on its members to ensure cooperation rather than conflict. And at the same time, he understands each individual as naturally driven by both erotic and aggressive impulses that cannot be satisfied directly without threatening social order. Those impulses in each of us must be either repressed or sublimated, or both, and that is a painful process. There is no way around this conflict between society's demands and the individual's wishes; it is at the heart of both individual personality development and the development of civilizations.

How does a person acquire the capacity to be moral, that is, to master his instinctual impulses? Freud describes the process whereby the soul of the child is modified to develop a conscience, or what he calls a "superego."[19] The child, utterly dependent and fearful of losing his parents' love, needs to master his oedipal impulses. He accomplishes this by identifying with his parents, internalizing their authoritative values as his own "ego ideal." He experiences the tension between this ideal and the actual performance of the ego as a sense of guilt.[20] The intensity of the self-incrimination he feels comes from his own aggression, and this is the surprising and important point. The natural aggressiveness that we must suppress cannot simply disappear. Inhibiting its external expression means turning it inward.

> From the point of view of instinctual control, of morality, it may be said of the id that it is totally non-moral, of the ego that it strives to be moral, and of the super-ego that it can be super-moral and then become as cruel as only the id can be. It is remarkable that the more a man checks his aggressiveness towards the exterior the more severe—that is aggressive—he becomes in his ego ideal. The ordinary view sees the situation the other way around: the standard set up by the ego ideal seems to be the motive for the suppression of aggressiveness. The fact remains, however, as we have stated it: the more a man controls his aggressiveness, the more intense becomes his ideal's inclination to aggressiveness against his ego. . . . But even ordinary normal morality has a harshly restraining, cruelly prohibiting quality.[21]

> [The super-ego] in the form of "conscience," is ready to put into action against the ego the same harsh aggressiveness that the ego would have liked to satisfy upon other, extraneous individuals. The tension between the harsh super-ego and the ego that is subjected to it, is called by us the sense of guilt; it expresses itself as a need for punishment. Civilization, therefore, obtains mastery over the individual's dangerous desire for aggression by weakening and disarming it and by setting up an agency within him to watch over it, like a garrison in a conquered city.[22]

The capacity for moral goodness in the form of the development of the superego is, at the same time, a source of painful psychic conflict. Moreover, an excessively harsh superego can also be the source of neurotic disorders — melancholia and obsessional neurosis in particular.[23] An excessive sense of guilt can lead people to do irrational things, sometimes even to commit crimes, in order to bring on the punishment that can relieve the pain of their guilt feelings.[24] As important as it is, conscience is nonetheless a decidedly mixed blessing.

Not surprisingly, Freud takes the position that people can be "too good" for their own good. He sharply criticizes moral ideals that he sees as unrealistically demanding, particularly Christian ideals such as "love thy neighbor as thyself," which he sees as tantamount to "love thine enemies." Universal love is an unreasonable demand: not everyone is equally deserving of love, and most important, universal love is impossible. Human aggressiveness is natural. The demand for universal love requires excessive repression and is still bound to fail. A community founded on universal love will not overcome its aggression altogether; it will express that aggression toward outsiders. The very fact that moral ideals are believed to be divine commands only makes matters worse, if your primary concern is to lessen the punitive requirements of the superego.

> It would be an undoubted advantage if we were to leave God out of it altogether and honestly admit the purely human origin of all the regulations and precepts of civilization. Along with their pretended sanctity, these commandments and laws would lose their rigidity and unchangeableness as well. People could understand that they are made, not so much to rule them as to serve their interests; and they would adopt a more friendly attitude to them, and instead of aiming at their abolition, would aim only at their improvement. This would be an important advance along the road which leads to becoming *reconciled to the burden of civilization.*[25]

People would do well to learn to be kinder to themselves when it comes to expectations for moral behavior.

The passage just cited makes Freud's aims clear, I think. He does not seek to increase man's compliance with moral precepts. Neither does he seek to release men from the pain of moral demands by encouraging libertinism. We are necessarily burdened with the moral demands of civilization; they serve our interests. Freud seeks only to reconcile us to our fate and to ease the burden by decreasing the psychic suffering it causes and by increasing psychic health. Psychic health is a person's ability to master his impulses and adjust to the reality of his situation. This is the task of the ego, which Freud compares to a rider on a horse (the id), attempting to control its direction.[26] To the extent that the rider, and not the horse, is in control, the person is free to direct his own life. The ego is able to gain greater control the better it recognizes the reality of its situation. An honest confrontation with the truth about oneself is an important part of this process. Self-knowledge, self-command, and psychic freedom are essential components of psychic health. And psychic health implies the ability to manage the inevitable conflicts between the ego and the ego-ideal enforced by the superego. Freud aims to reduce the suffering that arises from the demands of morality. This may not seem like an exalted goal (to patients skeptical of the benefits of analysis, Freud replied that they might gain much by transforming their "hysterical misery" into "common unhappiness"),[27] but it is a humane and even altruistic one.

Like Plato, Freud understands psychic health to be self-mastery in accordance with the truth about human nature. But it should be clear by now that, unlike Plato, Freud does not believe there is any reason to expect that improvements in psychic health will necessarily bring improvements in morality as well, particularly if morality means willingness to comply with the demands of social authority. Moreover, moral ideals that are out of reach, enforced with too much exactitude, or both, can take a severe toll in diminished psychic health and happiness. There is a paradox to morality. Moral rules develop to make it possible for human beings to reap the benefits of social life, particularly cooperative labor and love. In that sense they contribute to human happiness. Yet at the same time, each individual pays a price in happiness for the sake of morality. To the extent that there is a tension between morality and happiness, morality seems to have the upper hand in Freud's account. It has the superego and the sense of guilt as allies and hardly needs additional support. Happiness, on the other hand, could use the support that Freud offers from his version of what I have called an "ethic of psychic health." Nonetheless, Freud's children's stories rarely have entirely happy endings.

IMPLICATIONS

Does this brief discussion of the thought of Plato and Freud help us understand the relation between goodness and the health of the soul? From a Platonic point of view, a healthy soul seems to be both a necessary and a sufficient condition for goodness. Psychic health and virtue, maturity and morality, are one and the same. Many people today take a similar position, believing that increases in healthy self-esteem, for example, will lead to good behavior.[28] And there is some plausibility to this. Psychic capacities like self-command, impulse control, reality testing, confidence, trust, and many others are requisites of moral behavior. But Plato is not entirely successful in defending the identification of psychic health and goodness.

A more nuanced reading of Plato's *Republic* would reveal some of the complications of his position. The very first time Socrates makes an analogy between an individual and a city, the analogy that governs the argument of *The Republic*, he famously makes the case that a gang of robbers must be just among themselves in order to function. By analogy, he concludes that an individual could not be effectively and single-mindedly evil (*Republic*, 351c–352a). But the case is much less convincing for an individual than for a group. One can imagine, for example, a successful Mafia don who is confident, in command of himself, and fully mature in many respects. Such a person might well be described as healthy but evil. The example indicates that, at the very least, in addition to psychic health, sound moral judgment and the desire to be good are also required for morality.

Plato, of course, would not accept the example: no evil person could have a healthy soul. This is because Plato's conception of psychic health is a soul ruled by its rational part in accordance with nature. For Plato there is a truth about nature and about man's place in it that determines what human goodness is. To be ruled by the rational part of the soul is to be directed toward truth and goodness. For the philosopher, driven as he is by an erotic longing for the truth, sound moral judgment and the desire to be good can be safely assumed. Psychic health includes them. Throughout *The Republic*, Plato's identification of the health of the soul with virtue is far more convincing for the philosopher than it might be for ordinary folk. For them, the case that virtue is its own reward and that a well-ordered soul is a sufficient condition for goodness is less convincing. Adeimantus is right to ask whether the guardians in the ideal city of *The Republic* will be happy (*Republic*, 419a), and Freud would have asked the same question.

Freud maintains that psychic health and goodness conflict, and there is some plausibility to this as well. We have all experienced painful and compelling feelings of guilt and anxiety that can lead us to act against either our wishes or our better judgment in complying with social norms. Perhaps Freud emphasizes these kinds of conflicts because he was responding to a historical moment when the moral demands of the culture were particularly severe and their negative psychological consequences particularly obvious. Nonetheless, he is able to sustain his view of the conflict between psychic health and goodness only by construing goodness in a rather limited manner. Freud speaks of morals as the social imperatives meant to control our behavior. Goodness, then, is a matter of obedience, duty, compliance, and self-regulation. But what if we consider a more expansive notion of goodness—one that includes, for example, the capacity to forge loving relationships of various kinds that enrich the lives of all parties?[29] Certainly Freud recognizes the ways psychic health enables healthy relationships and is tied to the capacity for love. If this form of social bond and cooperation is included in the conception of goodness, alongside compliance with social norms, even Freud would have to admit that there is a positive relation between psychic health and goodness as well as a conflictual one.

There is no simple or categorical answer to the question of the relation between goodness and psychic health. We have already seen that psychic health is necessary for certain kinds of goodness. But it is not a sufficient condition: psychic health is also compatible with badness (the Mafia don again). Similarly, certain kinds of psychic unhealth can motivate good behavior, for example, through excessive guilt or a neurotically anxious desire to please. But at the same time, an unhealthy psyche can be the source of considerable evil: consider a person whose experience as an abuse victim leaves him unable to control his rage. Freud, who views healthy and unhealthy states of the soul on a kind of continuum, might argue that not only are each of these human types possible, but each of us individually in different ways at different times experiences each of the four possible combinations of goodness/badness and health/unhealth. An appreciation of this complexity emerges from a consideration of ethics of psychic health. It should lead to skepticism toward both sides of a contemporary argument over the relation of goodness and the health of the soul. Some claim that doing good will improve health, happiness, and flourishing. Others claim that improved happiness, health, and flourishing will produce goodness.[30] The realities are simply more complicated than either position allows.

What other implications does an "ethic of psychic health" have for how goodness is understood? Remember that I have identified as ethics of psychic health those approaches that either give precedence to psychic health where it is in conflict with goodness or adopt psychic health as the standard for recognizing what goodness truly is. Clearly there are a wide variety of positions that belong in this category, and I deliberately chose Freud and Plato to illustrate that divergence. I might have discussed Rousseau, who is similar to Plato in identifying psychic health as the standard for goodness but is unlike Plato in many other respects. Rousseau's ideal is one of integrity or psychic wholeness that is inseparable from goodness. What all types of good men and women share is integrity.[31] For Rousseau, evil emerges in the world as the result of a process of corruption that divides people against themselves. Similarly, I might have discussed Nietzsche, who, like Freud, views morality as a threat to psychic health but differs from Freud in rejecting any form of moral goodness that impedes strength, vitality, or greatness. But despite the variety and complexity of alternative "ethics of psychic health," they share some common elements and some common implications.

The first major implication of an ethic of psychic health concerns how moral development and moral education are understood. If goodness is a matter of the right ordering of the soul, as Plato would have it, it seems that moral development and personality development become one and the same. Goodness is fundamentally about who you are. Similarly, if goodness is about the development of the conscience and its relation to the other parts of the soul, as Freud describes it, moral development might best be conceived as a subset of personality development. Again, goodness has everything to do with who you are in a fundamental sense.

This is probably not a very controversial claim, but it does not seem to be the claim that informs most contemporary approaches to moral development and education. These tend to treat moral education as if it resembled other forms of education or training. Note that these approaches would be compatible with an ethic of altruism, where the underlying assumption is that children can be taught to share, to be concerned for the welfare of others, and so forth. Book titles like *How to Teach Values to Your Children* imply that values education is like learning math: a form of knowledge the child acquires as an addition to what he or she already is. Many character education programs have a similar appeal, though here it is habits, rather than knowledge, that are acquired through training. Any child can develop behaviors that are tolerant, respectful, responsible, or altruistic in an environment that habitually requires them. Last, there are programs that attempt to help children learn to make good choices, treating morality as a matter of acquiring decision-making skills.

Whatever the benefits of these approaches, they share a common defect. They treat moral development and education as if it takes place at a distance through something that adults do *for* children, or do *to* children, or *give* to children, but not as something that adults do *with* children. In contrast, consider Freud's discussion of the creation of an ego-ideal and its enforcement by the superego. The content of the ego-ideal will include social norms and rules, but it will be decisively shaped by who each particular child's parents are, who the child is, and the relationship between them. The child acquires a conscience through a process that takes place within a relationship with particular adults, occurring in every interaction between them. This means that moral education or development is not something that can be segregated or compartmentalized; it is not something acquired superficially; it is something that is going on continuously in the child's life in relation to others and at the level of his or her very being. And, importantly, this means that children's moral development cannot be separated from the moral maturity of the significant adults in their lives. Helping adults to continue to progress morally, to gain self-awareness or to overcome their own particular obstacles to empathy and so forth, might be the best thing we could do for children's moral development.[32]

The second major implication of ethics of psychic health is that they provide a standpoint from which to challenge common conceptions of goodness that draw on the dichotomy between egoism and altruism.[33] Egoism and altruism are often conceived as a continuum, with egoism at one pole and altruism at the other, so that the more one seeks to benefit oneself, the less one benefits others and vice versa. The model of giving that best captures this conception is philanthropy. One imagines a finite resource such that the giver's share is depleted by however much is given to another.[34] But there are many other ways of conceptualizing giving that do not pit the needs of the self and the needs of others against one another in a zero-sum game. Parental love is the most obvious example of a form of giving that can be fulfilling for the giver rather than depleting. Consider also expressing appreciation for gifts received; this too is a gift.[35] There is often reciprocity involved in giving that goes unrecognized in discussions of "altruism."

Moreover, egoism and altruism are not always mutually exclusive but are often conjoined in a variety of ways. Anna Freud characterized adolescents as "excessively egoistic, regarding themselves as the center of the universe and the sole object of interest, and yet at no time in later life are they capable of so much self-sacrifice and devotion." She observed that many very giving people come to identify themselves with those they help and thus give to others and to themselves simultaneously.[36] Drawing on studies of gentiles who rescued Jews from the Nazis, Neera Kapur Badhwar also challenges the usual dualism of egoism and altruism. "[The rescuers'] unambiguous sense of themselves as part of a common humanity gave them *both* an altruistic desire for affirming others *and* a self-interested desire for being true to this sense of themselves."[37] It was precisely the combination of egoism and altruism that allowed them to be wholeheartedly altruistic. Rousseau describes how children first come to care for others in response to those who care for them. His account of generosity and compassion explains both as extensions or developments of the basic sentiment of self-love.[38] Self-love is the foundation of goodness, not its enemy.

Instead of simply seeking to constrain egoism and encourage altruism, then, we ought to be trying to encourage healthy forms and discourage unhealthy forms of both. That, of course, requires the ability to distinguish between them. Does it matter whether altruism is accompanied by righteousness and bitterness or humility and contentment? Can we tell the difference between altruism and masochism, or a healthy ego and a narcissistic one? From the point of view of the "ethics of psychic health," the Giving Tree is the epitome of masochistic giving that only encourages the boy's narcissism. Might Socrates' altruism and apparent self-sacrifice serve as an alternative model? Consider that Socrates gives the Athenians something they need rather than everything they ask for. And his giving in no way diminishes him. It follows from his devotion to a certain way of life.

I began by asking, Is altruism good? And my answer is, Not always. Altruism is most likely to be excessive and unhealthy precisely when, thinking within the logic of the egoism/altruism dichotomy, its goodness is measured by the degree of self-sacrifice it demands. Kinds of self-sacrifice are not all alike. There is such a thing as "abject self-sacrifice":

> A person who leads such a self-sacrificial life has abdicated or never developed her own independent judgment and ends. If others did not wish to use her for their own ends, she would have nothing to live for. *Others* she sees as ends in themselves; herself, as only a means to their ends. Lacking a sense of self-worth, she has discounted the importance of her own interests. . . . It is this radical failure of interest in herself for her own sake—this radical lack of *self*—that explains why, in her, even altruism fails to be a virtue.[39]

Goodness requires recognizing the moral claims of the self as well as the moral claims of others.

A healthy altruism, by contrast, gives the self its due. Consider the biblical commandment, "Thou shalt love thy neighbor as thyself." The Reverend Joseph Butler, in 1729, commenting on this text in his sermons, argued not only that egoism and altruism are intertwined, but that appropriate self-love is also a moral demand.[40] In Kantian terms, to exempt oneself from the moral law is unjust. The point here is that this is true whether that exemption advantages *or disadvantages* oneself. Rousseau praises the Calvinist ministers of Geneva for their severity toward themselves and their gentleness toward others. But why are they not also deserving of gentleness?[41] He invokes an ideal of a person who is outraged at injustice toward others but indifferent when he himself is its victim. Why?[42] "To treat all people equally does not mean giving everyone but oneself equal concern."[43]

"Ethics of altruism" too often fail to recognize the claims of the self, and as a result they make the mistake of measuring goodness by the self-sacrifice it requires. So often, well-meaning people who are doing a great deal of good in the world torment themselves with doubt about the purity of their motives. If they find that serving others is relatively easy or even enjoyable, they wonder whether their giving "counts" as good. They wonder, "Isn't this just my way of being selfish?" Maybe it is; but why condemn this sort of selfishness?[44] Goodness should be measured not by the sacrifice required but by its contribution to human flourishing, one's own *and* others'. Imagine a physician who has been in private practice for thirty years and decides to work for Doctors Without Borders. She is assigned to Cambodia, where living conditions are difficult, but she finds the experience exciting and fulfilling—so much so that on her return she signs up for another assignment. Does her evident pleasure in this new role compromise the moral quality of her action? Would we prefer someone who did this sort of work out of a grudging sense of duty? Shouldn't we be aiming for precisely the sort of people who can find genuine satisfaction in helping others?

I hope it is clear that, by emphasizing the claims of the self, I am not encouraging selfishness and discouraging altruism. It would be perverse indeed to argue that what the world needs is more self-concern. In the Jewish tradition, there is no special merit in suffering as a result of giving and no need to impoverish oneself through charitable giving. But Maimonides warns that in the real world this is not the real problem, and one must not use this as an excuse for stinginess.[45] Similarly, I would not want to see the argument I am making used as an excuse for egoism. I have tried to show that the choice between egoism and altruism is a false one. An ethic of psychic health allows plenty of room for altruism and has the additional advantage of allowing us to distinguish between its truly beneficial forms and its harmful ones. Moreover, in emphasizing the claims of the self, I am not denying that responsibilities to others sometimes require real sacrifices. Everyone faces situations where primary obligations to others require us to forgo opportunities, desires, and needs of our own. But here it is important to recur to the difference between suffering and harm.[46] There is suffering that is not necessarily harmful, and there is sacrifice that falls short of "abject self-sacrifice." I argue not that there are no painful choices to be made, but only that we ought not to "commend in our everyday lives a love that seems so thoroughly to diminish the self."

Let me add one final reason that it is a mistake to view egoism and altruism as necessarily contending forces, with altruism identified with goodness and egoism considered as either immoral or amoral selfishness.

It leads us to neglect, misunderstand, and consequently underestimate cruelty. While it is true that seeking to benefit others (altruism) is opposed in some sense to seeking to benefit oneself (egoism), it is surely also opposed to seeking to harm others or taking pleasure in their pain (cruelty). But the altruism/egoism dichotomy blinds us to this second possibility. Here is what Hobbes had to say about cruelty: *"Cruelty, Contempt,* or little sense of the calamity of others, is that which men call CRUELTY; proceeding from security of their own fortune. For, that any man should take pleasure in other men's great harms, without other end of his own, I do not conceive it possible."[47]

Because Hobbes assumes that people act egoistically, to advantage themselves, he mistakenly identifies indifference with cruelty. Indifference is a particular form of selfishness, so it accords with Hobbes's assumption. But he cannot understand that people might "take pleasure in other men's great harms." Unlike Hobbes, I believe reality confirms that possibility far too often. Selfishness, after all, is not the worst of human evils. Moreover, we have seen that egoism and altruism are not simple opposites: benefiting others and benefiting oneself are often simultaneous. With this understanding in mind, rather than discouraging egoism and encouraging altruism, we might seek instead to combine their forces and enlist them in the battle against cruelty.

These are just some of the various reasons to expand our thinking beyond the dichotomy of altruism and egoism. We could be thinking differently about moral education, about what selfishness really is and is not, and about the many ways of giving to others. I have tried to show how an "ethic of psychic health" can open up these questions. At the same time, there is more than one "ethic of psychic health," and the relation between goodness and the health of the soul remains exceedingly complex. But *that* is the relation that must be understood if we ever want to fully understand the relation between one's own good and the good of others.

NOTES

1. Anna Freud calls this phenomenon "altruistic surrender." *The Ego and the Mechanisms of Defense*, rev. ed. (New York: International Universities Press, 1973), 132.
2. Shel Silverstein, *The Giving Tree* (New York: Harper Collins, 1964).
3. "The Giving Tree: A Symposium," *First Things*, January 1995, 22–45.
4. William Werpehowski, "Symposium," 41.
5. Aristotle, *Nichomachean Ethics*, 4.1119b.25–1122a.15, trans. Martin Ostwald (Upper Saddle River, NJ: Prentice-Hall, 1999).
6. Werpehowski, "Symposium," 41.

7. See below at note 45 for a comment on how giving is viewed in Judaism. Jacob Neusner and Alan J. Avery-Peck argue that altruism is a modern concept that would have made no sense within the framework of classical Judaism. See "Altruism in Classical Judaism," in *Altruism in World Religions,* ed. Jacob Neusner and Bruce Chilton (Washington, DC: Georgetown University Press, 2005).
8. "Babette's Feast" is another story that explores this tension, in Isak Dinesen, *"Babette's Feast" and Other Anecdotes of Destiny* (New York: Vintage, 1988).
9. For both points, see Charles Taylor, *A Secular Age* (Cambridge, MA: Belknap Press, 2007), 16–20.
10. For example, see Stephen Pot, Jill Neimark, and Otis Moss Jr., *Why Good Things Happen to Good People: How to Live a Longer, Healthier, Happier Life by the Simple Act of Giving* (New York: Broadway, 2008).
11. Susan Wolf, "Moral Saints," *Journal of Philosophy* 79, no. 8 (August 1982): 419–39.
12. Jean Hampton, "Selflessness and the Loss of Self," in *Altruism,* ed. Ellen Frankel Paul, Fred D. Miller Jr., and Jeffrey Paul (Cambridge: Cambridge University Press, 1993), 146.
13. Robert Coles, *The Moral Life of Children* (Boston: Atlantic Monthly Press, 1986), 157–200.
14. Søren Kierkegaard, *The Sickness unto Death,* trans. Alastair Hanay (London: Penguin, 1989), 80–81n. Here is an example of what I've called the second alternative discussed above.
15. Philip Rieff, *Freud: The Mind of the Moralist* (Garden City, NY: Doubleday, 1961), 353.
16. Laurence Cooper, in his comments on this paper at our conference, criticized how much my account of Plato's position makes the identity of goodness and psychic health seem automatic, rather than an achievement. He sees that identity as resulting from the education of the desire to be noble, a desire that Glaucon and Adeimantus both possess. That desire, which is rooted in natural passion, can explain how regard for oneself can lead one to care for others. Noble action is both self-regarding and self-forgetting.
17. See Stanley Hauerwas's chapter in this volume, where he paraphrases Raimond Gaita's argument that "Socrates meant not that a person who lives virtuously could not suffer, but that, even in their suffering people who see their life in the light of a certain kind of love, a love of philosophy, could not be harmed" (94).
18. At least for the philosopher, who turns out to be the just man. Whether Socrates' argument holds for the rest of us is not at all clear. See 34 below.
19. Bruno Bettelheim points out that Freud used the German word for "soul," but his English translator avoided the term, generally substituting "mind." Bettelheim, *Freud and Man's Soul* (New York: Alfred A. Knopf, 1983), 4, 12–13, 70–78.
20. Sigmund Freud, *The Ego and the Id,* trans. Joan Riviere, ed. James Strachey (New York: Norton, 1960), 26–27.
21. Freud, *Ego and the Id,* 44. Friedrich Nietzsche also sees the connection between cruelty toward the self and altruism: "Only the bad conscience, only the will to self-maltreatment provided the conditions for the *value* of the unegoistic." Nietzsche, *On the Genealogy of Morals,* trans. Walter Kaufmann (New York: Vintage Books, 1967), second essay, sec. 18, 88.

22. Sigmund Freud, *Civilization and Its Discontents,* trans. and ed. James Strachey (New York: Norton, 1961), 70–71.

23. Freud, *Ego and the Id,* 44–45.

24. Philip Rieff, ed., *Character and Culture* (New York: Collier Books, 1963), 179–81.

25. Sigmund Freud, *The Future of an Illusion,* trans. and ed. James Strachey (New York: Norton, 1961), 41; my emphasis.

26. Freud, *Ego and the Id,* 15.

27. Rieff, *Mind of the Moralist,* 358.

28. For critiques of this view, which also document its prevalence, see Roy Baumeister, Laura Smart, and Joseph M. Borden, "Relation of Threatened Egotism to Violence and Aggression: The Dark Side of High Self-Esteem," *Psychological Review* 103, no. 1 (January 1996): 5–33, and William Damon, *Greater Expectations: Overcoming the Culture of Indulgence in Our Homes and Schools* (New York: Free Press, 1996).

29. Self psychology, a post-Freudian development in psychoanalytic thinking associated with the work of Heinz Kohut, focuses on the formation of the self through relationships with others rather than on the management of instinctual drives.

30. See notes 10 and 28 above.

31. Ruth W. Grant, *Hypocrisy and Integrity* (Chicago: University of Chicago Press, 1997), 75–88.

32. Richard Weissbourd, *The Parents We Mean to Be: How Well-Intentioned Parents Undermine Children's Moral and Emotional Development* (Boston: Houghton Mifflin, 2009), chap. 5.

33. The term altruism was invented by Auguste Comte. The pair egoism/altruism has come to replace self-interest/benevolence, which was common in the eighteenth century. Thomas Dixon, *The Invention of Altruism: Making Moral Meanings in Victorian Britain* (Oxford: British Academy, 2008), recounts how the new term reshaped moral understandings in Victorian Britain.

34. Experimental studies of altruism invariably use this model. Typical examples are studies of "the ultimatum game" and "the dictator game," where altruism is measured by the amount of money subjects are willing to give to other subjects under various conditions.

35. See Dinesen, "Babette's Feast."

36. Such identifications are sometimes healthy and sometimes not. Coles, *Moral Life of Children,* 164–69.

37. Neera Kapur Badhwar, "Altruism versus Self-Interest: Sometimes a False Dichotomy," in *Altruism,* ed. Ellen Frankel Paul, Fred D. Miller Jr., and Jeffrey Paul (Cambridge: Cambridge University Press, 1993), 114.

38. "But when the strength of an expansive soul makes me identify myself with my fellow, and I feel that I am, so to speak, in him, it is in order not to suffer that I do not want him to suffer. . . . Love of men derived from love of self is the principle of human justice." Jean-Jacques Rousseau, *Émile,* trans. Allan Bloom (New York: Basic Books, 1979), 235n. See also 212–13, 220ff., and 291, where Rousseau speaks of "the temptation of doing good." For a contemporary discussion of why we so often fail to recognize the pleasures of kindness, see Adam Phillips and Barbara Taylor, *On Kindness* (London: Hamish Hamilton, 2009).

39. Badhwar, "Altruism versus Self-Interest," 117.

40. Joseph Butler, *Fifteen Sermons Preached at the Rolls Chapel* (Cambridge: Hilliard and Brown, 1827; reproduced, Virginia Theological Seminary, 2005), sermons 11 and 12.

41. "Letter to the Republic of Geneva," in *Jean-Jacques Rousseau, The Basic Political Writings* (Indianapolis, IN: Hackett, 1987), 31.

42. Grant, *Hypocrisy and Integrity*, 173.

43. Hampton, "Selflessness and the Loss of Self," 164.

44. As Laurence Cooper remarked in his conference comments, "The value of a self-interested action depends upon the value of the self."

45. My thanks to Rabbi John Friedman for this reference. Maimonides, Mishnah Torah, book 7, "Seeds," chap. 10.

46. See note 17 above.

47. Thomas Hobbes, *Leviathan* (New York: Collier Books, 1962), 53.

THREE

Are Moral Conversions Possible?

David B. Wong

The hopeful among us would like to believe in the possibility of moral conversion.[1] Here I discuss what warrant there is for hope. By "moral conversion," I mean a significant change for the better in an adult's moral commitments and actions, most typically a change from an unremarkable or poor moral record to an admirable one. Such conversions are often construed as triggered by an experience or a series of experiences that reveals to the agent something he had not seen or felt before. I use the term "conversion" with full awareness that to some it might suggest a religious conversion. I accept a parallel insofar as a moral conversion brings about a dramatic transformation in the way the agent construes the meaning of his life. I do not mean to suggest other parallels that might be drawn, based on the experience of some during religious conversion that they are taken, without any intention on their part, by something much greater than themselves, in a way that defies explanation by psychology or other human sciences. My approach is to ask whether moral conversions, as I have defined them, really happen, and how they happen if they do. These two questions are tied together. Whether we think such conversions happen depends on whether we think we have a plausible conception of how they happen. Moral conversions cannot be recorded as matters of objective observation, independent of what we think the agent's motivations were and how they changed. And most cases of apparent or possible conversion are subject to multiple interpretations of the agent's motivations and of what, if any, change occurred.

I will examine three cases of apparent moral conversion, try to interpret the agents' motives, and draw some speculative conclusions about moral conversion. The first case is from a film about a fictional drab functionary of the East German regime who ends up trying to save the people he is assigned to spy on. The film expresses our very human hopes for the possibility of conversion, but I shall discuss questions that critics have raised about its plausibility. My discussion will lead to the second case, the real-life story of Oskar Schindler, who is credited with saving the lives of over a thousand Jews during the Nazi occupation of Poland. Schindler's conversion highlights the effects of repeated exposure to evil and shows how his independence from authority structures, together with his charm and roguish character, may have suited him for deceiving, cajoling, and bribing Nazi officials in order to save lives. The third case is about a leader of the Ku Klux Klan who improbably became friends with a militant black activist during the desegregation of the public schools in Durham, North Carolina. The Klan leader's desire for social acceptance, his independence of mind, and his fundamental decency (I am very surprised to be writing these words!) play a key role in his conversion. I will weave reflections taken from these works with theoretical and empirical work on the nature of emotion and its relation to cognitive and perceptual capacities. We may not know enough to draw definitive conclusions about the possibility of moral conversion and how it works, but there is enough for some speculation that bears further investigation.

A FICTIONAL STASI MAN

The film *The Lives of Others* (2006) is about Gerd Wiesler, who works for the Stasi, the secret police of East Germany. Wiesler is assigned to find incriminating material on a prominent playwright and a distinguished actress who is the playwright's lover. He listens to their conversations, telephone calls, and lovemaking. Gradually he undergoes a transformation and tries to protect the couple from exposure to his own organization. We are left to infer what could have brought about such a change. Wiesler is depicted as a tightly self-controlled, by-the-book functionary who believes in the necessity and importance of his job. However, he learns that a government official had him assigned to the case so that the official could have the playwright's lover for himself. Wiesler becomes disillusioned with the Stasi and with his own role as the cat's-paw of a powerful man motivated by nothing more than grubby lust. He appears to be an excruciatingly lonely man with an eroding rationale for the job that has given purpose to his life. In this condition, it appears plausible that he is moved by the purpose of the people he is assigned to spy on. The imagined case of Wiesler illustrates clearly that aspect of moral conversion that parallels religious conversion: someone who has lost the only thing that gave meaning to his life finds new meaning in protecting those who are living out an alternative to the ideology of the regime. He eavesdrops on the playing of a "Sonata for a Good Man," of which it is said that anyone who really listens to it cannot be other than a good man, and he comes to have feelings for the actress that are mixed with the impulse to comfort and protect her. In the end, his efforts to protect the couple end very badly for the actress, but when the East German regime collapses and Stasi surveillance records are made available to their victims, the playwright discovers Wiesler's efforts to protect them. The film ends with Wiesler finding a book written by the playwright, dedicated to a "Good Man." When the clerk asks whether he wants the book wrapped as a gift, Wiesler smiles and says, "It's for me."

In an essay on the film, Anna Funder, author of a book on the Stasi, argues that it is a beautiful fantasy that could not have happened. One of her reasons is that totalitarian systems control their own agents through internal surveillance and division of tasks. Rather than assigning surveillance to a primary agent and a subordinate, as depicted in the film, the assignment is given to many agents, each charged with only a piece of the total operation; each piece of information is checked and cross-checked. No individual Stasi agent could have fooled the system in the way Wiesler did. Another of Funder's reasons for thinking the movie's events impossible is that in her experience no Stasi man ever wanted to save people from the system. Institutional coercion made them all into "true believers; it shrank their consciences and heightened their tolerance for injustice and cruelty 'for the cause.'" The director of the film, Florian Henckel von Donnersmarck, responded to such criticisms by saying that he did not want to tell a true story but rather tried to express belief in humanity and explore how someone might have behaved. In his "director's statement" accompanying press releases for the film, Donnersmarck wrote, "More than anything else, *The Lives of Others* is a human drama about the ability of human beings to do the right thing, no matter how far they have gone down the wrong path." Funder replied: "This is an uplifting thought. But what is more likely to save us from going down the wrong path again is recognising how human beings can be trained and forced into faceless systems of oppression, in which conscience is extinguished." Donnersmarck cited *Schindler's List* as a justification for his own film. But Funder quotes Dr. Hubertus Knabe, director of the memorial museum about the former East German regime, as commenting, "There was a Schindler. There was no Wiesler."[2]

The factors Funder cites do indeed seem to reduce the possibility of a real-life Wiesler, and they are not unrelated. The coercive, diminishing effect of an institution like the Stasi is heightened by mechanisms that reduce knowledge of what one is really doing and, at the same time, exact a high cost for indulging one's curiosity. Even the relatively optimistic movie includes an incident portraying the constant vigilance for wrong attitudes that pervaded the Stasi agency. In a relaxed moment, an agent starts to tell a joke about the government. When he hesitates, realizing that a superior is listening, he is encouraged to finish the joke and made to feel that it will be taken in good humor. The viewer later finds out that the joke was really on the agent when he and a by-then disgraced Wiesler find themselves together in the basement of a Stasi building, performing the mindless task of steaming open envelopes.

Work in psychology on how situations influence individuals' behavior seems to support the pessimistic side of the argument about *The Lives of Others*. Subjects of the famous Milgram experiments were led to believe they were taking part in an investigation of the effects of escalating electric shocks administered to a "learner" (hired by the experimenters to play the role) every time he gave a wrong answer to a test of learning and memory. The shocks were not real, but the learner, who deliberately kept making mistakes, acted as if the shocks were real and increasingly painful, up to voltage levels marked "danger: severe shock" and "xxx." In Milgram's first set of experiments, 65 percent of participants administered the maximum voltage, though many were extremely uncomfortable doing so; at some point every participant paused and questioned the experiment, and some said they would give back the money they were paid for participating. Only one steadfastly refused to administer shocks before the 300-volt level. Milgram gives a revealing summary of the experiment:

> I set up a simple experiment at Yale University to test how much pain an ordinary citizen would inflict on another person simply because he was ordered to by an experimental scientist. Stark authority was pitted against the subjects' [participants'] strongest moral imperatives against hurting others, and, with the subjects' [participants'] ears ringing with the screams of the victims, authority won more often than not. The extreme willingness of adults to go to almost any lengths on the command of an authority constitutes the chief finding of the study and the fact most urgently demanding explanation.
>
> Ordinary people, simply doing their jobs, and without any particular hostility on their part, can become agents in a terrible destructive process. Moreover, even when the destructive effects of their work become patently clear, and they are asked to carry out actions incompatible with fundamental standards of morality, relatively few people have the resources needed to resist authority.[3]

More recently, in Philip Zimbardo's Stanford prison experiment, Stanford undergraduates played the roles of prisoners and guards in a mock prison. The students quickly internalized their roles to the extent that one-third of the "guards" were judged to have exhibited genuine sadistic tendencies and many "prisoners" suffered emotional trauma. Zimbardo ended the experiment early, but only after a graduate student (who was later to become his wife) voiced strenuous moral objections. The similarities between the experiment and the torture and abuse that occurred in Abu Ghraib prison during the Iraq War were not lost on Zimbardo, who testified in defense of one of the prosecuted prison guards.[4]

Some philosophers have used studies such as the Milgram and Stanford experiments to question the viability of traditional ethical ideals of cultivating a stable good character. They argue that human character traits are liable to be extremely situation sensitive and hence that our ethical behavior is highly dependent on the right context.[5] But there were subjects in the Milgram experiment who disobeyed the authority figure, and student "guards" in the Stanford experiment who did not behave sadistically. Milgram himself offered an explanation of the unexpected frequency of compliance to authority in his experiments, which was the adaptive value of the capacity to fit into social hierarchy. This capacity, in Milgram's view, is activated when a person is placed in certain circumstances: for example, perception of a legitimate authority that seems relevant to the situation at hand (an experimenter in a white lab coat who greets participants and explains what is to be done), the absence of a competing authority, and entry into the authority system (a laboratory, a space the experimenter seems to "own").[6] Contrary to the radical situationist claim that there are no character traits,[7] Milgram's own explanation of the willingness to administer painful and apparently dangerous electric shocks suggests a kind of trait that evolutionary theory might lead us to expect in human beings. The trait of willingness to fit into social hierarchy is activated under certain conditions, and understanding those conditions might help us understand why some people disobeyed the experimenter and stopped administering shocks to the "bad" learner.

The one person who disobeyed and stopped before administering 300 volts is vividly portrayed as an extremely fastidious, crusty instructor of the Old Testament at a major divinity school. He is one of the few to question the experimenter's claim that it is "absolutely essential" to go on administering the shocks and that there would be "no permanent tissue damage" to the "learner." Moreover, it is not so much that he questions the necessity of obeying some authority: at one point he declares that he will "take orders" from the "learner" to stop, and when he later is told the point of the experiment and asked the most effective way to strengthen resistance to inhumane authority, he answers that taking God as the ultimate authority will trivialize human authority.[8] Indeed, in reading Milgram's various portraits of particular people who disobeyed and stopped and those who obeyed to the end, I am struck both by what they have in common—a tendency to comply with authority under the right conditions—and by the individuality that allows those who obey to the end to do so in different ways and with different attitudes toward what they have done, whereas others resist and stop administering shocks at various points in the learning trials. The individual enters into the explanation as soon as we inquire into why obedience or why disobedience. It cannot all be the situation, for the situation is a relatively crude factor that is filtered through the individual's perceptions and that interacts with his temperament and traits. The situationists may be right in holding that there are very few "global" character traits that persist over the widest variety of situations, but into this variety the individual does carry tendencies that are more likely to be activated given this or that kind of situation. There are at the very least such "local" character traits that crucially go into explaining what an individual thinks, feels, and decides to do.

The debate over the plausibility of *The Lives of Others*, however, draws attention to the importance of how situations *interact* with character traits and how they might constrain action that might otherwise follow from certain traits. Recall Funder's point that institutional coercion "shrank" the consciences of Stasi agents to the extent that she never encountered one who ever wanted to save people from the system. That institutional coercion was especially potent in its effect on agents in whom the motivation to fit into social hierarchy was already strong. And for those agents whose motivation was weaker, the internal surveillance of the Stasi agency provided the incentive of self-preservation.

The urge to fit into social hierarchy can result in a lot of good. In a study of those who rescued Jews in Holland and France during World War II, Michael Gross emphasizes the factors of organization, material support, and supporting social networks as necessary for sustaining rescue attempts, which in Western Europe were generally collective rather than purely individual efforts.[9] The historical record of such attempts reveals the key role of strong clerical and secular leaders who relied on their perceived legitimate authority to persuade and cajole prospective participants in Jewish rescue. Gross found that rescue leaders in Holland attributed their success to the general climate of trust in villages that eliminated the presence of traitors and the availability of material resources to reimburse villagers for their expenses. Both factors reduced the cost of action.

Situational factors, then, condition and constrain individual choice, motivation, and action, for good and evil. But the Milgram experiment, while suggesting the power of authority structures over many people, also reveals that not everyone is equally susceptible. As Hubertus Knabe observed, there was a Schindler, even if there was no Wiesler. It is a pity that the real is so often ambiguous and hard to read.

A REAL SCHINDLER WHO MUST
NEVERTHELESS BE INTERPRETED

The difficulty of overcoming oppressive structures that shrink the consciences of people who might otherwise experience a moral conversion increases one's interest in the actual story of Schindler, which became widely known through Thomas Keneally's novel *Schindler's Ark* (republished as *Schindler's List*), later made into a Hollywood movie. Keneally draws heavily from the remembrances of the people who were saved by Schindler or who knew him, as well as from Schindler's own accounts of the period, but even light fictionalizing raises the question of how much the novel reveals Schindler's inner life and motivation. A massive study by the historian David M. Crowe provides additional information.[10] In what follows, I want to engage in some (I hope) informed speculation about what happened to prompt what Schindler did in saving one thousand Jews.

Schindler was the son of a heavy-drinking, abusive father who eventually left his wife and family for another woman. Schindler detested his father, but he himself became a heavy-drinking womanizer who deceived his wife Emilie, fathering one and possibly two children by another woman.[11] Significantly, Emilie always admired his kindness and his willingness to help others. Schindler's family was Sudeten (southern) German and lived near Czechoslovakia. Keneally reports that Schindler grew up in a multiethnic neighborhood, next door to the family of a Reform or liberal rabbi, and was a playmate of the rabbi's two sons.[12]

Sudeten Germans constituted a significant cultural and political presence in Czechoslovakia, many of them supporting pro-Nazi parties. Schindler became an agent for Abwehr, the counterespionage and counterintelligence branch of the Wehrmacht (the German armed forces in Nazi Germany from 1935 to 1945). Abwehr made contact with Sudeten Germans in Czechoslovakia and established a network of agents in the country. However, the Germans' stance toward Czechoslovakia before World War II and their activities there were far from unified. Tensions and antagonisms among certain groups in the German military such as Abwehr, on the one hand, and the

German SD or Security Service and Gestapo or Secret State Police, on the other hand, played out in their actions toward a pro-Nazi Czech political party, the SdP. Abwehr backed the "traditionalists" in that party, who initially professed the intention to work within the Czech political system to protect the interests of Sudeten Germans. The SD and Gestapo supported the radicals in the SdP, who favored union of the Sudeten German areas in Czechoslovakia with Germany. Schindler seems not to have had any strong political convictions about these matters. He became involved with Abwehr initially through a liaison with a woman, then later for the money. As an Abwehr agent he grew to distrust the SD and the Gestapo, yet he learned to work with them because of their intelligence capabilities. He acquired ties with anti-Hitler Abwehr officers, including the deputy of the head of Abwehr. The deputy was very much like Schindler: elegant, dapper, daring, without fear, agile, and lacking caution.

At the start of World War II Schindler moved to Kraków in Poland to make his fortune. He soon acquired an enamelware factory and landed contracts to produce mess kits for the war effort. He also aimed to make massive amounts of money in the black market economy of occupied Poland. At the beginning of the war, Schindler had an impressive knack for knowing the right people and an ability to wheel and deal. He took lovers, and though he lied to his wife about his affairs, he made little effort to conceal them. At the end of the war he was still the same Schindler, but he had taken great personal risks and had used his talents and connections, his "friendships" with various SS officers, and his knowledge of whom to bribe to remove Jews from the Plaszów concentration camp for work and protection at his factory.

The contrast with Wiesler the fictional Stasi agent is provocative. Whereas Wiesler is an exemplar of the gray organization man, Schindler was a rule bender. He was equipped to deal with the structures of German occupation of Poland, but he was not a creature of that structure. He had the skills to manipulate actors within these structures, and this may have exempted him from many of the coercive, diminishing effects Stasi agents were subject to, even—or perhaps especially—those with the potential to question what they were doing. Very likely his ambiguous relationship with the SD and Gestapo in Czechoslovakia before the war had not only equipped him with contacts but also cultivated or strengthened his disposition to distrust structures of power yet work within them. In Milgram's terms, while Schindler "entered" the German authority structure in Poland, he had never fallen fully within its grip but rather maneuvered inside it and made deals. Perhaps no one but a charming rogue could have done what Schindler did, in the way he did it.

Yet how did he come to save a thousand Jews? Initially he hired Jewish workers because they were cheaper than non-Jewish Polish workers. Then he hired still more because they proved reliable and efficient. Later, Crowe describes how Schindler's motives appeared to shift.

> He convinced the monstrous Amon Göth, the commandant of the Plaszów forced labor camp, to allow him to build a sub-camp with barracks and other facilities for his Jewish workers. Schindler even provided housing for 450 Jewish workers from nearby German factories. He became the protector of his Jewish workers, keeping them healthy and well fed. When other factory owners began to shut down their factories and return to the Reich with their profits in the face of the westward march of Stalin's Red Army, Schindler arranged to open a new sub-camp and factory, Brünnlitz, near his home town of Svitay, where he employed over 1,000 Jewish workers, most of whom survived the war.[13]

By the time Schindler began to plan this transfer to Brünnlitz, Crowe writes, he was fully committed to saving not only the workers from his own factory but also those from other factories. Crowe states that it is difficult to pinpoint a moment when Schindler's sole or primary motivation became to protect his Jewish workers.[14]

Keneally constructs a dramatic moment to portray Schindler's conversion. Schindler views the liquidation of the Kraków ghetto from an adjacent hilltop. A toddler dressed in red compels his attention. A guard gently corrects her wandering path and nudges her back into line, but other soldiers are shooting women and children on the sidewalk. Schindler watches a mother and a young boy retreat from the slaughter under a windowsill, and with intolerable fear for them and "terror in his blood," he watches soldiers execute them.

> At last Schindler slithered from his horse, tripped, and found himself on his knees hugging the trunk of a pine tree. The urge to throw up his excellent breakfast was, he sensed, to be suppressed, for he suspected it meant that all his cunning body was doing was making room to digest the horrors of Krakusa Street.
>
> Later in the day, after he had absorbed a ration of brandy, Oscar understood . . . they permitted witnesses, such witnesses as the red toddler, because they believed all the witnesses would perish too.[15]

Though Keneally's description of this dramatic moment is fictional, it shows a good novelist's sense for how human beings are deeply affected by traumatic events. Consider recent work in psychology and neuroscience suggesting a two-track model of the way human beings process and react to information about their environments. Both tracks can appear in the complex course of having an emotion. One track enables human beings to process information very quickly, beneath the level of consciousness.[16] Emotions very often involve this fast processing, which takes the form of an assessment or appraisal of something or someone in terms of what matters to the agent (consider fear of an animal or anger at another person), along with changes in physiological state such as motor activity (facial expression) and changes in the autonomic nervous system (quickening of pulse, rise in blood pressure) that serve as signals to others ("I am not a threat" or "back off!"), as preparation for appropriate action (flight or fight), or both.

However, a slower, deliberate, and conscious mode of processing can occur as one is experiencing an emotion. Subsequent to the initial fast response to something or someone, one can reappraise the object of emotion, making specific discriminations of how or how much it is to be feared, for example. It may involve complex forms of reflection involving the self (Why am I feeling this way? or What's out there that's causing me to react like this?). This slower track can result in conscious choice or modification of the mode of action that is tightly connected to the fast response (an involuntary startle response to a loud bang may lead one to do an auditory and visual scan of the environment for possible threats and decide to take cover).

Keneally's description of Schindler's watching the slaughter with "terror in his blood," then sliding down from his horse to hug a tree, ready to throw up his breakfast, is a vivid way to convey the bodily response to an event with such horrifying emotional impact. His reluctance to yield to the urge to throw up manifests a reluctance to absorb more of the horror into his body. And the description of Schindler's subsequent reflective assessment of what he saw illustrates Jenefer Robinson's point that an emotion typically extends over time[17] and that the initial affective bodily response may focus attention on the apparent cause and reassess its significance — in this case that the slaughter will be ongoing and unrelenting.

Consider in this regard Antonio Damasio's well-known proposal that efficacious rational decision making with personal and social import (judging what to do in matters that affect one's welfare and that of others, and then acting on one's judgment, as opposed, say, to simply making a judgment in a hypothetical situation with no practical decision in the offing) requires an emotional component.[18] This component is based on the feeling of bodily changes, a "somatic marker," that gets associated with representations of scenarios that pose possible courses of action. For example, Damasio asks you to imagine being a business owner who must decide whether to meet with a possible client. The potential client can bring you valuable business but is the archenemy of your best friend. As you consider whether to meet, multiple imaginary scenes flash in and out of your imagination: being seen in the client's company and jeopardizing your friendship; not meeting and preserving the friendship; and so forth. Damasio's view is that you resolve the impasse not by performing a cost-benefit calculation on the available action options but by responding to your gut feelings, say, when you imagine your friend's face as he sees you with his archenemy.[19] The association of these gut feelings with imagined scenarios is a product of your individual learning from the consequences of past violations of trust. Somatic markers eliminate some options from consideration, disadvantage some, and highlight others positively. According to Damasio, the gut feelings themselves do not come from deliberation. Indeed, if they did they could not serve one of their primary functions of reducing the array of options we have to consciously consider and evaluate. Relative to all that the world throws at us, the amount of information and options our working memories can hold in conscious awareness at any given time is pitifully small. Somatic markers help us evaluate information and options beneath the level of consciousness.

In the light of Damasio's theory of somatic markers, Keneally's dramatization seems apt. In particular, the option of not doing anything about the slaughter became marked by violent sickness. It made not doing anything an option that was "silenced," one that could not be considered. John McDowell has written perceptively on the way a virtue in a person might manifest itself in certain situations, "silencing" other considerations rather than outweighing or overriding them. Considerations that would otherwise provide an agent with reasons for action thus lack practical significance when set against the considerations virtue requires that one attend to.[20] Being a good friend, then, might involve having negative affective valence attached to the thought of betraying one's friend and *silencing* the thought of financial gain, rather than merely outweighing or overriding it in a conscious cost-benefit calculation. If one is a good friend, in other words, certain actions toward one's friend become unthinkable—it makes one sick to one's stomach to think of doing them. Damasio's somatic marker theory might help explain why the negative valence attached to betrayal might silence an otherwise significant consideration of financial gain.

McDowell's example combines two powerful primal motivations that can be turned toward moral ends in human beings. The first motivation is attachment. Studies of the physiological mechanisms that might underlie an emotional concern for others have identified a role for the neurohormone oxytocin. In animals, oxytocin promotes attachment to offspring and between monogamous mammals and cohabiting sexual partners. Neuroscientists have speculated that the neural mechanisms underlying the motivating emotions of sexual pairing and child rearing also get recruited for other social bonding, such as friendship.[21] Human studies have shown that oxytocin promotes a temporary attachment between strangers, increasing trust, reciprocity, and generosity.[22] Anonymous charitable giving based on moral beliefs corresponds to activation of reward systems in frontolimbic brain networks that are also activated by food, sex, drugs, and money. Such giving is also linked to networks that control the release of oxytocin and another neurohormone, vasopressin, also implicated in attachment between monogamous mammals and cohabiting sexual partners. One speculation emerging from this particular study is that the capacity to feel attachment to social causes, such as donating to charity, emerged from a coevolution of genes and culture that allowed primitive reward and social attachment systems to operate beyond the immediate spheres of kinship, thus enabling human beings to form friendships, to trust and cooperate with strangers, and to directly link motivational value to abstract collective causes, principles, and ideologies.[23]

The other primal motivation suggested by McDowell's example is moral disgust. As well as feeling bad for a friend one has betrayed, one might very well feel disgust at oneself for betraying him. Humans share protodisgust reactions with nonhuman animals, all showing distaste and nausea from exposure to potentially toxic foods and odors, and these reactions clearly have adaptive functions.[24] In humans, nonsocial disgust gets extended to the social realm, resulting in social disapproval, moralistic aggression, and willingness to punish moral norm violators even at significant cost to oneself.[25] While such moralized disgust can have a positive and even essential function in sustaining social cooperation, it quite possibly also plays a role in primitive dislike of groups that differ from one's own in physical appearance or in cultural norms.

Consider now an act that provokes both empathy for another whom one is attached to and disgust at the perpetrator of the act. The effect of these combined primal motivations will be powerful. It may be no accident that human beings are often most effective in overcoming differences between themselves when united against a common enemy. Consider Keneally's depiction of the terror Schindler felt for the victims of the Kraków liquidation, combined with his nausea on witnessing the brutality.

Related to this point is something the real Schindler did say about his realization that he had to do something. In 1964 he was asked on German television why he had intervened on behalf of the Kraków Jews. Schindler said: "The persecution of the Jews in the General Government in Poland meant that we could see horror emerging gradually in many ways. In 1939 they were forced to wear the Jewish Stars and people were herded and shut up in ghettoes. Then in the years 1941 and 1942 there was plenty of public evidence of pure sadism, with people behaving *like pigs* [my emphasis]. I felt the Jews were being destroyed. I had to help them. There was no choice."[26] There was of course a choice that others made not to do anything or to do worse. But perhaps Schindler was saying that those options had been eliminated for him, given the effect of what he had seen. The real Schindler seems to have witnessed or heard of many acts of gradually increasing horror and then of pure sadism, and this seems the more plausible, if less dramatic, scenario of his conversion to a person committed to sheltering and then saving Jews in his factory. The option of not doing anything faded from his view rather than disappearing suddenly, perhaps as it became increasingly marked with brutality and compassion for the victims he was increasingly identifying with.

In an interview with the Canadian journalist Herbert Steinhouse, Schindler recounted two of the accumulated events that played this role. They took place in Schindler's Emalia enamelware factory and involved SS officers who came to inspect the factory.

> On one occasion, three SS men walked onto the factory floor without warning, arguing among themselves. "I tell you, the Jew is even lower than an animal," one was saying. Then, taking out his pistol, he ordered the nearest Jewish worker to leave his machine and pick up some sweepings from the floor. "Eat it," he barked, waving his gun. The shivering man choked down the mess. "You see what I mean," the SS man explained to his friends as they walked away. "They eat anything at all. Even an animal would never do that."
>
> Another time, during an inspection by an official SS commission, the attention of the visitors was caught by the sight of the old Jew, Lamus, who was dragging himself across the factory courtyard in an utterly depressed state. The head of the commission asked why the man was so sad, and it was explained to him that Lamus had lost his wife and only child a few weeks earlier during the evacuation of the ghetto. Deeply touched, the commander reacted by ordering his adjutant to shoot the Jew "so that he might be reunited with his family in heaven," then he guffawed and the commission moved on. Schindler was left standing with Lamus and the adjutant.

"Slip your pants down to your ankles and start walking," the adjutant ordered Lamus. Dazed, the man did as he was told.

"You are interfering with all my discipline here," Schindler said desperately. The SS officer sneered.

"The morale of my workers will suffer. Production for der Vaterland will be affected." Schindler blurted out the words. The officer took out his gun.

"A bottle of schnapps if you don't shoot him," Schindler almost screamed, no longer thinking rationally.

"Stimmt!" To his astonishment, the man complied. Grinning, the officer put the gun away and strolled arm in arm with the shaken Schindler to the office to collect his bottle. And Lamus, trailing his pants along the ground, continued shuffling across the yard, waiting sickeningly for the bullet in his back that never came.[27]

It is difficult to avoid the conclusion that a series of emotionally compelling experiences contributed to Schindler's conversion. These experiences helped produce both a change in Schindler's motivation to save people from the Nazis and a change in his beliefs about what he morally had to do. Sometimes people acquire new motivation to do what they already believe they morally must do. It might be thought that Schindler's case fits this description because of his history of kindness and willingness to help others.[28] These traits indicate a capacity for compassion that made him receptive to the horrors he witnessed and enabled him to conclude that he had no choice but to try to help people who would otherwise be murdered. But a willingness to help others daily in "normal" life does not amount to a willingness to risk one's life and fortune to save innocent lives. Nothing Schindler did before or after the war supports attributing to him anything like such a standing moral project. What he did during the war seems to have been a more particular response to what was happening around him, and though he believed in the rightness and necessity of what he did, that belief seemed to be as much a product of his emotional experiences as was his motivation to act on it.

Any plausible explanation of Schindler's conversion must include the mixture and ambivalence of his motives and their evolution over time. When he first brings Jews into his Emalia factory, evidence of Schindler's self-interested calculation is apparent. Even when he later becomes clearly committed to saving lives at great risk and cost to himself, his regular reference to "his"[29] Jews reveals how his actions might have fed into a kind of self-serving image he held of himself. One might take this as evidence that his motives did not at all contain concern for the people whose lives he saved, but this is to deny the complexity of human beings. Mixed motives can support one another and the actions they give rise to, so that neither the self-concerned nor the other-concerned motives need bear the weight of supporting those highly risky actions (see Ruth Grant's contribution to this volume on the issue of mixed motives). Still, the evolution of Schindler's motives is important for conceiving of his conversion as genuine. The risks he took and the length of time he stayed in the game of saving lives stave off the cynical conclusion that he was *merely* serving himself.

Schindler's "freelance" relationship with power structures also seems relevant in explaining his conversion. Rather than entering and being enveloped by Nazi power structures as Stasi agents were later to enter and be enveloped in the East German power structure, Schindler's history with Abwehr demonstrates a relative independence from authority structures that perhaps left him better able to absorb and to act on the full import of what he witnessed in Poland. Schindler's independence furthermore involved a capacity to deal with authority and use it for his own ends. His "entrepreneurial" qualities, his love of risk, his charm, and his ability to connect with powerful Nazi officials in an "old boy" fashion made it possible for him to conceive a way to help that very few others could have envisioned. Our abilities, or the lack of them, form our vision of what is practically possible for us, and that vision deeply affects what we see as right or wrong for us to try to do.

Nechama Tec attempts to identify characteristics generally shared by Christian rescuers of Jews in Nazi-occupied Poland (she mentions Schindler only once, in passing).[30] She distinguishes between "normative" altruism, which is helping behavior that is demanded, supported, and reinforced by one's society, and "autonomous" altruism, which is helping behavior that is not socially demanded, supported, and reinforced. Her conclusion is that most Christian rescuers in Poland had autonomous motivation, and moreover that they displayed a sense of being socially marginal (of not being fully integrated with their environment but of standing apart from it) and a desire to help others based on values learned in the family.[31] Schindler certainly displayed a sense of marginality with respect to the Nazi authority structure, but his hard-drinking, womanizing, and abusive father hardly laid the groundwork for the "family values" that Tec characterize as typical of rescuers' backgrounds.[32]

It would be premature, however, to conclude that moral conversion depends on a sense of being apart from one's social environment. In their well-known study of rescuers in Western and Eastern Europe, Samuel and Pearl Oliner found in Western Europe many who would fit into Tec's classification as normative altruists — ones who rescued in compliance with the social norms of individuals or groups close to them.[33] Michael Gross's study of rescuers in Holland and France also points to a more diverse array of motivations. Employing Lawrence Kohlberg's framework of stages of moral development, Gross found that a considerable number of rescuers had "conventional" motivations such as the desire to comply with social norms — for example, being aware that friends and neighbors were helping and fearing that they would disapprove if they did not help too. Another motivation was considering it important to listen to local authorities in the church or the resistance — and desiring to comply with religious norms — and fearing God's punishment or thinking that Christians have a special obligation to protect Jews. Even those rescuers who cited motivations that Kohlbergian theory would label as more advanced or "postconventional," such as the duty of democratic citizens to defend civil rights and social justice, tested as cognitively "immature." They tended to view justifications cast in terms of civic responsibility, rights, and justice as having greater legitimacy than other sorts of justifications only when they agreed with the positions being justified. Gross suggests that some rescuers' reference to such justifications might reflect their socialization into democratic norms but not necessarily greater cognitive development in moral judgment.[34]

Reflection on the varied results reported by Tec, Gross, and the Oliners supports the conclusion that circumstances strongly influenced the character profile of who became rescuers. In Poland, anti-Semitism was relatively intense and well entrenched, and Jewish rescue was not generally socially reinforced; moreover, Nazi control of that country was stronger than in Western Europe (and even here the strength and nature of Nazi control varied nationally and even locally). In that context, it makes sense that there would be fewer rescuers and that they would tend to display the sense of social marginality that Tec attributes to them. The situation in Poland contrasted with that in parts of Western Europe where social and religious norms favored Jewish rescue, and where weaker Nazi control made it more possible and somewhat less dangerous to engage in rescue (though of course still risky in varying degrees). The studies I have cited do not focus on rescuers who underwent the kind of conversion Schindler did, but it is reasonable to infer that, if situational factors influence the type of person who becomes a rescuer, they can influence who undergoes conversion.

Moreover, Schindler's relative independence from authority does not refute the more general point that individual character interacts with situational factors. Gross's point that Jewish rescue efforts typically depended on organization, infrastructure, and material resources is relevant here.

Ironically, many of these external necessities came from the German military, because Schindler's factories were thought to be essential for the war effort, and because Schindler's character enabled him to manipulate the system. Situational factors that interact with an individual's character also include other people. We cannot leave out the ways others were partners with Schindler in the project of saving lives. Focusing on Schindler springs from a desire to find "heroes" who demonstrate and model the hopeful belief in humanity that the director of *The Lives of Others* wanted to honor. Focusing on Schindler *alone* corresponds to a romantic conception of heroes as all the more courageous because they act alone. This is false to Schindler's story. To fully explain why Schindler acted as he did, moreover, the role of those Jews who conspired with him in saving lives is crucial. For example, Schindler admired and respected Itzhak Stern, the accountant who worked with him in the factory, for his ethical values and fearless willingness to help.[35]

Then there is Emilie, who demonstrated tremendous courage and a much less ambivalent commitment to saving lives than Oskar did. In a memoir she wrote with the aid of Erika Rosenberg, Emilie Schindler tells of an event that took place during the last weeks of the war when Oskar was away in Kraków. Emilie encountered Nazis transporting 250 Jews to a death camp, crowded into four railroad cars. She persuaded the Gestapo to send these Jews to the factory camp "with regard to the continuing war industry production." She recalled that they found the door bolts frozen solid, the men and women inside emaciated as skeletons and having to be carried out like so many carcasses of frozen beef. Throughout that night and many following, Emilie worked unceasingly on nursing them back from the brink, and most survived.[36] After the war, and after her separation from Oskar, Emilie lived in Buenos Aires, alone and in poverty until a German Argentinean newspaper reporter wrote that while Oskar, "Father Courage," had not been forgotten, Emilie, "Mother Courage," had been.[37]

It should be noted here that the *type* of conversion Schindler underwent, that is, the type of moral excellence he came to realize, is relevant to understanding how it happened. Lawrence Blum, in a seminal essay on moral exemplars, identifies Schindler as an exemplar of the *moral hero*: one who becomes engaged in a moral project of bringing about a great good or preventing a great evil; who acts to a great extent from morally worthy motives that are substantially embedded in his psychology (showing a depth of moral commitment and centrality within the system of his various motivations); who carries out the project in the face of risk or danger; and in whom unworthy desires, dispositions, sentiments, and attitudes are relatively absent.[38] The moral hero is different from another kind of exemplar who appears in the writings of Iris Murdoch, whom Blum calls the Murdochian paragon: one who lacks the moral project of a hero but who acts from morally worthy motives substantially embedded in her psychology and in whom there is relative absence of unworthy motives. As Blum interprets Murdoch's paragon, this person is good, humble, and selfless and displays a greater absence of unworthy motives than the moral hero. The hero's moral project counterbalances a more impure set of motivations. Furthermore, the hero's project need not persist over all or most of his life, though it should last for a substantial period. By contrast, the paragon's state of moral excellence must show greater persistence.[39]

Conversion to being a moral hero might be a significantly different process than conversion to being a Murdochian paragon. A person might be able to become one type of exemplar but not the other. Indeed, it seems difficult to envision the Schindler we know from World War II converting to the excellence of humility and selflessness for most of the rest of his life. It would have required a far greater, and far more unlikely, transformation of his character. The story of how Schindler became a moral hero, when seen with more detail, with less emphasis on his persona as a charming rogue, on the one hand, and as a man who risked his life and fortune to save lives on the other, appears less than miraculous. The conversion becomes intelligible as a fortuitous overlapping of character and circumstances: the basic capacity for compassion that his wife admired in him; his unusual independence from authority; the eye for moneymaking opportunities that led him into the factory venture; the charm that enabled him to manipulate Nazis officials; the organizational infrastructure of his factories; the German support of these factories that allowed him to shelter Jews in plain sight and keep them reasonably healthy; and others such as Itzhak Stern and Emilie Schindler with whom he collaborated and who also reinforced his compassion and courage. In Schindler's case, the discontinuities that make his story one of moral conversion are underlain by continuities that help to make the conversion intelligible.

A KLANSMAN'S CONVERSION

Here is another story involving a mixture of emotionally transformative experiences, continuities of character, other people who played important roles, and situational factors that helped turn a person in a morally better direction. It involves the agent's attitudes toward authority, but in this case the attitudes are substantially different from Schindler's. This story involves a friendship that developed between C. P. Ellis, the exalted cyclops of the Durham, North Carolina, Klavern of the Ku Klux Klan, and Ann Atwater, the most militant black woman in Durham. Of this pair of friends, I concentrate on Ellis because his change was by far the more dramatic (which of course does not imply that Atwater was less admirable). The context in which Ellis's and Atwater's friendship developed was Durham's attempt to desegregate its public schools in the 1970s. The two were elected to cochair a charrette, a series of meetings created to promote communication between black and white parents whose children attended a newly integrated school. Ellis more or less fell into this situation, not initially motivated by goodwill but more out of a desire to increase the respectability of the Klan, to keep an eye (and not a benevolent or helpful one) on the unfolding desegregation process, and to represent the "white" point of view.

Osha Gray Davidson's telling of Ellis's transformation includes an illuminating historical context that concerns the changing class structure of the Klan.[40] The Klan arose in 1866, created by white southerners of the higher social classes. Its leaders needed the support of lower-class whites, and to get it they encouraged the perception that whites were united against a common enemy, that the KKK, for example, would protect their families from the blacks.[41] By the time Ellis found the KKK, the upper-class whites had found more respectable organizations to join. The KKK was left to lower-class whites sharing a past of poverty and failure and a common enemy. The Klan served as an extended family and offered the promise of better days with white supremacy.[42] That for Ellis the Klan answered a strong need for acceptance and recognition is clear from a passage in which Davidson describes his feelings during the induction ceremony: "As he looked out at the rows of men welcoming him, he felt the old shame of poverty, failure, and purposelessness melt away. A lifetime of being an outsider was over. He felt blissfully submerged into a new and yet familiar community. The Klansmen were the descendants of failed farmers and broken mill hands just like himself."[43]

Ellis not only found a home in the Klan but was surprised to find that others respected him, and as he gained confidence, he spoke out more forcefully. He did not actively seek the leadership role, but once he became the exalted cyclops, he concluded largely on his own that the Klan should not worry so much about secrecy and should start effectively communicating its views. He went to city council meetings to take the Klan public.

When he begins participating in the charrette, things do not start out harmoniously. At the organizational meeting, C. P. shouts that the problem with Durham schools is "niggers." Ann Atwater shoots back that the problem is "stupid crackers like C. P. Ellis in Durham."[44] The organizer of the meeting, Bill Riddick, perceives Ellis as "hurting and hurtful, possessed of all the tedious, creaking, accumulated hatreds of the South, and yet guileless and—Riddick believed—essentially honorable, Klansman or not."[45] After agreeing to cochair the steering committee of the charrette, Ellis has a revelatory dinner meeting with Atwater:

> That she was capable of sitting in a chair in a restaurant and eating food was a revelation to him. Ann had ceased being human to C. P. years before; she existed only as a symbol of everything he hated about her race. . . . But Ann doing something so ordinary as eating a meal in a restaurant—this was beyond C. P.'s powers of imagination. . . . He could hear the grinding of her teeth, feel the warmth emanating from her body. He sniffed, and swore he caught the scent of her hair. It certainly wasn't sexual attraction that churned inside of him, but it wasn't exactly disgust either. Unable to bear the confusion of feelings any longer, C. P. offered some excuse and hurried from the restaurant.[46]

Davidson stresses Ellis's turmoil as he gets hostility from his fellow Klansmen and as a teacher taunts his son for having a Klansman father who loves "niggers." In a meeting of the charrette, Ellis becomes particularly interested in the comments of a black woman who charges that teachers and the school administration treated her children as if they were stupid troublemakers. He had been about to say the same thing about his children, that they were treated badly because they were "poor white trash." This experience happened repeatedly throughout the day. For the first time, he really listened to black people and was stunned to hear, over and over, his own concerns coming from their mouths: "When arguments among kids erupted at school, it was the working-class children—black and white—who were always blamed and punished."[47]

This led Atwater and Ellis to talk about how hard it was to raise children without much money, about how they were always having to tell their kids that they were just as good as kids from middle-class homes, and never to be ashamed of who they were. At the same time Atwater and Ellis confessed to each other they had to hide their own shame about not being better providers. They talked about the teachers' never letting their kids forget that they came from impoverished households. Their stories were so familiar that they could almost be interchangeable.

> C. P. couldn't believe what he was hearing. But even more amazing to him was what he was saying—and to whom. He was sharing his most intimate grievances, all of his doubts and failures, with the hated

Ann Atwater. The militant he usually referred to with a sneer as "that fat nigger." And yet, here they were, talking like old friends. As if she wasn't black at all, or he wasn't white, or as if all that didn't *matter*. He looked at her and it was as if he was seeing her for the first time. He was stunned by what he saw. Mirrored in her face were the same deeply etched lines of work and worry that marked his own face. And suddenly he was crying. The tears came without warning, and once started, he was unable to stop them. Ann was dumbfounded, but she reacted instinctively by reaching out and taking his hand in her own. She tried to comfort him, stroking his hand and murmuring, "It's okay, it's okay," as he sobbed. Then she, too, began to cry.[48]

Ellis came to the realization that it was not blacks who were holding poor whites down but wealthy white factory owners and businessmen, such as James "Buck" Duke, founding figure of Duke University. Ellis called for poor whites to unite against their real enemies, and with that he lost his place in the Klan.

As in Schindler's witnessing the vile and murderous acts of Nazis, emotionally transformative experiences seem to have played a key role in Ellis's conversion. Indeed, evoking emotion is the purpose of a charrette, conceived as a series of hours-long face-to-face meetings of a diverse group of people for working out their differences. In organizing the Durham charrette, Bill Riddick recognized that the "trick was to draw out people's deepest longings and fears, their frustrations and their dreams—while preventing these raw and antipodean emotions, once exposed, from combusting into violence."[49] One might think that Ellis's transformation as a result of these meetings was primarily cognitive and not emotional—coming to believe that black people eat in restaurants just like white people; that black people's children are victimized in schools just like poor white people's children; that both black and poor white parents feel shame for not being able to protect their children from such victimization; that "respectable" white people are happy to have poor whites as allies against blacks but not happy to have them as social equals. But Davidson's descriptions of the occasions when these insights hit home bring out the visceral nature of Ellis's realizations. It would be misunderstanding the nature of Ellis's conversion to regard it as primarily cognitive or to regard emotional transformations as mere consequences of cognitive gains. Ellis's intense emotional experiences broke down defenses against those insights. We have an emotional investment in preserving beliefs that give us comfort and security, and correspondingly we have an investment in overlooking, ignoring, and denying what undermines those beliefs. In the Klan, Ellis found a community that accepted and respected him, then looked to him for leadership. In the charrette, Ellis in effect found a new community that recognized him as a leader and with which he was able to share his "deepest longings and fears." Without that kind of experience, it is doubtful that the crucial changes in mere belief would have taken hold.

As in Schindler's case, character plays a crucial role in conversion. In contrast to Schindler and his relation to authority structures, what strikes one about Ellis is his earnestness, the satisfaction he evidently got from the Klan as a kind of extended family, and the desire to earn respectability that appears in people who are denied respect. Though Ellis might have seen himself as "socially marginal" in relation to respectable white society, he yearned for acceptance, not for manipulating authority structures to achieve his own ends. Before his conversion, his anger over his low status was directed at scapegoats in the black community, but Bill Riddick turned out to be right in seeing Ellis as "guileless" and "essentially honorable."[50] Furthermore, there is Ellis's capacity for independent thought. He recognizes that Klan meetings are simply the venting of resentment and anger and seeks to be proactive in reaching out to the "respectable" layers of Durham society. More important, he is able to recognize what he shares with Ann Atwater and the other black parents in the charrette. Another person might have noted the similarity but dismissed it by thinking that the black children and parents *deserved* the treatment they got from the schools. Perhaps Ellis's decency lay in his ability to now see a black person, formerly considered a kind of alien being, as another human being in much the same predicament as himself. Finally, Ellis's anger did not go away; it was redirected more accurately at the upper reaches of southern white society. Like Schindler, Ellis was capable of both compassion and moralized disgust. These are continuities of character that underlay his transformation.

There is also the set of situational factors that helped set up this transformation. Durham, along with the rest of the South, was changing. Integration became inevitable, at least for those who could not afford to send their children to private schools or move to parts of the metropolitan area where there weren't many black families. The national and local movements toward desegregation resulted in organization, infrastructure, and material resources that leaders could deploy. In his outreach for respectability, it is not miraculous that Ellis could have become involved in this community effort to deal with desegregation. As I indicated earlier, the social structure of the Klan was changing: the "higher-class" whites were more eager to distance themselves from working-class whites, thus increasing the possibility that someone as independent-minded as Ellis could see who was really keeping working-class whites down. Unlike Wiesler in *The Lives of Others*, who seemed thoroughly a creature of the Stasi authority structure, and unlike Schindler, who was suited to manipulate authority structures for his own purposes, Ellis sought recognition and respect in a society whose authority structures were changing, and that allowed him to recognize how he and others like him had been used and deceived.

And there are others who played crucial roles in Ellis's transformation. Bill Riddick, whom Davidson credits with acute psychological perceptiveness and extraordinary persuasive powers, saw the honorableness in Ellis and first raised the possibility of having him cochair with Ann Atwater. Riddick perhaps saw that Ellis would turn in a fundamentally new direction if he was given responsibility for making things go well.[51] Ellis's insights into who was keeping whites like him down were prompted by events such as the time the black militant Howard Clement, to whom he responded angrily at the meeting, spoke respectfully to him afterward and wanted to shake his hand. This reminded Ellis that a white city councilman had talked strategy with him over the phone and met with him secretly but deliberately crossed the street to avoid having to greet him publicly and shake hands.[52] Again in contrast, Joe Becton, a black city official, invited Ellis to meet publicly with him and in fact insisted that all his interactions with the Klan leader occur in the open. And most of all there was Ann Atwater, who was extremely surprised to see that Ellis was afraid to attend a charrette meeting at a predominantly black school in a black neighborhood. She, of course, was used to seeing the Klan as a terrorizing force, but when she realized that Ellis felt he needed protection against black people, she reacted with humor instead of anger: "Don't you worry about that, C. P. I'll protect you."[53] And indeed she did. When Ellis set up an information table to distribute Klan literature at a school fair and some black teenagers angrily threatened to destroy the exhibit, Ann came over and in no uncertain terms turned them back.

One might think that in emphasizing the role of others in the individual's achievement of moral excellence, I am diminishing the role of personal responsibility.[54] If recognizing personal responsibility simply means endorsing the idea that individuals should do what is right for them to do even if others fail, I can hardly dissent from such an idea. But I am skeptical that solemn reminders to "take personal responsibility" will have much effect on their own. Even conscious awareness that one is personally responsible to do something may be overrated. If our moral upbringing has been adequate, much of the good we do will be habitual and unself-conscious. At a time of crisis when we ask ourselves what responsibilities we have, the efficacy of the answers we give to ourselves might crucially depend on our emotional responsiveness and which other people are with us. I do not deny that accepting one's personal responsibility has a role in achieving moral excellence, but we would do well to recognize its limits and realize that people can support one another in taking responsibility.

THE VISION AND HABITUATED CHARACTER THAT UNDERLIE MORAL CONVERSION

To close, let me compare the tentative conclusions of these studies with a philosophical conception of moral conversion—of vision that becomes unclouded. Moral reality is there to be seen, and those who cannot see it have their vision obscured. For the philosopher-novelist Iris Murdoch, who holds something like this conception, selfishness clouds moral vision (see Romand Coles's contribution to this volume for an articulation of Murdoch's conception of moral vision in relation to the environment). This vision is a matter of seeing people clearly and fairly, with "just and loving" attention.[55] To love someone is to struggle against selfishness so as to be fair, to see that person in all his or her particularity, not just the parts one wants to see but everything there is. For Murdoch this struggle is first and primarily a private internal struggle for the individual, because it is the fantasies one imposes on others that one must recognize for what they are.

To illustrate these themes, Murdoch tells the story of M, who has previously judged her daughter-in-law D to be "pert and familiar, insufficiently ceremonious, brusque, sometimes positively rude, always tiresomely juvenile. M does not like D's accent or the way D dresses. M feels that her son has married beneath him."[56] Murdoch asks us to imagine that this is a set of opinions M has kept entirely to herself. M has not let on in the slightest to anyone else about her view, and particularly not to D. And now she is reconsidering and asking whether she has been old-fashioned and conventional, prejudiced, narrow-minded, and snobbish. So M says to herself, Let me look again. Since M has not confided her feelings about D to anyone, especially to D, nothing that has occurred in the interaction between them has prompted M to reconsider her view of D. M's struggle to see D fairly is a purely private one. So M looks again and now finds D to be not vulgar but refreshingly simple, not undignified but spontaneous, not noisy but gay, not tiresomely juvenile but delightfully youthful.

I want to stress, to be fair to Murdoch, that she is not presenting the case of M and D as a case of *moral conversion*. I am sketching her general picture of the moral life and then inferring what that picture implies for the nature and possibility of moral conversion—the idea that at least some cases depend on dispersing the clouds of selfishness obscuring one's vision of what is worthy of one's love and care. Surely there is truth in this idea. Schindler sees what is happening to the Jews, unlike many others, who very well might have self-interested reasons for not seeing clearly or not looking further because they suspect that what they find will put them in an awkward position. A crucial event in C. P. Ellis's conversion is when he sees Ann as a human being, eating just as he does. He also *hears* Ann and other black people speak about their shame and knows it to be the same as his shame. He also has self-interested motivations to sustain his clouded vision and hearing.

On the other hand, Murdoch's exclusive emphasis on *perceiving* the moral reality of the other is seriously misleading if it leaves out the necessity of emotional impact, the sickening process that left Schindler concluding that he had no choice but to act, or the emotional catharsis in which Ellis and Ann affirmed their shared vulnerability, shame, and inability to protect their children. To adequately name a felt solidarity like that seems to require more than the metaphors of seeing and hearing accurately. Of course, Murdoch would add the words "just" and "loving" to "attention." I would need to add, then, that such words must point to something substantially independent of vision, something that grips the body and prepares it to see and to respond to what it sees. The words cannot merely *qualify* vision to identify merely a kind of perception. I have cited work in psychology and neuroscience to suggest that human moral motivation depends on tapping primal drives such as attachment and disgust. The metaphor of clear vision may mislead us about the gritty roots of morally inspired judgments and choices. Human beings capable of seeing what is worth loving in others and responding in an appropriate way are *embodied* creatures whose primal drives spring from the emotional equipment that evolved to sustain reproduction and child rearing. Without such primal drives and the very complex elaboration, refinement, and transformation of these drives through culture, socialization, and personal experience, there is no moral nobility. There would be nothing to see clearly that could also motivate.

Murdoch stresses the role of art in helping us see clearly what is of worth in the world. So does *The Lives of Others,* in implying that a pivotal moment in Wiesler's conversion was listening to a sonata for a good man. For me this was the least persuasive element of the film. This is not to deny that art might have transformative effects (as can natural beauty; see the Coles contribution to this volume), but it can happen only in a context where it can grip the body and prepare it to respond. The most plausible suggestion of the film, on the other hand, is that a man who becomes utterly disillusioned with the cause that has given his life its sole meaning and purpose will grasp at an alternative and defend a life of connection, as demonstrated by the artists he is assigned to spy on. Disillusionment with what has given life meaning also plays a role in Ellis's conversion, as well as anger and a sense of betrayal toward the upper-class whites he came to see as using him and others like him. In both these cases, the agent's vision becomes clearer, but there is much more that happens: emotional turmoil, despair, anger, and a newfound connection with others prepare the way for better vision and grip the body, preparing it to respond.

The point about connection leads to my second point, that it seems seriously misleading to leave out the roles others can play in the kind of feeling attention that can bring about moral conversion. It seems theoretically possible to see clearly all by oneself as a result of a purely internal struggle, but it is a mistake to valorize this possibility, because surely there are others from whom we have much to learn and much to gain in the way of inspiration and support. Third, selfishness in any clear sense of the word is not by any means the only problem. The human impulse to submit eagerly to social hierarchy is deeply rooted and widespread, if not universal. The impulse can be wedded to selfless sacrifice (see the Grant contribution to this volume, on the moral liabilities of selflessness) as well as to craven self-service. Fourth, the circumstances surely do play a role in which of a person's character traits help or hinder moral conversion. Before and after the war, Schindler never did anything that approximated the moral value of his actions during the war. Fifth, circumstances also play a role in what kind of person can do good. It is difficult to imagine a man with Schindler's traits playing a constructive role during something like the Durham desegregation crisis; and it is equally difficult to imagine a C. P. Ellis succeeding in Schindler's circumstances. As I noted earlier, a person's capabilities and resources shape his vision of what can be done, and this in turn shapes his judgment of what he should do. The relevant capabilities and resources are relative to the circumstances in which they can be exercised. All this is so much more than overcoming selfishness and attaining clear vision.

So, is moral conversion possible? My conclusion is that it is, and in ways that make it less mysteriously heroic but simply human, and still supportive of hope. I stress that it is *hope* that is warranted, not optimism, for the same kind of processes that result in a Schindler or an Ellis could produce conversion to moral vice rather than excellence. Wiesler initially saw the meaning of his life in serving the East German regime. Ellis initially found his community and meaning for his life in the Klan. These points weigh against optimism, which is premised on the assumption that the odds are on one's side. Hope is focused on what is possible, not necessarily probable. But hope can spur efforts to better understand what might make for conversions to excellence. The stories of conversion examined here suggest inquiry into the ways moral education can engage emotion as well as critical reflection and inquiry. The stories further suggest that we would do well to recognize what a complex and varied phenomenon moral excellence is—how one form of excellence that builds on a particular person's strengths can be suitable for one set of circumstances but not another set. And the stories suggest we need to wean ourselves from the moral romance of the lone hero. If we pursue these lines of inquiry, we may have warrant in the future for something more than hope. But for now, hope will have to be enough.

NOTES

1. I have greatly benefited from comments from Sin Yee Chan and Ruth Grant on the version of this essay presented during the conference "In Search of Goodness" at Duke University, from comments from other participants at the conference, and from an audience at Kent State University, where I delivered a later version as the Veroni Lecture for 2009.

2. Anna Funder, "Tyranny of Terror," *Guardian*, May 5, 2007, http://books.guardian .co.uk/review/story/0,,2072454,00.html, accessed May 19, 2008. Her book on the Stasi is *Stasiland: True Stories from Behind the Berlin Wall* (London: Granta Books, 2003).

3. Stanley Milgram, *Obedience to Authority: The Unique Experiment That Challenged Human Nature* (New York: Harper, 2004), 24. A recent partial replication of Milgram's experiments was done by Jerry M. Burger at Santa Clara University. See "Replicating Milgram: Would People Still Obey Today?" *American Psychologist* 64, no. 1 (2009): 1-11. Only a slightly lower rate of conformity was found. The replication was only partial because current ethical guidelines required that the simulated shocks go up to (only) 150 volts instead of the 450 volts in the original experiments. Study of Milgram's data led the author to conclude that willingness to administer 150 volts was a good predictor of one's willingness to go all the way to 450. However, since the replication was only partial, it is open to debate whether there is full confirmation of Milgram's conclusion for the present.

4. Philip Zimbardo, *The Lucifer Effect: Understanding How Good People Become Evil* (New York: Random House, 2008).

5. See Gilbert Harman, "Moral Philosophy Meets Social Psychology: Virtue Ethics and the Fundamental Attribution Error," *Proceedings of the Aristotelian Society* 99 (1998-99): 315-31, and Harman, "The Nonexistence of Character Traits," *Proceedings of the Aristotelian Society* 100 (1999-2000): 223-26; see also John Doris, *Lack of Character: Personality and Moral Behavior* (Cambridge: Cambridge University Press, 2002).

6. Milgram, *Obedience to Authority*, 138-40.

7. Gilbert Harman in particular makes this radical claim. See note 5.

8. Milgram, *Obedience to Authority*, 48-49.

9. Michael L. Gross, "Jewish Rescue in Holland and France during the Second World War: Moral Cognition and Collective Action," *Social Forces* 73, no. 2 (1994): 463-96.

10. David M. Crowe, *Oskar Schindler: The Untold Account of His Life, Wartime Activities, and the True Story Behind the List* (New York: Basic Books, 2004).

11. Ibid., 8.

12. Thomas Keneally, *Schindler's List* (New York: Simon and Shuster, 1993), 34.

13. Crowe, *Oskar Schindler*, 139-40.

14. Crowe states at one point (177) that Schindler's motivation did become one of working "solely to save his Jewish workers," but then in the next sentence he states that he had "business as well as moral reasons." His dream was that his factory at Brünnlitz could supply postwar Europe with pots and pans, with his Jewish workers at the core of his labor force.

15. Keneally, *Schindler's List*, 129-30.

16. J. Bargh and T. L. Chartrand, "The Unbearable Automaticity of Being," *American Psychologist* 54 (1999): 462-79; J. A. Bargh and E. L. Williams, "The Automaticity of Social Life," *Current Directions in Psychological Science* 15 (2006): 1-4.

17. Jenefer Robinson, *Deeper Than Reason: Emotion and Its Role in Literature, Music, and Art* (New York: Oxford University Press, 2005), chap. 3.

18. Antonio R. Damasio, *Descartes' Error: Emotion, Reason, and the Human Brain* (New York: Penguin, 2005), chap. 8. As in most science that is new, there is controversy over how far Damasio's evidence supports his hypotheses about the workings of emotion and their role in decisions. For some analyses of the controversy, see Alan G. Sanfrey and Jonathan D. Cohen, "Is Knowing Always Feeling?" *Proceedings of the National Academy of Science* 101, no. 48 (2004): 16709-10; Tiago V. Maia and James L. McClelland, "A Reexamination of the Evidence for the Somatic Marker Hypothesis: What Participants Really Know in the Iowa Gambling Task," *Proceedings of the National Academy of Sciences* 101, no. 45 (2004): 16075-80; Giovanna Columbetti, "The Somatic Marker Hypotheses, and What the Iowa Gambling Tasks Do, and Do Not, Show," *British Journal of the Philosophy of Science* 59 (2008): 51-71. Whether the details of Damasio's theory are right as a theory of rational decision making and the role emotion plays in it is less important for my purposes that his more general theme that motivation for acting on our judgments of what we believe to be right depends on those judgments' being connected to a more primal source of motivational energy.

19. Damasio, *Descartes' Error*, 170-71.

20. John McDowell, "Are Moral Requirements Hypothetical Imperatives?" in *Proceedings of the Aristotelian Society*, suppl., 52 (1978): 26-28.

21. See C. S. Carter and E. B. Keverne, "The Neurobiology of Social Affiliation and Pair Bonding, in *Hormones, Brain, and Behavior*, 5 vols., ed. D. W. Pfaff et al. (San Diego, CA: Academic Press, 2002), 1:299-337.

22. See C. S. Carter, L. Ahnert, K. E. Grossman, S. B. Hrdy, M. E. Lamb, et al., *Attach-

ment and Bonding: A New Synthesis (Cambridge, MA: MIT Press, 2006); T. R. Insel, "A Neurobiological Basis of Social Attachment," *American Journal of Psychiatry* 154 (1997): 726-35; P. J. Zak, "The Neuroeconomics of Trust," in *Renaissance in Behavioral Economics*, ed. Roger S. Frantz (New York: Routledge, 2008); P. J. Zak, "Trust: A Temporary Human Attachment Facilitated by Oxytocin," *Behavioral Brain Sciences* 28 (2005): 368-69; P. J. Zak, R. Kurzban, and W. T. Matzner, "Oxytocin Is Associated with Human Trustworthiness," *Hormonal Behavior* 48 (2005): 522-27; M. Kosfeld, M. Heinrichs, P. J. Zak, U. Fischbacher, and E. Fehr, "Oxytocin Increases Trust in Humans," *Nature* 435 (2005): 673-76; P. J. Zak, R. Kurzban, and W. T. Matzner, "The Neurobiology of Trust," *Annual of the New York Academy of Science* 1032 (2004): 224-27; P. J. Zak, A. A. Stanton, and S. Ahmadi, "Oxytocin Increases Generosity in Human Beings," *PLoS ONE* 2, no. 11 (November 2007): e1128. doi:10.1371/journal.pone.0001128.

23. See Jorge Moll, Frank Drueger, Roland Zahn, Matteo Pardini, Ricardo de Oliveira-Souza, and Jordan Grafman, "Human Fronto-mesolimbic Networks Guide Decisions about Charitable Donation," *Proceedings of the National Academy of Sciences of the United States of America* 103 (2006): 15623-28. That is, human beings biologically evolved into creatures that become attached to cultural norms specifying abstract causes and principles by way of the same motivational mechanisms that attach them to food, sex, drugs, money, mates, and children. The more reflective and reasoned attachments of human beings piggyback motivationally on the most primitive layers of the motivational system.

24. Paul Rozin and Jonathan Haidt, "Disgust," in *Handbook of Emotions*, ed. Michael Lewis and Jeannette M. Haviland (New York: Guilford Press, 1993), and Paul Rozin, "The Process of Moralization," *Psychological Science* 10 (1999): 218-21.

25. W. F. Arsenio and E. A. Lemerise, "Aggression and Moral Development: Integrating Social Information Processing and Moral Domain Models," *Child Development* 75, no. 4 (2004): 987-1002; Jorge Moll, Ricardo de Oliveira-Souza, and Paul J. Eslinger, "Morals and the Human Brain: A Working Model," *NeuroReport* 14, no. 3 (2003): 299-305, and Dan Jones, "Moral Psychology: The Depths of Disgust," *Nature* 447, no. 7146 (2007): 768-71.

26. Quotation from a German documentary made in 1964, quoted at http://www.deathcamps.info/Leyson/Schindler.htm, accessed March 8, 2009.

27. Herbert Steinhouse, "The Real Oskar Schindler," *Saturday Night* 109, no. 3 (April 1994): 43-49. Text reproduced at http://www.writing.upenn.edu/~afilreis/Holocaust/steinhouse.html, accessed November 23, 2008.

28. Sin Yee Chan suggested this possibility in commenting on a draft of this chapter.

29. The pronominal reference is in the interview with Steinhouse.

30. Nechama Tec, *When Light Pierced the Darkness: Christian Rescue of Jews in Nazi-Occupied Poland* (New York: Oxford University Press, 1986), 5.

31. Ibid., 152-53. She cites Perry London's earlier work that supports similar conclusions but that also identifies a third characteristic, a love of adventure. See Perry London, "The Rescuers: Motivational Hypotheses about Christians Who Saved Jews from the Nazis," in *Altruism and Helping Behavior*, ed. J. R. Macaulay and

L. Berkowitz (New York: Academic Press, 1970), 241-50. Tec believes that adventurousness is just a form of marginality, although she simply asserts this and does not argue for it.

32. Crowe, *Oskar Schindler*, 3-4, notes that very little information is available about Schindler's early family life. Most of his information seems to have come from Emilie, who blamed her father-in-law for her husband's worst traits. Crowe gives no information on what role Schindler's mother played in Oskar's upbringing.

33. Samuel P. Oliner and Pearl M. Oliner, *The Altruistic Personality: Rescuers of Jews in Nazi Europe* (New York: Macmillan, 1988), 142-77, 257. The other motivation that frequently played a role, according to the Oliners, was empathic arousal.

34. Gross, "Jewish Rescue in Holland and France," 473-81.

35. Crowe, *Oskar Schindler*, 102.

36. Emilie Schindler, with Erika Rosenberg, *Where Light and Shadow Meet: A Memoir*, trans. Dolores M. Koch (New York: W. W. Norton, 1997), 90-91.

37. Crowe, "Jewish Rescue in Holland and France," 541.

38. Lawrence Blum, "Moral Exemplars: Reflections on Schindler, the Trocmés, and Others," in *Moral Perception and Particularity* (New York: Cambridge University Press, 1994), 75. Blum acknowledges some uncertainty about whether Schindler fully satisfies all the criteria for being a moral hero. For example, he worries that Schindler was a bit too taken with his self-image as savior of "his" Jews, but he argues that his attachment to that self-image did not run as deep as his concern for the welfare of others.

39. Ibid., 78-79. His description of the Murdochian paragon is drawn primarily from her book of philosophical essays, *The Sovereignty of Good* (London: Routledge and Kegan Paul, 1970).

40. Osha Gray Davidson, *Best of Enemies: Race and Redemption in the New South* (Chapel Hill: University of North Carolina Press, 2007).

41. Ibid., 126-27.

42. Ibid., 188.

43. Ibid., 123.

44. Ibid., 253.

45. Ibid., 255.

46. Ibid., 263.

47. Ibid., 274.

48. Ibid., 276.

49. Ibid., 249.

50. Ibid., 255.

51. I owe this interesting point to Romand Coles and Suzanne Shanahan.

52. Davidson, *Best of Enemies*, 242-43, 255.

53. Ibid., 267.

54. Sin Yee Chan raised this issue in her comments.

55. Murdoch, *Sovereignty of Good*, 34.

56. Ibid., 16.

FOUR

What Good Is Innocence?

J. Peter Euben

What good is innocence?[1] Is it a good at all? And if it is, what sort of good is it? Should we talk about innocence and innocent people, or do we need to specify a particular realm of discourse about innocence: legal, political, theological, psychological, sociological, or some amalgam of these? Is innocence a state of being, a stage of life, or an aspect of life? We can lose innocence, but can we regain it? Is innocence a matter of choice, or is it prior to choice? And is there something paradoxical about analyzing innocence, since not being able to analyze is a characteristic of innocence? E. B. White once complained that analyzing comedy is like dissecting a frog: at the end of the process the subject is dead. Is something like that true of innocence as well?[2]

The question What good is innocence? is complicated by "our" ambivalence toward innocents and innocence. On the one hand, innocents seem literal-minded, childlike, and naive, lacking the capacity for irony and playfulness, oblivious to the impact their actions have on others or, indeed, on themselves. In Bakhtinian terms, innocents read the world homophonically and monologically. Billy Budd, the subject of this essay and a quintessential innocent, cannot begin to fathom *Billy Budd*. But this hardly settles the question whether this is a "good" thing or not if reading the novel requires, as the narrator implies, a "sinister dexterity." Such dexterity is the price paid by those who have encountered evil. But this implies that lost innocence is a precondition for writing and even reading *Billy Budd*.

On the other hand, even sophisticates contemptuous of innocence are not immune to its allure. Thus the attractions to the simplicity of childhood,[3] youthfulness, and spontaneity; the longings for Eden, golden ages, island utopias, heavenly cities, simpler times and places; the celebration of moral purity and political certainties; the romance with nature and noble savages. Sometimes these longings are strategic endorsements made by the knowing few on behalf of the unsophisticated many. Outrage at the injustice and suffering a heartless God permits, if not secretly condones, is present in Robespierre and the Terror, Ivan and his grand inquisitor, Max Weber's chiliasts who would scourge the world with one final act of violence to end all future violations, and Sartre's Hugo in *Dirty Hands*, who is warned by Hoederer, "Your purity resembles death."[4] We knowing ones, we writers and readers, we ironists, must shield the superstitious many from the truth. We know there is no redemption, no ultimate meaning to suffering, no final alignment of human purpose with nature or God, but they do not. The radicalness of Machiavelli, Isaiah Berlin argued, was in his undermining the assumption that "somewhere in the past, or the future, in this world or the next, in the church or in the laboratory, in the speculations of the metaphysics or the findings of the social scientist or the uncorrupted heart of the simple good man, there is to be found the final solution to the question of how men should live."[5]

Disbelief in redemption is one of the defining aspects of Greek tragedy. For the tragedians, "innocence" and childhood end with the recognition that human beings are mortal; that every moment of our lives is shaped by a fate we have chosen and that has been chosen for us. For those who forget, ignore, or are enraged at these limits, retribution is fierce and inevitable; incurable diseases and unrelenting pain, humiliation, the desolation of cities and families, dismemberment, transfigurations, and premature, dishonorable death.

* * *

I was drawn to this question, What good is innocence? less by Plato, Augustine, Rousseau, Kant, Nietzsche,[6] and James Baldwin,[7] who directly address it, than by Greek tragedy, more specifically by Euripides' *Bacchae*. It is an odd inspiration and an admittedly circuitous route to the issues contained in *Billy Budd*, especially since the Greeks had no word for evil or, indeed, for innocence, and Melville's allusions to Greek figures and texts are episodic at most, while allusions to Christianity are all-pervasive. So why Greek tragedy, and why this particular one?

The *Bacchae* tells the story of the god Dionysus returning to Thebes disguised as a human, initially asking, then demanding, acknowledgment of the divinity of his mother, Semele. His cousin, the young King Pentheus, not only refuses but, outraged at the stranger's leading the women out of Thebes, attempts to imprison him. But these women, now under the god's spell, are running free in the fields and mountains outside the confines of the city and the supervision of men. Indeed, as the transgression of boundaries, dissolution of hierarchies, and abrogation of public laws and forms intensifies, the chorus provides an ironic counterpoint with a celebration of the old ways, simple wisdom, and conventional rituals. With a bit of political license we could regard the Sparagmos—the upcoming ritual sacrifice and dismemberment of Pentheus—as an example of revolutions as portrayed by Thucydides.

Except that the scene on the mountain before the sacrifice is bucolic. Milk, honey, and wine miraculously appear with the touch of a *thrysus*. Women suckle baby gazelles and wolves, while "slithering snakes"[8] lick the excess milk off their cheeks. In this place and at this moment divisions between species have no more standing than hierarchies of class and status do. But life-giving nature is not all of nature, and a moment is only a moment, because an inclusive ecstatic community, such as the one created by Dionysus, can be instantly transformed into a vengeful horde of killers. Thus, when the men of Thebes seek to curry favor with their king by detaching his mother, Agave, from the other bacchants, the nurturing mothers turn on them with a fury that almost destroys them. The cattle they tend are not so lucky. Some women tear calves in two with their bare hands, while others claw heifers to pieces. Enraged bulls fall stumbling in the midst of their charges, to be immediately stripped of flesh and skin. The forest drips with blood.

The near fate of these men anticipates the final fate of Pentheus. Refusing to heed Dionysus's counsel, then his warnings, Pentheus continues to try to capture and destroy him. The god's revenge is to lure the king out of the city to see what the king thinks will be unlimited coupling that includes his mother. To get a clearer view yet remain hidden, Pentheus, now transformed from an aggressively masculine king to a coquettish, effeminate, genderless, prurient he-she, climbs a tree. But Dionysus calls to his maenads and points to the intruder. All hell breaks loose. His mother, thinking her son is a lion, tears him apart limb by limb. All join in "tearing his flesh, his ribs clawed clean of flesh and every hand was smeared with blood as they played ball with scraps of Pentheus's body" (1136). It all ends with Agave impaling his head on her wand in triumph. Her return to Thebes, sanity, and the recognition that the lion she boasted of vanquishing is her son is one of the most affecting scenes in Greek tragedy.[9] As the messenger concludes, "All the victory she carries home is her own grief" (1147).

There are no bacchants in *Billy Budd*, no god whose gift of wine eases the pain of everyday grief and provides a respite from the knowledge of death. Nor, obviously, does the play evince Hebraic or Christian theology. No comparable gloss is possible for a novel as densely layered as *Billy Budd*, so my attempt at one must flatten the theology and politics of the story. On its surface (which has its own limitations and integrity), it is a tale of a British seaman taken from his merchant vessel and impressed into the Royal Navy, where Billy Budd (repeatedly called the "handsome sailor") exists in a state of innocent grace that both inspires and seduces the audience, with one notable exception. For that man, there is no charm or goodness in who and what Billy is and does. Indeed, so disgusted and perverse is Claggart that he manipulates Billy's innocence to charge him with mutinous intentions. Stunned by the charge, Billy, whose one blemish is stuttering and who thus is unable to answer the charge, strikes Claggart dead. Captain Vere, who is attracted to Billy and who knows he is (or was) innocent, insists on a speedy trial and on Billy's death. The angel, he says, must hang.

But who exactly is Billy Budd? What exactly has he done? Can he keep his innocence? And what are we to make of the silences and murmurings that stud the story, Billy's end, and the end of the novel?

Given that the *Bacchae* and *Billy Budd* are written in such radically different times, cultures, and genres, what is the point of introducing the novel with a Greek drama? And why this novel and this play?

I chose these two texts precisely because their radically distinct social ontologies help dramatize a set of themes having to do with my question about innocence. For one thing, both works suggest a dialectic in which an obsession with form incites violation of what is explicitly endorsed. In the *Bacchae*, Dionysus transforms the hypermasculine young king into a coquettish "girl." Everything Pentheus thought himself not to be, everything he defined himself against, everything he sought to banish, imprison, and vanquish as foreign, is revealed to be at the center of his being. The more he fights, the more he succumbs; the more he attempts to distance himself from Dionysus the more he is seduced by him. In *Billy Budd* the practice of impressing and oppressing sailors intensifies the fear of mutiny, which in turn produces an atmosphere fraught with secrecy, fear, and conspiracy. In such circumstances, chaos and anarchic revolution battle continuously but also feed the obsession with form and repression.[10] For another thing, Billy and Claggart are almost always presented as opposites, the one standing for innocence and good, the other for evil and "sophistication," in the most pejorative sense of the word. Yet both are products of nature who have no history, though historical narratives are projected onto them. And each has a complicated relationship with what he is not, as that is present in the other. Billy could certainly "use" Claggart's guile to forestall being a victim of the corporal punishment that so traumatized him (even though it is Claggart he has to fear); and Claggart has what one might call a love-hate relationship with Billy. He admires Billy's natural grace, beauty, and ease of bearing but has contempt for the innocence that makes those possible. He would be Billy, or at least have Billy, if he could, but he is enraged by Billy's obliviousness. If he cannot have him or be him, he must kill him.

I chose these works because each dramatizes a logic of sacrifice. Perhaps "logic" is too strong a word, and perhaps the discrepancies between the play and the novel are too great to sustain a comparison. After all, Billy's sacrifice is more or less done by the book, adhering to procedures of martial law, or so Vere would have us believe.[11] Dionysus's sacrifice of Pentheus, on the other hand, is vengeful, full of blood and guts, at once sprawling and out of control. Yet there is form to the Dionysian sacrifice of Pentheus (and Thebes), and preverbal and prerational Dionysian forces drive Vere's attachment to form and institutions. If we think of Foucault's *Discipline and Punish*, we could argue that the *Bacchae* is the world of Damiens that appears to be the irrational precursor to Billy Budd's more "civilized" form of punishment.

There is another dimension to the logic of sacrifice as it works itself out in *Billy Budd*. There is a debate over whether Melville was on the side of resistance or acceptance when it came to various forms of inequality, whether and to what extent he sympathized with revolution or institutions, *The Rights of Man* or the man-of-war, innocence or sophistication. But to insist that Melville choose between these mutually exclusive alternatives that Billy and Claggart are imagined to represent not only obscures the pathos of the novel (regarded as Melville's last will and testament) but "regrettably . . . celebrates the sacrificial logic Melville strives to keep at bay."[12] The text survives "in fragile equilibrium," as do the characters and situations that constitute it. The volatility of the novel's content is mirrored in its tortured gestation.

Billy Budd is a challenge. It is not clear what to make of the discrepancies between author and narrator, or of the way the latter interrupts the story to remind us how difficult his project is and how far afield he must go to make sense of various characters and events. What follows if, as he says, rational reflection is itself innocent in the face of innocence and evil? If all stories, including his, have what he calls "ragged edges" that point beyond whatever completion seems achieved, what interpretive and political lesson should we draw? Such perplexity is increased by there being three endings to the novel, and by the uncertain status of what may be alternative forms of communication just outside the register of official audibility. Do stuttering, murmuring, and the shrouded cries of men and animals in the novel constitute a critical subtext, one able to contest the forms power deploys to "impress" the right history and political memory? Does this form of communication—if that is what it is—capture or express what Adorno referred to as the "cross-grained, opaque and unassimilated material" that "has outwitted the historical dynamic?"[13] Or is it simply incomprehensible babble?

* * *

In what follows, I focus on the pivotal incident in the novel: Billy's lashing out at Claggart when Claggart slanders him in front of Captain Vere. The "reason" Billy did what he did, the narrator informs us, is that, despite being perfect, he had one defect: "Under sudden provocation of strong heart-feeling his voice, otherwise singularly musical, as if expressive of the harmony within, was apt to develop an organic hesitancy, in fact more or less of a stutter or even worse" (19).[14]

What can we say about this "organic hesitancy"? One thing is that Billy's defect, "the calling card of the envious marplot of Eden," is a sign that nothing human can be perfect. Another is to note Vere's role in bringing about the defect. Remembering a schooldays incident, Vere recognizes Billy's predicament and tries to encourage him. "There is no hurry my boy. Take your time, take your time" (61). But this paternal care when coupled with the awesome authority the captain already has—remember that part of Billy's fury at Claggart is that the master-at-arms defamed him in front of his captain—just intensifies the pressures until the only relief possible is the lethal blow. And when Vere says, "Struck dead by an Angel of God but the Angel of God must hang" (62), we know that everything that comes after is something of a "show trial." Then there is the narrator's suggestion, made more explicit elsewhere, that what is outside reveals what is inside, that the body is an eye to the soul, and that, more particularly, a handsome soul must lie within the "handsome sailor." But if such harmony is problematic, as it turns out to be, then what is on the surface is as much an obstacle for understanding as a foundation for it. And this presumably is as true of the novel as of the characters in it.

But how did we get to this crossroads? Who are these characters? What exactly have they done, and what do they represent? These questions cannot be fully answered because we know nothing about the origins or history of Billy Budd and John Claggart. If they are without histories, what then do they "stand for" (in both senses of the phrase)? One answer is that Billy Budd embodies perfect innocence, John Claggart absolute evil as part of his "natural depravity," and Captain Vere the worldly authority that recognizes the theological and moral complexity of events but elides such considerations in the name of political responsibility and duty. The most provocative version of this reading is offered by Hannah Arendt.[15]

For Arendt, Billy is Christ returned to Earth, a figure whose goodness is so perfect that "it is beyond virtue." Claggart is the exact opposite: a man who embodies an absolute evil beyond vice. The paradox is that absolute goodness, no less than absolute evil, is dangerous and unmanageable in the public realm. In her Aristotelian idiom, the polis exists between beasts and gods, and while humans may partake of both, they cannot be either if the political realm is to exist.

Arendt goes on to argue that goodness, though it is stronger than evil, shares with it the elementary violence inherent in all strength, a strength that is detrimental to all forms of politics. Ventriloquizing Melville, she asks us to imagine the foundation of political life as if Abel slew Cain. "Don't you see," her Melville continues, "that from this deed of violence the same chain of wrongdoing will follow, only that now mankind will not even have the consolation that the violence it must call crime is indeed characteristic of evil men only." Replacing original sin with original goodness, as the French revolutionaries did, leaves us, politically speaking, in exactly the same condition. In Arendt's version, the central figure of the tragedy is Vere, who is aware that only virtue, but not absolute goodness, is capable of being embodied in lasting institutions.

As forceful and provocative as Arendt's version is, it is not wholly persuasive. Her reading ignores or underplays complications that confound the oppositions and contrasts her argument relies on. First there is the question of Billy's innocence and purity. Billy has been approached about joining a mutiny but does not report it, in part because he cannot wholly comprehend what he is being asked to do. But he knows enough about the seriousness of the moment to stutter. Thus the question Vere poses in the confrontation with Claggart about whether Billy had been involved in mutinous activity ratchets up the pressure on Billy. Second, there is a dress rehearsal for the pivotal incident. On *The Rights of Man*, someone named Red Whiskers continually provokes Billy for no apparent reason. At first Billy "forebore" and "reasoned with him in a pleasant way." This failing, he hit Red Whiskers and almost killed him. The punch transformed Red Whiskers, who, along with almost everyone else, "now loves Billy and joins the others in doing favors for him" (13–14). *The Rights of Man*, as a ship and as a doctrine, apparently works only when someone with an authority sanctioned by natural goodness is present as an exemplar. In this regard innocence *can* be recaptured in a way that does not destroy politics.

Moreover, Billy's innocence is a kind of blankness that cannot bear the weight of the symbolism Arendt (and the narrator) attribute to him. When it is not just a blankness, when it seems to exercise real authority, that authority is grounded in violence. Then there is Billy's horrified reaction to a flogging.

So traumatic is the experience that Billy "resolved that never through remissness would he make himself liable to such a visitation, or do or omit aught that might merit even verbal reproof" (33). That he lacked the capacity to realize this does not quiet the suspicion that Billy's life henceforth may be driven by a Hobbesian wariness in order to forestall any possibility of so harsh a punishment. It may even be that the violence of the punishment is an anticipation and explanation of the violence he visits on Claggart, whose responsibilities as master-at-arms connect him with floggings.

If Billy does indeed expend energy in reading situations that might lead to flogging, it follows that he might also be using a physical beauty, natural authority, and innocence to help ensure his immunity to such beatings. But innocence used cannot be innocence, at least not in the sense in which the narrator and commentators regard Billy as innocent. Penultimately there is the way Billy is likened to Achilles, Heracles, and Apollo. But the first two are Greek heroes known for their violence, and Apollo is linguistically linked to the verb *apollumi*, meaning "to destroy." That the narrator mentions nothing about this suggests that one theme of the novel is the way violence is suppressed and how history is rewritten to ensure this.

Finally, Arendt's triangulation of Billy, Vere, and Claggart is suspect because Billy is too many things to too many people to be tagged and sorted. He is a Christ figure and Adam before the Fall; Baby Budd and an upright barbarian with a heroic countenance; a man whose example transformed *The Rights of Man* from a violent near anarchy into a community; and a beautiful man (or man-woman) who is an object of erotic desire if not obsession. The narrator describes Billy's physical features in loving detail; Captain Vere wants to find a place for Billy near him so he can see Billy more often; the men love to do "womanly" chores for him; and even Claggart desires him. Indeed, as I suggested, Claggart's hatred of Billy is in no small part based on the resentment of unacknowledgeable erotic desire.

* * *

Supposedly Billy knows none of this because he is, the narrator says, "innocent of the serpent's wiles." But this innocence creates a barrier against what we regard as the thinking and experience necessary for adulthood.

Billy's virtue—he is without vanity, envy, or corruption—leaves him oblivious to the impression he makes on others. Such obliviousness precludes reading social nuance, thus leaving him vulnerable to what he fears most. Blinded by his lack of sophistication and worldliness, he is—unsurprisingly—unable to fathom, let alone anticipate, the corruption that lies in wait for him.

Because Billy is incapable of recognizing irony, satire, paradox, allusion, or double meanings, he cannot read the novel in which he is the principal antagonist, which means that those who recognize and use such "knowingness" come from another world. What, then, is someone as innocent as Billy to do with that world?

Billy may be without any physical flaw, but his one imperfection, stuttering, is lethal. If he did not stutter, none of this would have happened, yet everything that has happened prepares for it, and all that does happen results from it. Stuttering is a manifestation of Billy's innocence of evil, a prelude to violence, and an expression of the narrator's need for legitimacy. If there were no stuttering, there could be no story, or at least no story of the kind the narrator thinks he is telling (and the author thinks he is writing). Billy's imperfection, the narrator says, vouches for the seriousness of his tale, as against romances that deal only with perfection. However much we may rail against the serpent's wiles and resent our imperfections, they are what make us interesting and worth writing about, or even able to write at all.

If we ask why Billy stutters, the answer seems clear enough. Confronting a radically unfamiliar and unexpected situation in a place he has never been before, forced to speak in front of those from whom he has only taken orders, unable to defend himself and with the memory of flogging indelibly in his mind, Billy is overcome by emotion and lashes out in frustration and rage. But this is only part of the answer.

It is only part of the answer because the novel invites us to look at the conditions of power that create and sustain situations in which people become stutterers. The political situation of the sailors is reprehensible. The men are taught to obey, their lives are rigidly confined both spatially and temporally, they are described as childlike and subject to harsh punishment for the slightest infraction. Their condition resembles slavery.

But to pathologize the life of impressed seamen is to overstate the case in two ways. The first is that it does not apply to Billy Budd. Except for the flogging, he seems oblivious to his environment. Second, to pathologize the condition is to miss the way stuttering, broadly understood, exists in "normal" circumstances. What conditions leave us helpless or baffled, furious yet impotent, unable to express our resentment and rage or move beyond repetition of an initial consonant or initial thought? What, if anything, does stuttering have to do with speech, silence, and whispers, inarticulateness and compulsive talking, hesitancy and question marks at the ends of assertions? When and with what consequences do we feel ourselves outsiders in a discourse whose assumptions remain unstated and whose exclusions are normalized?

Those conditions extend to the novel itself insofar as *it* stutters. In his essay on stuttering,[16] Gilles Deleuze distinguishes between a character's stuttering in speech and a writer's stuttering in language. On both levels stuttering, murmuring, and stammering create what he calls an "atmosphere of disequilibrium," the phrase Nancy Ruttenberg uses in her analysis of *Billy Budd*.[17] I think Deleuze's point also applies to the *Bacchae*, but it is the novel that concerns us here.

In *Billy Budd* the narrator expresses a desire simply to tell the truth. But he finds himself dogged by what seems to be an independent narrative that appears to "warp his efforts, turning his own offering into a chronicle of misgivings featuring double negatives, self-cancelling statements, and obfuscating syntax." As for telling the truth, the narrator must explain how a lie (Claggart's accusation against Billy) becomes the truth. But no such explanations are offered, in part because the narration frequently proceeds by fits and starts, appearing to provide information when in fact it is withdrawn or has its authority undercut. Why, for example, is the narrator unable to explore the ironies about Billy's condition that the text provides? Why, at the critical encounter, does he turn away from considering the moral signification of the blow in favor of detailed description of where on Claggart's body the blow fell? Does the narrator stutter for the same reason Billy does? Is *he* innocent? Might *he* also be seduced by Billy?

There is another reason not to pathologize the condition of the sailors in regard to stuttering: it is not necessarily a sign of insufficiency. Stuttering can signal the presence of an absence, mark a loss, hint at a way of speaking that exists on the fringe of official sanctioned discourse, or amount to a withholding of love, power, and closure.[18]

That *Billy Budd* has no fewer than three last chapters—the death of Vere, the authorized version of Billy's death, and the mystification of Billy in the book's concluding song—can be taken as a kind of stuttering. Consider, too, the narrator's assertion (or excuse) that the "symmetry of form attainable in pure fiction cannot so readily be achieved in a narration essentially having less to do with fable than with fact." Truth, he goes on, "uncompromisingly told will always have its ragged edges, hence the conclusion of such a narration is apt to be less finished than an architectural finial" (87). This introduces his apology that though the story should end with the end of Billy's life, it has a life after Billy's death; three lives, as it turns out.

But for all this, the stuttering that matters is Billy's; the act that matters is the violence Billy's frustration, rage, and shame drive him to commit; the decision that matters is Vere's when he narrows the meaning of events to expedite judgment. Vere's decision—the fact of it, the circumstances surrounding it, and the rationale offered for it—suggests that the *Bellipotent* is as much a ship of state as a ship of war. And despite Vere's temperance, it is a state founded on slavery (we are told there were "good masters") *and* the fear of rebellion and revolution that slavery threatens.

The French Revolution is all over *Billy Budd*. Edmund Burke and Thomas Paine are constant presences in the novel. They are there as background for two recent mutinies, the first standing against abuses, the second committing them, or so the narrator says. The Revolution and the memory of mutiny are responsible for the deaths of all three protagonists (Vere is killed in battle with the French ship *Atheist*). But, as I suggested, the kind of men and citizens this ship of state requires and promotes are infantilized by a hierarchy that demands unconditional obedience. The narrator calls the sailors shaped by such a world "juvenile." These juveniles laugh at the joke of a superior with "counterfeit glee" (36), not because it is funny but because it comes from a superior, a reminder of the bit slave owners put in the mouths of "uppity" slaves, who were thus forced into a permanent "smile." In this, and in the general hyperattentiveness of sailors to their superiors, it is clear that Billy is not the only one anxious to anticipate the moods of those who might impose a flogging. Such hierarchies of power were maintained not only by a kind of terror but by what Hannah Arendt (in *Eichmann in Jerusalem*) calls "language rules."[19] With these rules, impressment becomes an "alternative form of enlistment in the King's service," and guns become peacemakers. In such circumstances the men are silenced, left dumb to murmur inarticulately.

The language rules apply most directly to the way the past is written by the powerful, who seek to erase events as part of a moralizing narrative. A few weeks after the execution, the official *Navy Chronicle* renders an account of events where Claggart emerges as the moral hero stabbed "vindictively to death" in an "assassination" by a man who is said to be an alien passing as an Englishman (an outside agitator?) and to be thoroughly *depraved* (my italics). Claggart, on the other hand, is praised for his respectability and his patriotism. This publication is the only human record that attests to the kind of men Claggart and Billy were (89–90).

As I said earlier, this is an exaggeration, because silences can be much more than silent. In this case, silence writes over an underground form of communication it cannot hear. The narrator emphasizes the silence at the moment of execution but "hears" that silence disturbed by "a sound not easily to be verbally rendered" (85). The source's "seeming remoteness" is in fact close at hand. The "murmurous indistinctness" comes from the men massed on deck. To the narrator the sound is inarticulate, of dubious significance, no more than a "capricious revulsion of thought or feeling mobs are liable to make." But the sound may also be a silent protest against Billy's execution and the "order" that brought it about. Vere recognizes it as such, which is why he commands the boatswain to pipe down the starboard watch to "pierce" the "ominous low sound" and reestablish discipline. The likening of the whistle to "the shriek" of a sea hawk suggests that nature herself joins the protest.

The ominous low sound that punctuates the surface order with intimations of revolutionary violence is, as we saw with Pentheus, called forth by the very obsession with order that seeks to quell it at all costs. The murmurings of the men are too inchoate to be a counternarrative of events, but they do provide an alternative story and an alternative kind of story. This story is sung (Billy is likened to a nightingale), poetic and formless when weighed against the forms so dear to Vere. These murmurings contain memories of Billy outside sanctioned versions.

The spar from the *Bellipotent* was kept by a foretopman and became an honored trace of Billy's life and death. To the men it was "a piece of the cross" (90). Despite their ignorance of the secret facts of the event, his comrades kept alive Billy's memory—including his innocence. The final song of the third ending ("Billy in the Darbies"), which concludes the book in the sense of being its last pages, is sung by a mate of Billy's.

Whatever else they are, Billy's life, death, and "resurrection" constitute a biblical parable. Vere calls Billy an "Angel of God" even after he kills Claggart, and the narrator likens Billy and Vere to the story of Isaac and Abraham. Preparing to die, Billy is tranquil. Like a slumbering child in the cradle, Billy's death ends the circle of his life, which began as a foundling discovered in a silk-lined basket. Finding him serene and happy, the chaplain regards himself as superfluous. What he has to offer Billy does not need, and what Billy needs is nothing at all. More particularly, Billy cannot comprehend the idea of salvation or of a savior. But this indifference, rather than separating him from Christ, only brings him closer, since Billy is imitating "the generation" that first followed the Son of God (81). The parable of Billy's life includes his "ascension," the "otherworldly" stillness as he dies, and the responsive human murmur joined by the inarticulate birds "which flew screaming to the spot" where Billy entered the ocean, their encircling motions and outstretched wings providing a "croaked requiem" for the handsome sailor (86).

The chaplain who visits Billy to administer the final rites does not regard Billy's innocence as tarnished by the killing of Claggart. How could he, given the history of Christianity, a religion of love that has become a religion of violence? Indeed, the chaplain acknowledges the contradictory demands of his vocation. A chaplain "is the minister of the Prince of Peace serving the host of the God of war—Mars." But why then is he there? Of what use can he be even for those who cannot attain the innocence of a Billy Budd? "Because," the narrator says, "he indirectly subserves the purpose attested to by the cannon; because he too lends the sanction of the religion of the meek to that which practically is the abrogation of everything but Brute Force" (81).

* * *

Arendt is mostly right in regarding Vere as the center of the novel's *human* tragedy. Having a past, he is less a symbol than Billy and Claggart, who are forces of nature. The narrator admits his difficulties in grasping the combination of traits found in Billy and Claggart, but Vere is a man of this world, so the narrator knows his way around *this* character, at least.

Vere is introduced as an egalitarian who dislikes the self-importance of elites. While others object to the poor having any place or power, Vere considers their status dispassionately instead of ideologically. Such commitments are reflected in his own persona of modesty, the fact that he possesses "striking but not sterling qualities," and his resolute nature. If you were to see Vere out of uniform you could never guess who he is and what he does.

Vere is a reader, mostly of history and biographies and accounts of real events and people, both ancient and modern. Like Machiavelli, he uses such study not only to distill principles of action, but to discover institutional forms appropriate for political and military order. Such reflections are often unappreciated by his peers, who regard his breadth of reading and allusion as superfluous—thus his nickname, "Starry Vere." Finally, he is the only character who, seeing the incident comprehensively, can move between the various discourses of innocence. He knows what is at stake politically, ethically, and theologically as well. For these and other reasons, the narrator and Arendt regard Vere as the "moral touchstone" of the novel. But I am not so sure.

There is something disconcerting, even unseemly, about the anxiety Vere displays in wanting to get the trial and execution over with. Of course he has compelling reasons: a superior officer has been killed by a subordinate at a time when memories of mutiny remain fresh. Billy may be an angel and an innocent before God, he goes on, but a drumhead court is not a theological forum or a church. Billy may be a good man, but moral considerations are mere distractions from what matters: the pragmatics of the situation and the facts of the case. In these circumstances we are, Vere insists, servants of the king first and our conscience only afterward. No personal attachment can be allowed to interfere with the law. That law may be pitiless, but its forms are the only consideration we can entertain, or we will all be lost.

But this is hardly the whole story. As I noted earlier, his fellow officers do not agree with him and indeed raise questions about both the legality of the proceedings and Vere's sanity. Several believe that he should wait until the ship joins the fleet and leave the decision to the admiral, that anything else violates the formal procedures Vere is so intent on maintaining. In regard to his reading history, we know from the official version of Billy's death (as from the Rodney King trial)[20] how facts can be made unreal and the real become fictionalized if one has the power and skill to do so. And if such history is the ground of the institutional forms Vere endorses, then those forms are no less problematic than Arendt's triangulation of Vere, Claggart, and Billy, or the opposition between innocence and violence.

As for Vere's sanity, it is hard to escape the suspicion that his anxiety to reduce all considerations to legal ones is at least partly a defense against his own affection for Billy: that he is afraid a single breach of forms that support a wall between public and private will mean the collapse of everything. The question is whether, as in Euripides, these banished feelings—his paternal and erotic attachment to Billy—do not drive the anxiety and pace of the trial and execution as much as explicitly political and military considerations do. "Where," the narrator asks, "does sanity and insanity begin and end?" The differences, we are told, are "imperceptible." Remember, too, that reason is used most adroitly by the madman Claggart.

Seeing Vere in those terms puts a different spin on his death. That death is the subject of a second "final" chapter. Vere is killed fighting a French ship of the line named *Atheist*. On his deathbed he *murmurs* (my emphasis), "Billy Budd, Billy Budd" (88), a phrase his attendant regards as inarticulate and the narrator assures us was not said in remorse. But again, I am not so sure.

So is Vere a moral touchstone? Is he a good man, one who knows what sort of goodness is right for specific areas of life as well as life as a whole? Up to a point he is. But beyond that point, or perhaps along with it, he becomes a moral object lesson. At least that is so if I am right about his unseemly rush to execute Billy Budd on exclusively pragmatic grounds. Perhaps his being both a touchstone and an object lesson applies to Billy as well. But what can be said about Claggart?

According to the narrator, almost anything and almost nothing. Anything because there is so little about him that fits our categories and expectations and so much about his motives and form of perversity that we are ignorant of. Confronting this situation, we are tempted to fill in the historical and moral blanks, if only to satisfy our need for coherence and sanity. Nothing because Claggart remains an enigma no matter how many times and how many ways he is approached. Indeed, the narrator confesses the insufficiency of conventional notions of knowledge and human nature in helping to grasp how it is that Claggart unites traits that usually stand opposed and separates traits that are normally found together. Unlike other men of evil, Claggart has "no vulgar alloy of the brute" in him. Instead, he is dominated by a certain intellectuality, embraces a surface respectability, and eschews small sins and vices and everything mercenary and avaricious (and Dionysian) (41–42).

The most forbidding aspect of Claggart is his relation to reason. Claggart presents himself as a man of even temper and dignity, a reasonable man subject to the laws of reason. But in fact his heart riots against that law, deploying reason "ambidexterously" to accomplish the irrational. Toward this wantonness of malignity that would "seem to partake of the insane, he will direct a cool judgment, sagacious and sound."

Vere may be driven to near madness by his conflicting feelings and commitments surrounding the incident, but Claggart is the true madman. His lunacies are unpredictable, his hatreds at once spontaneous and random; and however trivial the cause of his outrage, the consequences of it are momentous. What makes this man evil is not vicious training, corrupting books, or licentious living, as we would expect, but "nature herself." His evil, we are told, is a "depravity according to nature."

But of course Billy's innocence is also according to nature, which suggests an affinity or intimacy between the two men that was part of Arendt's point about the novel and mine about the *Bacchae*. In these terms, Billy is a mirror image of Claggart. That may be why Claggart is the only person (apart from Vere) who truly understands "the moral phenomenon presented by Billy Budd" (43). Claggart not only appreciates Billy's innocence, he longs to imitate it when he is not at war with it. He admires the charm of innocence, the courageousness of its free and easy manner, its power to move men and inspire their confidence and affection, and its indifference to petty vices. But there is something in him, some elemental evil put there by nature that he cannot overcome. Powerless to be innocent, he is intent on eliminating innocence. In this Claggart suggests Nietzsche's man of *resentiment*. "Having no power to annul the elemental evil in him, apprehending the good but powerless to be good," possessing a nature "surcharged with energy," Claggart's only recourse is "to recoil upon himself"[21] and "like the scorpion for which the Creator alone is responsible, act out to the end the part allotted to it" (42).

But if there is no *reason* for what Claggart does; if, like the scorpion, he is God's responsibility, what sort of moral universe are we in, and what conception of innocence and goodness operates within it? What grounds do we have to condemn Claggart or, for that matter, to praise Billy? These not only are hard questions, they are, the narrator assures us, dangerous ones as well. Dangerous because to understand the kind of man and evil Claggart represents we must cross a moral abyss (38) from which we may never return. "To pass from a normal nature to him [Claggart]," an "honest scholar" tells the narrator, one must cross the "deadly space between" without assurance that once entering such a labyrinth one can emerge at all or with the same sanity (38).

* * *

But the crossing also describes what it means to learn from experience, to grow up, to become worldly. The loss of innocence, for all its risks, is a necessary condition for reckoning with the responsibilities of citizenship in a way foreclosed both by perpetual innocence and by intimidation of the sort used to keep the sailors in permanent tutelage. This means that "corruption" in the sense of the knowingness that enables us to read *Billy Budd* is an achievement as well as a loss, politically and literarily. That it isn't for Billy is one reason I find his incorruptibility after he kills Claggart so disconcerting. His purity may not be death as Sartre's character claims, but it is implicated in violence and death.

I want to resist wholesale acceptance of the progressivist narrative that innocence is a rite of passage to adulthood and worldliness. I want to resist it because progressivist narratives, no matter how self-reflective, often rest on nostalgia, as in solemn invocations to accept the burdens of worldliness. I want to resist the narrative because, as Nietzsche's project reminds us, it is possible to become innocent in a sophisticated way. Similarly but less ambitiously, we understand what people mean when they say, "I saw it [a Rembrandt or political possibilities] for the first time." Perhaps having read about Rembrandt's use of light or about the Diggers or Polish Solidarity, what had been ordinary becomes fresh and exciting. In this register, innocence includes our capacity for surprise and wonder, our ability to see anew, and a wellspring of energy, hope, and imagination against what world-weariness counts as sophistication.

I want to resist the progressivist narrative for two other reasons. It is hardly surprising that someone can be innocent about some things and sophisticated about others. It is only a little more surprising that someone would be innocent and sophisticated in the same sphere of life. More surprising still is that one can be innocent and worldly about the same thing at the same time. Take Oedipus of *Oedipus Tyrannus* as an example. Here is a sophisticated, masterful, courageous, and perceptive man who cannot recognize the significance of his own name, or see his feet. For all his knowingness, he is oblivious to the impact and meaning of his actions; things stare him in the face, but he is blind to them. Uttering clear imprecations upon the killer of Laius, who happens to be himself, he is actually speaking in tongues. His orders, demands, and assertions are radically incomplete, only half-articulated despite their lucidity, compromised by murmurs of violation beneath surface respectability.

At one point the narrator in *Billy Budd* says we must go back to Plato to understand depravity according to nature. The phrase "natural depravity" is not in Plato,[22] but I want to invoke his name (as well as Freud's) to suggest a final reason to resist the progressivist narrative. Here, each character has a place in our soul.[23] Claggart is part of us, that part of our being that surfaces in our nightmares, the hyperaware, scheming, resentful part that frightens all who glimpse it, including ourselves. We did not know we were capable of such thoughts. What do we do with them—repress them, make them public and subject to "analysis" (in both senses), "work through" them? How do we keep Claggart from killing Billy and lying to Vere? Billy too is a part of our souls. At its best that part is incorruptible and fresh, enabling a natural ease and authority among others. But its obliviousness and lack of self-reflexiveness makes such virtues potentially lethal. Arendt has a point. "Vere" is the pragmatic, temperate part of the soul, exploring what is possible, calculating in the best sense, endorsing institutions and practices that would contain the worst of Claggart and Billy. He would mediate in the world and soul as he does in the novel. But for reasons adduced before, his claim to do so is suspect. In *The Republic*, one person or type of person or part of the soul is given the responsibility to rule. But not in *Billy Budd*. For better or worse, it dumps the problem of authority in our laps, as is to be expected in a book with multiple endings, a story with jagged edges built around a theme of stuttering. "The meaning of a text," Hans-Georg Gadamer writes, "surpasses its author not occasionally but always. Thus understanding is not a reproductive procedure but . . . always also a productive one."[24]

NOTES

1. David Wong, George Shulman, Roxanne Euben, and Bronwyn Lewis were invaluable interlocutors in the writing of this essay.

2. E. B. White and K. S. White, eds., *A Subtreasury of American Humor*, Modern Library ed. (New York: Random House, 1948), xvii.

3. The celebration of childhood as the quintessential moment of innocence is persuasive only if you have never read Freud or had children of your own.

4. Jean-Paul Sartre, *"No Exit" and Three Other Plays* (New York: Vintage International, 1989), 220.

5. Isaiah Berlin, "The Originality of Machiavelli," in *Against the Current: Essays in the History of Ideas*, ed. Henry Hardy (Princeton, NJ: Princeton University Press, 2001), 76.

6. This is not entirely true. It is Nietzsche, after all, who reveals the violence of form and regards Dionysus as mediating between the natural and the civilized, the bestial and the human realms. Indeed, one could read Nietzsche's project from *The Birth of Tragedy, The Uses and Abuses of History*, and *The Genealogy* to *Zarathustra* as a search for and an attempt at a sophisticated innocence.

7. There is much to be learned in juxtaposing Melville's ideas of innocence with Baldwin's idea of innocence in "Many Thousands Gone." See James Baldwin, "Many Thousands Gone," in *Notes of a Native Son* (Boston: Beacon Press, 1984), 24–45. For Baldwin it is the claim of innocence that constitutes an outrage. As he puts it, "It is the innocence which constitutes the crime." See James Baldwin, "My Dungeon Shook: Letter to My Nephew on the One Hundredth Anniversary of Emancipation," in *The Fire Next Time* (New York: Vintage International, 1993), 6. On these and related matters see George Shulman, *American Prophecy: Race and Redemption in American Political Culture* (Minneapolis: University of Minnesota Press, 2008).

8. I am relying (with a few minor emendations) on the Arrowsmith translation found in David Grene and Richmond Lattimore, *Euripides V* (Chicago: University of Chicago Press, 1959).

9. It is also "over the top." The line between tragedy and parody in Euripides can be very thin, like the line between sanity and insanity in *Billy Budd*.

10. See Nancy Ruttenberg, "Melville's Handsome Sailor: The Anxiety of Innocence," *American Literature* 66, no. 1 (March 1994): 83–103. Ruttenberg's essay is the most perceptive I know on the subject of innocence in *Billy Budd*. But her insistence on generating increasingly comprehensive and sophisticated explanations of events and characters plays into the logic of sacrifice she criticizes.

11. Ibid., 85.

12. I should state by way of apology and explanation that I am not a Melville scholar and that the more of that scholarship I read the more convinced I become that I am

not. I have not read all of Melville or his correspondence and occasional pieces. Nor have I read extensively in the literature that debates the origins and gestation of the novel. And though I have explored the connections between Melville and Emerson (especially the latter's essay "The Poet") and Whitman (especially *Leaves of Grass*), these are not the focus of this essay.

13. Theodore Adorno, "Can One Live After Auschwitz?" in *Can One Live After Auschwitz? A Philosophical Reader*, by Theodore Adorno, ed. Rolf Tiedemann, trans. Rodney Livingston and others (Stanford, CA: Stanford University Press, 1969), 67.

14. All page references are from Herman Melville, *"Billy Budd" and Other Tales* (New York: Penguin, 1961).

15. Hannah Arendt, *On Revolution* (New York: Penguin, 1963), 81–88.

16. Gilles Deleuze, "He Stuttered," in *Essays Critical and Clinical* (Minneapolis: University of Minnesota Press, 1997), 107–13.

17. Ruttenberg, "Melville's Handsome Sailor," 95.

18. On two ways silence can be "constitutive," see Keenan Ferguson, "Silence: A Politics," *Contemporary Political Theory*, no. 1 (2002): 1–17, and John Zumbrunnen, *Silence and Democracy: Athenian Politics in Thucydides' History* (University Park, PA: Penn State University Press, 2008).

19. Hannah Arendt, *Eichmann in Jerusalem: A Report on the Banality of Evil* (New York: Penguin Books, 1994), 69, 85–86.

20. See Kimberlé Crenshaw and Gary Peller, "Reel Time / Real Justice," in *Reading Rodney King, Reading Urban Uprising*, ed. Robert Gooding-Williams (New York: Routledge, 1993).

21. Friedrich Nietzsche, *On the Genealogy of Morality*, ed. Keith Ansell-Pearson, trans. Carol Diethe (Cambridge: Cambridge University Press, 1994).

22. The word *kakophoia*, meaning "bad nature, badness in nature, or what is unnatural," was present in the Academy, though it appears nowhere in Plato. See Plato, *Complete Works*, ed. John M. Cooper, assoc. ed. D. S. Hutchinson (Indianapolis, IN: Hackett, 1997), 1685.

23. See Michael Paul Rogin's original reading of the novel with his psychoanalytic elaboration of how each aspect of the soul functions in *Subversive Genealogy: The Politics and Art of Melville* (New York: Alfred A. Knopf, 1983).

24. Hans-Georg Gadamer, *Philosophical Hermeneutics*, ed. with intro. David Linge (Berkeley: University of California Press, 2008), 5.

FIVE

God and Goodness

A THEOLOGICAL EXPLORATION

Stanley Hauerwas

SETTING THE PROBLEM

Then someone came to him and said, "Teacher, what good deed must I do to have eternal life?" And he said to him, "Why do you ask me about what is good? There is only one who is good. If you wish to enter into life, keep the commandments." He said to him, "Which ones?" And Jesus said, "You shall not murder; You shall not commit adultery; You shall not steal; You shall not bear false witness; Honor your father and mother; also, You shall love your neighbor as yourself." The young man said to him, "I have kept all these; what do I still lack?" Jesus said to him, "If you wish to be perfect, go, sell your possessions, and give the money to the poor, and you will have treasure in heaven; then come and follow me." When the young man heard this word, he went away grieving, for he had many possessions.

Then Jesus said to his disciples, "Truly I tell you, it will be hard for a rich person to enter the kingdom of heaven. Again I tell you, it is easier for a camel to go through the eye of a needle than for someone who is rich to enter the kingdom of God." When the disciples heard this, they were greatly astounded and said, "Then who can be saved?" But Jesus looked at them and said. "For mortals it is impossible, but for God all things are possible." (Matthew 19:16-26)

Jesus does not answer the question as posed. The young man asked him what good deed he must do to gain eternal life. He seems to be asking a question we might identify as "ethical." Jesus, however, restates the question to suggest that metaphysical issues are at stake: "Why do you ask me about what is good?" Jesus's response to his own question, however, makes matters even more confusing because he suggests that the question is not about "what" but about "who."

I confess I find this exchange between Jesus and the young man—a young man who will turn out to have many possessions—puzzling. But that is probably the way it should be. Iris Murdoch's observation that "goodness appears to be both rare and hard to picture" certainly seems right.[1] Was Jesus trying to help the young man understand how difficult it is to "picture goodness"?[2] It is tempting to think Jesus was trying to make a philosophical point, but something more seems to be at stake. For he tells the young man that if he wishes to enter into life, which seems a more inclusive concept than the young man's question about "eternal life," he should keep the commandments. There must be some relation between goodness and keeping the commandments, but it is not immediately clear what that relation might be.

The young man reasonably responds by asking which commandments he should keep. Given Jesus's reframing of his question, we might have expected him to begin with the first commandment of the Decalogue. For surely God is "the only one who is good." But instead Jesus names the commandments of the Decalogue that deal with our relations with one another.[3] If the only one who is good is God, why does Jesus not begin with the commandment that we should have no other God than the one who brought Israel out of Egypt?

Even more puzzling, to the list derived from the Decalogue Jesus adds that we are to love our neighbor as ourselves. Paul writes to the church in Rome (Romans 13:8–10) suggesting that the same commandments Jesus commends to the young man are summed up by "Love your neighbor as yourself," but that is Paul, and this is Jesus. Later Jesus is asked by a Pharisee to identify the greatest commandment. He answers with the commandment that we should love God with all our heart, soul, and mind and our neighbor as ourselves (Matthew 22:34–40). And so it seems strange that he makes no such linkage in his reply to this young man. Even if such a linkage had been made, one wonders what the connection is between loving God, keeping the commandments, and loving one's neighbor.

Matters become even more complex with the young man's declaration that he has kept all the commandments Jesus enumerates but still thinks he must lack something. Jesus tells him to sell everything he has, give the proceeds to the poor, and then come and follow him. Is this a condition for being good that applies only to this young man? Or is Jesus suggesting anyone who wants to be good must be dispossessed? Moreover, what finally does following Jesus have to do with the one who alone is good? Jesus's declaration to the disciples concerning the status of the wealthy seems to suggest that goodness depends in some way on God; that is, "for God all things are possible." Is Jesus suggesting that he is the "who" that alone is good?

Christians are sure there is a relation between God and goodness, but we have never been sure how to spell it out. Platonism has often seemed like an attractive way to display the relation between God and goodness. Christians have read Plato's account of the impossibility of "picturing" the good as an anticipation of the Christian insistence that only God is good. Plato's account of the good, moreover, implies that there is a mystery about how someone may actually be good that suggests something like the Christian understanding of grace.

One cannot help but hear, for example, the Platonic resonances in Augustine when he says in *The City of God*,

> Thus we say that there is only one unchanging Good; and that is the one, true, and blessed God. The things he made are good because they were made by him; but they are subject to change, because they were made not out of his being but out of nothing. Therefore although they are not supreme goods, since God is a greater good than they, still those mutable goods are of great value, because they can adhere to the immutable Good, and so attain happiness; and this is so truly their Good, that without it the creatures cannot but be wretched.[4]

Such a view can lead and has led some to think that Christians, and in particular Augustine, subordinate all earthly loves, including love of neighbor, to the love of God. However, as Eric Gregory has recently argued, Augustine's distinction between what is to be enjoyed and what is to be used is finally not determined by his Platonism, because Augustine's Platonism is Christologically determined.[5] There can be no love of God, according to Augustine, apart from love of neighbor, but that is not to say, as Gregory observes, "that explicit love of God involves nothing more than love of neighbor."[6]

But what does it mean for goodness, even understood as love of the neighbor, to be Christologically determined? How is the love of God, the love that determines how goodness is understood, inseparable from what it means to "follow me"? To follow Christ, moreover, has meant that Christians have at times found it necessary to sacrifice all worldly goods including life itself rather than betray what they took to be necessary to follow Christ. Whatever it may mean to be good from a Christian perspective cannot avoid the possibility of martyrdom.[7]

That there is some essential connection between death and goodness is not a thought peculiar to Christians. Raimond Gaita, a philosopher who does not share my theological commitments, has argued that there is a necessary connection between how good people regard their deaths and how they understand the way they should care for their neighbor. By directing attention to Socrates' contention that nothing can harm a good man, Gaita develops an account of goodness that challenges modern accounts of altruism that conflate harm and suffering. When harm and suffering are not properly distinguished, Gaita suggests, this leads to a condescending stance toward those whose suffering cannot be eliminated.

Before turning to Gaita, I need to make it clear that I am not trying to argue that any satisfactory account of goodness requires belief in God. Such a project I take to be a theological mistake. It is a mistake often made by Christians faced by the loss of the status and intelligibility of Christian convictions in recent times: thus the attempt to show that if you do not believe in God the world will go to hell in a handbasket. I think we are long past the point where the truth of what Christians believe should depend on Christianity's being necessary to sustain the ethos of our "civilization."

By engaging Gaita, however, I hope that the analysis of goodness I develop will be of interest to those who do not share my theological convictions. That I write for myself and Christians, however, is an attempt to respond to a problem identified by Charles Taylor. Taylor observes that Platonism and Christianity, in spite of their considerable differences, shared the view that the good was known through the self-mastery made possible by reason in the case of Platonism and, in Christianity, by the transformation of the will by grace. Yet each tradition, according to Taylor, has been secularized primarily by being identified with the ideal of altruism.[8]

According to Taylor, most modern people assume that the highest form of ethical idealism is altruism. Because altruism is assumed to be the ideal, selfishness is then assumed to be the lowest form of morality. Such a high view of altruism means that those identified with dedication to others or the universal good are regarded with admiration and even awe. Such dedication has obvious roots, Taylor suggests, in "Christian spirituality" and no doubt is compatible with Christianity, but "the secular ethic of altruism has discarded something essential to the Christian outlook, once the love of God no longer plays a role."[9] Though Taylor does not explicitly draw the conclusion, I think his account of our lives makes it clear that the current identification of Christianity with altruism hides from most Christians that they have learned to live as if God does not exist.[10]

That is a position I hope to render problematic. My strategy is not to argue that what it means to be good depends on belief in God, but rather to show how goodness and God cannot be distinguished in the life and work of Jean Vanier. "Showing" is the heart of the matter. Gaita argues that if we are to see what goodness looks like it will depend on the unanticipated ability of some to be present to the afflicted without regret. Without people who have so learned to be with the afflicted, we are unable to see the humanity their affliction threatens to hide. I hope to show how such a "seeing" is made possible by the work of Jean Vanier.

RAIMOND GAITA ON GOODNESS

I am attracted to Raimond Gaita's account of goodness because his analysis betrays the influence of thinkers from whom I have also learned much—that is, Ludwig Wittgenstein, Rush Rhees, and Iris Murdoch. As might be expected from one so influenced, Gaita develops his case slowly and with attention to what we say. He attends to what we say because according to Gaita there cannot be an independent metaphysical inquiry into the reality of good and evil that could underwrite or undermine our most serious ways of speaking.[11] So he begins his investigation of what we might mean by good by directing attention to Socrates' address to the jury in the *Apology*: "You too gentlemen of the jury, must look forward to death with confidence and fix your minds on this one truth—that nothing can harm a good man either in life or after death."

Gaita observes that this passage is seldom discussed by Plato scholars because they assume that Socrates' claim about harm and what it means to be good is not relevant for understanding Plato's more developed metaphysics of the good. But Gaita lingers on Socrates' charge to the jury, arguing that Socrates meant not that people who live virtuously could not suffer but that, even in their suffering, people who see their life in the light of a certain kind of love, a love of philosophy, could not be harmed.

Socrates' understanding of goodness, Gaita suggests, astonished Aristotle, who thought Socrates' claim was irresponsible. For Aristotle, who certainly thought a person of virtue could endure great suffering, recognized that there might come a time in life when people's suffering was so great that they could not help but think it would have been better never to have been born. Gaita characterizes Aristotle's reaction to Socrates as the "most serious in the history of philosophy."[12] Yet Aristotle understood that he could only react to Socrates, because no argument in itself could count against Socrates' claim.

Yet Aristotle objected to Socrates' view because he assumed that a certain kind of humanism was at stake. It is a humanism that Gaita characterizes as a "non-reductive naturalism," committed to the view that what one counts as harm depends on one's ethical perspective. Aristotle, in contrast to Socrates, was attempting to defend what Gaita describes as an urbane humanism. From Aristotle's perspective, a Socratic point of view is but "high-minded indecency" if it fails to acknowledge that some lives are so steeped in appalling and ineradicable affliction that they are irredeemably ruined.

To explain why he thinks Aristotle represents such a view, Gaita raises the question "whether we can see those who have no share in what gives our lives sense as our moral equals."[13] We would like to think we do, but, drawing on Simone Weil, Gaita suggests that our reaction to those we do not believe share our moral lives is one of condescension. Weil observes: "We have the same carnal natures as animals. If a hen is hurt the others rush up to peck it. Our senses attach to affliction all the contempt, all the revulsion, all the hatred which our reason attaches to crime. Except for those whose soul is inhabited by Christ, everybody despises the afflicted to some extent, although practically no-one is conscious of it."[14]

Gaita is not questioning that most of us do not believe the afflicted should be despised or condescended to, but the question is whether we understand ourselves in believing it. He suspects we share with Aristotle the rejection of Socrates' claim that a good man cannot be harmed because we do believe it is possible for misfortune irredeemably to ruin the life of even a virtuous person. Such a view, according to Gaita, is based on the "sense of necessity which is internal to the judgment that there are lives such that it would have been better for those who suffer them if they had not been born."[15]

Gaita, however, argues that it is just at this point that we see the profound difference between Socrates and Aristotle. For Aristotle did not see, as at least Plato seemed to gesture, that "there was goodness beyond virtue and evil beyond vice."[16] Such goodness Socrates not only possessed, but saw in others. In contrast to Aristotle, Socrates thought no amount of suffering could negate the good. Thus Socrates' claim that a good man cannot be harmed. Such a view of the good, Gaita observes, is essentially mysterious given our limited epistemic and logical powers. The task of philosophy is to provide conceptual space for acknowledging such a mystery.

According to Gaita, there are three requirements philosophy must meet if a space is to be left for an account of the good that respects this mystery. The concept of what is essentially mysterious must be connected to a certain conception of experience; the concept of experience must be connected with that of being bound in testimony; and "we must give a serious place to the concept of love, Goodness and purity."[17]

All Gaita can do, therefore, is to provide examples that display the pressure to claim, as Socrates did, that a good person cannot be harmed.[18] The example he provides is Mother Teresa of Calcutta. He does so because it is said that she showed those who were appallingly afflicted "a compassion that was without a trace of condescension." That her compassion was without condescension means Mother Teresa was able to care for the afflicted "without a trace of the thought that it had been better if the person for whom she felt compassion had never been born, even if they suffered affliction of the most protracted, severe and ineradicable sort."[19]

Her compassion was a denial that the affliction could, or even at a certain limit must, make a person's life worthless. Mother Teresa's love had a purity that can only be characterized as a gift. So it is not an achievement that on Aristotelian grounds might be found in a virtue such as courage. Rather, her love is born of a humility that makes it of a different order. We stand in awe of such a love, but our wonder is determined not by her achievements but by the light her love throws on the afflicted. "The wonder which is in response to her is not a wonder at her, but a wonder *that human life could be as her love reveals it*."[20]

Gaita argues that it is a mistake, however, to try to retain the sense of what is revealed by the love Mother Teresa exhibits by constructing a metaphysics that would secure it.[21] He argues that his account of her compassion requires no metaphysical underpinning and in particular the "metaphysical underpinning that is often associated with Christianity."[22] He does not deny that Mother Teresa says she would not be able to do what she does were it not for the love of Jesus, but Gaita says he does not even have to ask what that means, much less believe it. Rather, we can retain a sense of what her compassion reveals by attention to similar things that are absolutely good. "We know them only as they are revealed in the light of pure love."[23]

But that is not Gaita's last word on the matter. He returns to the question of goodness in his book *A Common Humanity: Thinking About Love and Truth and Justice*, first published in Australia in 1998.[24] He begins a chapter titled "Goodness Beyond Virtue" with a story of working as a ward assistant in a psychiatric hospital when he was a seventeen.[25] It was in the early 1960s, and the ward was more like a prison than a hospital. The patients were judged incurable, so they were often subjected to inhumane treatments such a being washed down with mops after they had soiled themselves. Friends and relatives had long since ceased to visit them, and they were often treated brutally by those charged with their care.

There were some psychiatrists who worked to improve their condition in the name of the inalienable dignity of even patients. Gaita admired the psychiatrists' commitment to their patients, but, he observes, it probably did not help to appeal to their inalienable dignity, because such an appeal depends too much on appearances. The appeal to someone's "dignity" is too easily undermined by the complete loss of any "humanity."

However, Gaita reports, one day there came to the ward a nun whose demeanor toward the patients—the way she spoke to them, her facial expressions, the inflections of her body—was in marked contrast to that of even the psychiatrists Gaita admired. For like Mother Teresa she was without condescension.[26] She was able to interact with the people suffering from mental illness without any thought that it might be better had they never been born.

Gaita says he does not know how important it might have been that she was a nun. Her behavior might have been a function of her religious belief, but, because he argues that beliefs can explain behavior independent of their truth or falsity, nothing follows from how her behavior was connected to her beliefs. More important is how her behavior was shaped by the reality it revealed, that is, the full humanity of those whose afflictions had made their humanity invisible. Therefore no justification of her behavior is required because "the purity of her love proved the reality of what it revealed."[27]

Such love, according to Gaita, depends on the conviction that there exists goodness beyond virtue and evil beyond vice. True love requires that every human being, as Hannah Arendt argues, be regarded as "infinitely precious." To learn to love others and regard them as infinitely precious, Gaita suggests, requires training exemplified in the lives of the saints.[28]

Gaita acknowledges that religious traditions have spoken most simply and deeply about such a view by declaring all human beings sacred. But he contends that the language of love nourished by the love of saints can stand independent of speculation about supernatural entities. What grew in one place can flourish elsewhere. He reports, however, that there is one question put to him by a theologian whose answer he is not sure of.[29] The theologian asked whether the kind of love shown by the nun could exist in the prolonged absence of the kind of practices that were part of her religious vocation. In response Gaita says: "Iris Murdoch said that attention to something absolutely pure is the essence of prayer and is a form of love. If she is right, then the answer to Hauerwas' question will depend on whether with the demise of religion, we can find objects of attention that can sustain that love, or whether they will always fail us. I don't know the answer."[30]

Nor do I know the answer. I certainly have no reason to suggest that Gaita's account of goodness as noncondescending love is unintelligible if God does not exist. But then the question has never been about God's existence—it is about ours. Gaita is quite right to think that if Mother Teresa and the nun he encountered at seventeen did not exist we quite literally would be less human. They did exist, however, and it at least makes sense to ask if and how they and the goodness they reveal make sense if the God they worship does not exist.

That may well be far too abstract a way to put the question. For the God they worship is not some abstraction but rather a reality known through participation in a community across time and space. What I suspect Gaita misses is the role friendship plays in lives like that of Mother Teresa and the nun he so admires. In particular, Mother Teresa and the nun were not afraid to be befriended by those they served. To suggest why friendship is so important for the development of such goodness, I want to introduce another life that exhibits the kind of love Gaita thinks so defining of goodness.[31] The name of that life is Jean Vanier.

JEAN VANIER ON BEING BEFRIENDED BY THE DISABLED

Jean Vanier is the founder of the movement known as L'Arche ("the ark"). L'Arche is now a reality around the world in which people who are called mentally handicapped live with those who are not. A L'Arche home is just that, a home. The core members of the home are the mentally handicapped. Those who are not mentally handicapped are called assistants. Assistants do not live in the home to care for the mentally handicapped, they are there to be with the core members in the hope that they can learn to be friends.

In a lecture at Harvard titled "Through Their Wounds We Are Healed," Vanier told the story of how he, the son of a prominent family in Quebec, came to live with the mentally disabled. This is his story:

> I was thirteen when I joined the British navy during World War II. My adolescent years were taken up in the world of efficiency, controlling and commanding others. I was a technician of destruction. My last ship was the Canadian aircraft carrier, "The Magnificent." However, after a few years, I felt called by Jesus to take another path, the path of peace. I left the navy and did a doctorate in philosophy in Paris. I started teaching philosophy at the University of Toronto. Then through a priest-friend, I had the good fortune of meeting people with mental disabilities.
>
> In 1964 I took from an asylum two men, Raphael and Philip, and we began to live together. I did not know I was founding the first of many L'Arche communities. I simply felt called to live with these two men who had suffered rejection and a lot of inner pain and perhaps with a few others like them. When I had begun living with them, I soon started to discover the immense pain in their hearts. When we talk of the poor, or of announcing the good news to the poor, we should never

idealize the poor. Poor people are hurt; they are in pain. They can be very angry, in revolt or in depression.[32]

Vanier wrote his dissertation at the Catholic Institute of Paris on Aristotle. He would later write a favorable book on Aristotle's ethics, but he was critical of Aristotle's understanding of character friendship as possible only between equals.[33] He was critical of Aristotle's account of friendship because Aristotle failed to provide the resources necessary to account for what Vanier felt living with the mentally disabled had given him. Limited though they may be, unable to read or write, moving slowly or clumsily, many unable to speak, walk, or eat on their own, according to Vanier they have been an incredible gift to him. For if you are open to them, if you welcome them, "they give us life and lead us to Jesus and the good news."[34]

Vanier reports that when he began to live with Raphael and Philip he discovered their deep cry for communion. From their loneliness and pain they cried for love and friendship. Such a cry is often present when we visit people in institutions. Through the look in their eyes the men and women say to us, "Will you be my friend? Am I important to you? Do I have any value?" Some may be hiding away in a corner, taking cover behind bars of self-hatred; still others may be banging their heads on the wall, but they are crying for love, friendship, and communion.[35]

According to Vanier, when these people are welcomed from their world of anguish, brokenness, and depression, when they gradually discover they are loved, they are transformed. Their tense and angry bodies become relaxed and peaceful. Such discoveries Vanier says have helped him understand what it means to live in communion with someone. "Communion means accepting people just as they are, with their limits and inner pain, but also with their gifts and their beauty and their capacity to grow: to see the beauty inside of all the pain. To love someone is not first of all to do things *for* them, but to reveal to them their beauty and value, to say to them through our attitude: 'You are beautiful. You are important. I trust you. You can trust yourself.'"[36]

Vanier confesses that communion did not come easily to him. For one taught from an early age to be first, it is not easy to be asked by Jesus to share your life with those who have little culture. Only as he began to live with Raphael and Philip did he discover the hardness in his heart. They were crying out for friendship, and Vanier did not know how to respond because of the forces in him that, as he put it, "would pull him up the ladder." Yet he tells us that over the years the people he lives with in L'Arche have been teaching and healing him.

That he has been undergoing such training leads Vanier to observe that the people who come to L'Arche because they want to serve the poor are able to stay only once they discover that they are the poor. They must discover that Jesus came to bring good news to *the poor*, not those who *serve* the poor. According to Vanier, if you are called to live with wounded people, you must discover that God is present in the poverty and wounds of their hearts. He continues:

> God is not present in their capacity to heal but rather in their need to be healed. We can only truly love people who are different, we can only discover that difference is a treasure and not a threat, if in some way our hearts are becoming enfolded in the heart of the Father, if somewhere God is putting into our broken hearts that love that is in God's own heart for each and every human being. For God is truly in love with people, and with every individual human being. This healing power in us will not come from our capacities and our riches, but in and through our poverty. We are called to discover that God can bring peace, compassion and love through *our* wounds.[37]

Vanier reports that when he reads the gospels he is always moved by how Jesus lives and acts, how he enters into a relationship with each person he encounters. He asks, "Will you come with me? I love you. Will you enter into communion with me?" But his invitation to follow him is an invitation that forces us to make a choice. If you choose to follow him it means refusing to go in a different direction. If you choose to follow Jesus you will receive the gift of love and communion, but at the same time you will discover you must say no to the ways of the world and accept loss.[38]

Gaita wonders at the compassion Mother Teresa displays because it is without a trace of condescension. He is quite right, moreover, that to be free of condescension is remarkable because, as Weil insists, we *do* despise the afflicted, though we are seldom conscious of doing so. We despise them I think because, as Vanier suggests, we fear them. We fear and hate them for revealing our own weaknesses, our powerlessness to "make them strong." In the face of our helplessness some are even led to think it would be better that such people not exist. Compassion, particularly when it takes the form of altruism, can become murderous.[39]

SHOWINGS

"The wonder"—that is, the wonder Gaita suggests Mother Teresa should elicit in us—is not to be directed at her. Rather, it is the "wonder that hu-

man life could be as her love reveals it."[40] Jean Vanier would not wish that
we react to his life with "wonder" or awe. Any wonder would rightly be in
response to the humanity revealed through those who have befriended him.
He and his friends reveal our humanity, a goodness that we could not have
known possible without their "showing."

Jesus did not answer the young man's question concerning what deed
he must do to inherit eternal life. Instead, he commanded him to sell his
possessions, give the money to the poor, and follow him. To learn to follow
Jesus is the training necessary to become a human being.[41] To be a human
being is not a natural condition but requires training. The kind of training
required, moreover, has everything to do with death. To follow Jesus is to go
with him to Jerusalem, where he will be crucified. To follow Jesus therefore
is to undergo a training that refuses to let death, even death at the hands of
enemies, determine the shape of our living.

To learn to live without protection is to learn to live without possessions.
To be dispossessed, however, cannot be willed. To try to be dispossessed is
to be possessed by the will to be dispossessed. Rather, as Jean Vanier's life
reveals, to be dispossessed comes by being made a friend of those who have
no possessions. They have had to learn to live without possessions. Jean
Vanier had to learn from them how to live without the protections we think
possessions provide. To learn to live this way is to learn that death is not the
worst thing that can happen to us. The worst thing is to never have challenged our presumption that it would be better that Jean Vanier's friends
should have never been born.

Iris Murdoch observes that the "notion that 'it all somehow must make
sense'" seems necessary to preserve us from despair. The difficulty, according to Murdoch, is how to entertain such a consoling notion in a way that
does not hide from us the pointlessness of our living. She argues, therefore,
that "as soon as any idea is a consolation the tendency to falsify it becomes
strong: hence the traditional problem of preventing the idea of God from
degenerating in the believer's mind."[42] I do not think that belief in God
somehow makes "it all make sense." I do believe that the life and work of
Jean Vanier make sense of believing in a God who alone is good.

NOTES

1. Iris Murdoch, *The Sovereignty of Good* (New York: Schocken, 1971), 53.
2. Hilary Putnam, I think rightly, argues that Wittgenstein's attack on philosophers
   for being in the grip of a picture does not mean that he opposes pictorial thinking
   or thinks it is always a mistake. Wittgenstein does not think we can or should avoid
   pictures, but too steady a diet of one picture can get in the way of thought. Thus

Putnam argues that Wittgenstein's view is that religious people do employ pictures and draw certain consequences from them, but they are not the same consequences we draw when we use similar pictures in other contexts. The trick is locating the differences. See Hilary Putnam, *Renewing Philosophy* (Cambridge, MA: Harvard University Press, 1992), 156–57.

3. I think it a mistake, however, to separate the so-called second table of the Decalogue from the commandments dealing with our relationship with God. Aquinas rightly argued that the commandments are inseparable, which means that honoring father and mother depends on a people who have learned to have no other God than the one who delivered Israel from Egypt. For a more extensive account of the relation between the commandments, see Will Willimon and Stanley Hauerwas, *The Truth About God: The Ten Commandments and the Christian Life* (Nashville, TN: Abingdon Press, 1999), and Stanley Hauerwas, *Sanctify Them in the Truth: Holiness Exemplified* (Nashville, TN: Abingdon Press, 1998), 37–59. Jesus's naming the commandments that deal with the neighbor is a nice confirmation of Herbert McCabe's contention in *Law, Love, and Language* (London: Continuum, 2003) that it is not that God reveals the Ten Commandments to us, but that the Ten Commandments reveal God to us (57). McCabe's remark, I think, is where one must begin to think through the so-called Euthyphro question concerning the relation between the gods and piety.

4. Augustine, *The City of God*, trans. Henry Bettenson (Hammondsworth, UK: Penguin, 1976), 12, 1 (472).

5. Eric Gregory, *Politics and the Order of Love: An Augustinian Ethic of Democratic Citizenship* (Chicago: University of Chicago Press, 2008), 319–62. For a particularly insightful account of Augustine's "Platonism," see John Peter Kenney, *The Mysticism of Saint Augustine: Reading the Confessions* (New York: Routledge, 2005). Kenny observes that "Augustine understands divine transcendence according to his own logic, which owes its inspiration to the *libri Platonicorum*, but which turns out, upon inspection, to be a departure. He too is emphatic in asserting a level of intelligible reality beyond the sensible world. The intelligible/sensible distinction is fundamental to the theological narrative throughout the *Confessions*. Yet it is also, in the end, superseded by the distinction between the creator and the created" (124).

6. Gregory, *Politics and the Order of Love*, 322. Therefore, in spite of Augustine's worries about how friendship can distract from the love of God, Gregory rightly, I believe, suggests Augustine never abandoned his view that particular friendships are the school of virtue where compassion and social trust are learned (356–57).

7. Chris Huebner provides an insightful account of martyrdom as a challenge to the modern account of identity in *A Precarious Peace: Yoderian Explorations on Theology, Knowledge, and Identity* (Scottdale, PA: Herald Press, 2006), 189–202. Martyrs, from Huebner's perspective, constitute the paradigm of the Christian just to the extent that they do not know who they are until God tells them. Martyrs cannot seek martyrdom, not only because they rightly do not desire death, but because they do not want those who would kill them to be murderers. Accordingly, the church understands martyrdom to be a gift, not an accomplishment. Martyrs therefore are neither heroes nor victims. They are martyrs. See also Craig Hovey, *To Share in the*

Body: A Theology of Martyrdom for Today's Church (Grand Rapids, MI: Brazos Press, 2008), and Joshua Whitfield, *Pilgrim Holiness: Martyrdom as Descriptive Witness* (Eugene, OR: Cascade Press, 2008). Whitfield calls attention to an early Christian martyr named Sanctus whose body was so brutalized that it no longer was identifiable as a human body. Repeatedly questioned by his torturers about who he might be, he would say only, "I am a Christian." A reminder that whatever it might mean for Christians to be good, their primary identity is determined by a narrative in which what most mean by "good" is rendered secondary.

8. Charles Taylor, *Sources of the Self: The Making of Modern Identity* (Cambridge, MA: Harvard University Press, 1989), 21–22.

9. Ibid., 22.

10. In a sermon on Matthew 22:34–46 titled "Loving Yourself," Samuel Wells advises those who have always been told they should always live for others as a way to avoid being selfish that when they hear the words "Love your neighbor as yourself" they should swap the words round and say "Love yourself as your neighbor." They should do so because we ought to regard ourselves as the first among all the neighbors God calls us to love. Wells observes that the language of altruism never grasps this because it assumes we must choose between loving ourselves and loving others. "But God loves every one of us while still loving each of us as if we were the only one. We're able to love others because of the way God loves us. And to accept that love, we have to learn to love ourselves." Sermon Preached in Duke University chapel on October 26, 2008. For an argument that altruism and egoism are mistakenly understood as contending forces, see Ruth Grant's paper in this volume.

11. Raimond Gaita, *Good and Evil: An Absolute Conception* (London: Macmillan, 1991), 192. Of course one of the problems with Gaita's "method" is who the "we" is.

12. Ibid., 193.

13. Ibid., 195.

14. Quoted in ibid., 195. I explored a similar observation made by Adam Smith about those who had gone mad in Stanley Hauerwas, *Suffering Presence: Theological Reflections on Medicine, the Mentally Handicapped, and the Church* (Notre Dame, IN: University of Notre Dame Press, 1986), 174–75. Also relevant is the chapter "To Love God, the Poor, and Learning: Lessons Learned from Saint Gregory of Nazianzus," in Stanley Hauerwas, *The State of the University: Academic Knowledges and the Knowledge of God* (Oxford: Blackwell, 2007), 187–201. That chapter is my attempt to show the importance of Gregory's great oration on the significance of leprosy for constituting the Christian city. Gregory sees quite clearly that the sadness that constitutes the lives of lepers is their "sense that they are actually hated for their misfortune." They cannot help, moreover, identifying with such hate, leading them to regret their own existence. Drawn to lie beside one another, Gregory describes, as "a wretched union born of disease, each contributing his own misfortune to the common fund of misery, thus heightening each other's distress; pitiful in their affliction, more so in the sharing of it." "Letter 182" in *The Fathers Speak: St. Basil the Great, St. Gregory of Nazianzus, St. Gregory of Nyssa*, trans. Georges Barrois (Crestwood, NY: St. Vladimir's Seminary Press, 1986), 48.

15. Gaita, *Good and Evil*, 197. In *The Philosopher's Dog* (London: Routledge, 2002), Gaita makes the relation between how we regard our deaths and the deaths of others clearer than he does in his earlier work. He says, "Because animals have no reflective knowledge of death, they cannot dread it and if they could, they could not take comfort from the fact that they are not alone in their mortality. It is a fact utterly basic to human life that we are consoled by knowledge that others suffer as we do and must die as we must. At first sight that might seem like unsavory consolation, achieved by taking pleasure in the miseries of others. Really, it is not or, at any rate, mostly it is not. We are creatures who seek to make sense of our lives and the sense we make is never entirely private. What sense we make of our particular lives is always in large part sense we make of the human condition. The need to make sense of death is obviously driven not only by a response to one's own suffering, but also by a more general need to understand what it means to live a human life, and what death shows us about that meaning" (71–72).

16. Gaita, *Good and Evil*, 202.

17. Ibid., 203.

18. Gaita has an interesting comment on Ludwig Wittgenstein's remarking to his housekeeper as he was dying that she was to "tell them [his friends] that it has been a wonderful life." Gaita observes that Wittgenstein was not rendering a judgment that might be reconsidered but rather was expressing gratitude for his life considered as a certain kind of whole. Gaita argues that Wittgenstein's remark rightly means, "We cannot *flatly* say of any life, not even a life in which there had been much suffering, that it could have been better if only it had been blessed with more fortune. A human life can be seen under the aspect of that kind of unity which gives it a kind of completion, and indeed a kind of perfection, which resists any such appraisal. I think that is what Aristotle meant when he said a happy life was 'complete and lacking in nothing'" (*Good and Evil*, 198–99).

19. Ibid., 203.

20. Ibid., 206.

21. I suspect Gaita is reflecting the influence of Murdoch's claim that "the good has nothing to do with purpose, indeed it excludes the idea of purpose. 'All is vanity' is the beginning and end of ethics.' The only genuine way to be good is to be good 'for nothing' in the midst of a scene where every 'natural' thing, including one's own mind, is subject to chance, that is, to necessity. That 'for nothing' is indeed the experienced correlate of the invisibility or non-representable blankness of the idea of Good itself" (*Sovereignty of Good*, 71).

22. Gaita, *Good and Evil*, 214.

23. Ibid.

24. Raimond Gaita, *A Common Humanity: Thinking About Love and Truth and Justice* (London: Routledge, 2000). David Parker provides a fascinating reading of Gaita's work, and in particular his memoir, *Romulus, My Father*, to suggest that Gaita represents the exhaustion of the paradigm of autobiography that configures identity around ethnicity, gender, class, race, sexual preference, and natural language. Gaita is trying to react against the multiculturalist ethos by showing how goods that tran-

scend boundaries of difference can shape lives. Parker treats Gaita's work as one illustration of his general contention, a contention shaped by Taylor's *Sources of the Self*, that "the good is an inescapable framework for understanding any human agent and therefore for any writer of life narrative." See David Parker, *The Self in Moral Space: Life Narrative and the Good* (Ithaca, NY: Cornell University Press, 2007), 6. Parker argues that Gaita's account of his father is the key to the philosophical position he develops just to the extent that Gaita depicts his father as one who would sooner suffer wrong than to do it (135). Parker argues, however, based on Gaita's text, that Gaita has not been able to escape the particularistic language that depends on difference.

25. Gaita's attraction to Mother Teresa and the nun he encounters in the psychiatric hospital is understandable, but I wonder why he did not also consider those whose "goodness seems beyond virtue"—who have not led virtuous lives but have done extraordinary things. I am thinking of people like Oskar Schindler. That Gaita does not treat people like Schindler seems all the more surprising because Thomas Keneally, the author of *Schindler's List*, like Gaita, is Australian. Graham Greene gave classic expression to "goodness beyond virtue" in *The Power and the Glory*, introd. John Updike (New York: Penguin Books, 1990).

26. Gaita, *Common Humanity*, 17-18.

27. Ibid., 21.

28. Ibid., xix.

29. I was the theologian who asked the question that Gaita is not sure how to answer. I do not remember when or where I asked him about where such lives might come from once the practices that shaped the nun are no longer in existence. Some years ago we spoke at a conference in Australia, but that was well before he had published *A Common Humanity*. When I asked the question matters little, but I think its form is important. For note that I did not ask him about "beliefs," but rather asked about the practices that constitute belief.

30. Gaita, *Common Humanity*, xx.

31. The role of examples for characterizing goodness is crucial yet is a complex matter not easily analyzed. In the same passage by Murdoch that I quote toward the beginning of this chapter, concerning how hard it is to picture goodness, she comments further that goodness "is perhaps most convincingly met with in simple people— inarticulate, unselfish mothers of large families—but these cases are also the least illuminating" (*Sovereignty of Good*), 53. Such a comment may betray someone who lives in a world isolated from "simple people." Once you get to know them, simple people often turn out to be anything but "simple." But more important, Murdoch does not explain why "such cases" are the "least illuminating." Is it because she thinks, in Charles Taylor's terms, that the kind of goodness they display is inarticulate? If so, why is being articulate necessary for being good? I suspect goodness does require being articulate, but there are diverse ways to be articulate that Murdoch (and Taylor) may not have appreciated. In *Sources of the Self*, Taylor contrasts an honor ethic with the ethic of Plato to show that the former does not require the same philosophical articulateness as Plato's (20-21). Yet "I am a Christian" is prob-

ably closer to the "inarticulate warrior" than it is to Plato's philosophical account of the good. In *The Self in Moral Space* Parker argues that Taylor rightly contends that we "are all almost necessarily living by many more forms of the good than we can be aware of," which makes it all the more important that we "bring to focus the suppressed structures of value that constitute the ethical lives that we moderns cannot avoid living" (175).

32. Jean Vanier, *From Brokenness to Community* (New York: Paulist Press, 1992), 11–12.

33. The dissertation was "Happiness as Principle and End of Aristotelian Ethics." The later book is *Made for Happiness: Discovering the Meaning of Life with Aristotle*, trans. Kathryn Spink (London: Darton, Longman, Todd, 2001).

34. Vanier, *From Brokenness to Community*, 9. Hans Reinders provides the best account we have of how Vanier's work changes the way we must think of friendship. In particular Reinders argues that L'Arche requires as the prerequisite of friendship that we learn to receive the gift of unconditional love. That gift of unconditional love, Christians believe, is bestowed on us by God. For we believe that the "final end of our existence is to be reunited with God: friendship is the proper name of this reunion. The theological warrant for this claim is that the Christian story of God is about the promise that he will not abandon his creation, even when his creatures, for one reason or another, do not know how to find him. To restore us to the possibility of that reunion, God became one of us and gave himself to save us. This is, in essence, the story of God with human beings as Christians understand it. We learn from this story what living as human beings created in the divine image entails. Those who believe that this story reveals the truth about their existence will live lives in the promise of a gift that exceeds all other gifts: being one with God. Since they know that this promise is grounded in God's self-giving and does not in any way depend on their own doing, believers will know that living their lives in truth is possible only because of God's unconditional love. Friendship with God is a gift that is only his to give." Hans Reinders, *Receiving the Gift of Friendship: Profound Disability, Theological Anthropology, and Ethics* (Grand Rapids, MI: Eerdmans, 2008), 351.

35. Vanier, *From Brokenness to Community*, 14–15.

36. Ibid., 16.

37. Ibid., 20–21.

38. Ibid., 10.

39. See for example my chapter "Killing Compassion" in Stanley Hauerwas, *Dispatches from the Front: Theological Engagements with the Secular* (Durham, NC: Duke University Press, 1994), 164–76.

40. Gaita, *Good and Evil*, 206.

41. I am indebted to Romand Coles for this way of putting the matter.

42. Murdoch, *Sovereignty of Good*, 56–57.

To Make This Emergence Articulate

THE BEAUTIFUL, THE TRAGIC SUBLIME, THE GOOD,
AND THE SHAPES OF COMMON PRACTICE

Romand Coles

Commenting on Richard Wright's *Native Son,* James Baldwin argues that a literature more capable of informing initiatives beyond white supremacy, on the one hand, and self-destructive rage on the other, would need "to make this tradition articulate."[1] By "this tradition" he meant the myriad ways that for centuries blacks have both been marked by and given expression to their "long and painful experience"; their "battle waged" to survive; their struggle to create and pass on quotidian customs of care, pedagogy, and community that have enabled a modicum of freedom and relational dignity in a racist polity bent on extinguishing these practices. The hope for engendering a people more capable of living better and resisting—perhaps even transforming—the evils of the dominant order hinges on the pedagogy of powerful memories of how they had best done so thus far—without pretending to have passed beyond the place "where all men are betrayed by greed and guilt and bloodlust and where no one's hands are clean."[2] The chance for goodness in a world where, as Walter Benjamin put it poignantly, "the tradition of the oppressed teaches us that the 'state of emergency' in which we live is not the exception but the rule"[3] hinges on both powerful narratives recollecting the ways the squeaky-clean "goodness" of United States exceptionalism has been integrally entwined with the extinction of "many thousands gone" (the title of Baldwin's essay) and the ways (especially) black people have struggled for survival and dignity under the talons of this order.

By striving "to make this tradition articulate," then, Baldwin attached himself not to the dominant national teleology, but rather to a tenuous historical gathering of countermoves, always in a state of discerning, recovering, creating, and articulating themselves in a struggle to emerge beyond the barriers that established "goodness" poses to the possibility of goodness. In order to strike the tragic register that is appropriate in this context, let me put it thus: If Benjamin is right that "the state of emergency" is the norm (and surely Baldwin thinks he is), then goodness might be thought of always in terms of "arts of emergence"—emergence from emergency and impending catastrophe. Of course, "emergence" resonates with Kant's notion of enlightenment as "man's emergence from his self-imposed tutelage." This resonance is intentional. It is useful to read Baldwin and the account of emergence I offer in this essay less as "counter-enlightenment," and more as an exploration of understandings, sensibilities, and practices of an alternative enlightenment: modes of seeing, feeling, thinking, imagining, and possibly becoming better. Yet Baldwin's emergence is profoundly different from Kant's. For Baldwin, emergence is a task permanently linked to articulate memory of how the past's blindness and brutality continue to erode our present efforts, as well as to a sense of how quotidian social and political arts are indispensable to its possibility.

Goodness is often thought of in terms of innocence, whether of a person or of a collectivity; whether of the present or of a future soon to be attained; whether origin or goal. Yet "innocence" is one of the dirtiest words in Baldwin's lexicon.

> American white men still nourish the illusion that there is some means of recovering the European innocence of returning to a state where black men do not exist. This is one of the greatest errors Americans can make. . . . The American vision of the world—which allows so little reality . . . for any of the darker forces in human life, which tends until today to paint moral issues in glaring black and white—owes a great deal to the battle waged by Americans to maintain between themselves and black men a human separation which could not be bridged. . . . [T]his vision of the world is dangerously inaccurate, and perfectly useless. For it protects our moral high-mindedness at the terrible expense of weakening our grasp of reality. . . . anyone who insists on remaining in a state of innocence long after that innocence is dead turns himself into a monster.[4]

In contrast to the illusions of past, present, or soon-to-be-realized innocence, Baldwin calls us, "in great pain and terror . . . to assess the history which has placed one where one is and formed one's point of view"; "to enter into battle with that historical creation, Oneself, and to recreate oneself according to a principle more humane and more liberating"; "to wrestle with it, and finally accept it in order to bring myself out of it."[5] "More" is the operative word here: emergence is the permanently intransigent practice of seeking to acknowledge the despicable in order to wrestle our way beyond its grasp and move toward something better. As soon as we think we have arrived, or are nearing arrival, or are the best approximations of innocence, the odds are overwhelming that we will become much worse.

On the other hand, Baldwin thinks that acknowledging our entanglements opens us not to despair, but rather toward a more expansive notion of love and even "God." "I conceive of my own life as a journey toward something I do not understand, which in the going toward makes me better. . . . Love is a battle, love is a war; love is growing up."[6] Baldwin seeks to make this emergence articulate.

This constellation of insights forms the backdrop that haunts and guides my present efforts to articulate how we might live less poorly—and perhaps even better, which I take to be the task at the heart of goodness. In particular, I seek to make articulate some of the aesthetic, sensual aspects of this emergence in relation to some of the specific practices in which this struggle is under way in my new home in Flagstaff, Arizona. I take Iris Murdoch to be an indispensable interlocutor for this effort, not only because she takes the question of "how to become better" to be elemental to our understanding of the good and goodness, but because she maintains an intransigent eye toward the infinite value of the contingent, the inexpungable character of messiness, the proximity of blindness and tragic death, and the vitality of an ethical imagination that is at once rooted in and reflectively expressive of everyday traditions wherein lies the drama of the human thing. I begin with a brief discussion of Murdoch's account of what it might mean to theorize about goodness, before I turn to the task of actually doing so (with and beyond her reflections) from the vantage point of some emblematic emerging practices.

* * *

> What we require is a renewed sense of the difficulty and complexity of the moral life and the opacity of persons. . . . We need more concepts in terms of which to picture the substance of our being; it is through an enriching and deepening of concepts that moral progress takes place. Simone Weil said that morality was a matter of attention, not will. We need a new vocabulary of attention.[7]

For Murdoch, moral progress is less a matter of choice than the result of "patient, loving regard, directed upon a person, a thing, a situation" that yields something like "obedience": a perception that is so textured, developed, and vivid that much of our response seems inexorably oriented and constrained by the way things appear.[8] If this is so, the hope of becoming better hinges on seeing better, improving our aesthetic relation to the world. Such "refined and honest perception"—a "patient and just discernment of what confronts one"—is a "moral discipline."[9] A vital condition of such discipline is the presence of rich conceptual and imaginative vocabularies that solicit and inform it, at once orienting our vision and reminding us how little and how poorly we typically see.

Murdoch thinks most modern accounts of cognitive and moral action lead us far astray, and she offers instead a vision of the good profoundly inspired by Plato. While her concept of the good evokes goodness as an unending struggle toward a transcendence that both magnetizes our striving and forever remains inexhaustible in relation to our efforts, Murdoch does not claim that the truth status of her account rests on a transcendent vision. Instead, she speaks of a "non-metaphysical transcendence" revealed immanently in our ordinary experiences "connected with the attempt to see the unself."[10] She conceives of this theory as "a kind of inconclusive nondogmatic naturalism, which has the circularity of definition characteristic of such theories."[11] Moral pictures and concepts are rooted in our sense of the important facts of moral experience, while these "facts" are in turn illumined and Sovereignty of Good concealed by our moral vocabularies. "At deep levels, metaphor and perception merge. Perception is a mode of evaluation."[12] Hence "the development of consciousness in human beings is inseparably connected with the use of metaphor. Metaphors are . . . fundamental forms of our awareness of our condition."[13] Plato's metaphors—for example, the good, the sun, the fire, and the cave—are all forms of awareness that are both rooted in and supportive of our emergence from various states of unawareness. They are ways of attending to attention.

This circularity might seem to damn us eternally to pure arbitrariness, especially in light of Murdoch's profound sense of the "contextual privacy of language": the extent to which linguistic subtleties develop as "words said to particular individuals at particular times . . . grouped round a common object," whether this be a person, a thing, or a situation encompassing many of both.[14] Yet whether we are damned or not, she argues, depends significantly on the metaphors of cognition we employ as well as on the facts they do or do not illuminate. Thus metaphors that figure us as possessors of self-evident reason, pure choice, or radical linguistic constructivism tend to render invisible any gap between cognition and world and thereby short-circuit reflection that might lead to more just cognition. They constitutively "ignore certain facts, and . . . impose a single theory which admits of no communication with or escape into rival theories."[15] In contrast, Murdoch's metaphors draw our attention to the commonness of erroneous perception and thinking, and to the ways we ordinarily recognize the character of moral advance precisely in the movement beyond what appears retrospectively as error. They disclose that prospectively we must open cognition to an ever yet unknown beyond, and they beseech us to discipline our attention toward this inexhaustible reality. In this way we might unwind a vicious circularity to the richer possibilities of a circle that opens through patient and vulnerable labor to "facts" and "rival theories" beyond its grasp.

The basic idea comes to this: What we naturally share are often less the common perceptions of ordinary objects, contexts, or traditions and more the inexhaustibility, complexity, and contingency of all these, as well as a common need to develop vocabularies, imagery, body practices, sensibilities, and habits that call us to tend carefully to life and a world thus characterized. Our hopes of inhabiting the world less poorly—or better—hinge on how far we cultivate such sources in ways that propel our emergence from the fantasies that reduce the world to our energetic egos (individual or collective): on how far I emerge from a flattened world and into "the progressive revelation of something which exists independent of me."[16]

On Murdoch's reading, this task is extremely difficult, given the energy and machinery of the human ego. Collectivities frequently compound these problems by organizing myopia and violence that tap into and systematically reinforce our at once sleepy and energetic propensities toward reductionist fantasy. What is at stake thus is often resisting and emerging from perverse cultures—fantasy machines—of death. These stakes, in turn, require not simply our individual efforts but also collective pedagogies, practices, and modes of organizing that cultivate our capacities to perceive, imagine, and think about others and the world in better ways.

Of course it is well known that Murdoch—especially in her later writing—was highly suspicious of politics and sought mightily to confine the powers of the state. Moral development happened beneath the level of politics understood as a statist enterprise. Yet this did not lead her to infer that it was thus a purely or even primarily individual project. We have already seen that our egoistic fantasy machines require the cultivation of vocabularies and pedagogical practices that, on the one hand, allow such fantasies to be called into question and, on the other, enhance our capacities for attention to a world that exceeds our grasp. For these reasons she supported pedagogical projects such as silent meditation in schools, which she believed might aid the cultivation of characters capable of becoming better. Beyond "schooling" in the more usual sense of this term, however, Murdoch thought that people's moral progress required the careful work of particular people gathered in relation to particular issues and places, in ways that cultivated language and habits conducive to attention. For these reasons, she wrote that the "distinction [between morals and politics] . . . can be blurred as we find ourselves moving the political model away from its most obvious home in the governing of a state . . . [and toward consideration of] political situations in villages and 'political' situations in families."[17] In these contexts we may develop languages, arts, and pedagogies of tending to "'ordinary' truth. . . . Flourishing in this environment are innumerable concerns and respects for innumerable others which civilization and morality and religion and enlightened politics have gradually and not without difficulty developed: concern for the contingent individual, as a social unit, as a human person, as idea, as work of art, as plant, as animal, as planet."[18] Such associational schools of attention are essential to the possibility of moral progress for human beings, because rich vocabularies are key to perception and cognition; and these tend toward abstraction and fantasy unless they develop reflectively as (to repeat her phrase) "words said to particular individuals at particular times . . . grouped round a common object." There is no pure attention—no pure reception—of the world, others, the beautiful, the sublime. There are only experiences entwined with communities learning to say what they see, as well as how to be called to attentive silence and more words and silence . . . in the face of a world that exceeds our vision.

* * *

Murdoch's articulation of our hope for better possibilities hinges on a sense of our relation to the world that far exceeds the accent of the discussion above on reflective cognitive striving. Indeed, her conception of the good is rooted in—and seeks in turn to cultivate—an affective-aesthetic engagement with the "unself" that engenders an energetic crosscurrent in the midst of the hyperactive productions of the ego. This is evident in Murdoch's discussion of the beautiful—unflinchingly passionate and austere.

"Goodness and beauty are . . . largely part of the same structure," yet, following Plato, "beauty is the only spiritual thing which we love immediately by nature." For both the artist and the good person, the virtue aimed at is "selfless attention to nature: something which is easy to name but very hard to achieve."[19] Yet while selfless attention is very hard to achieve in either case, our relation to the beautiful is more obviously and powerfully aided by an instinctual pleasure that overcomes our so often self-focused character. Of a "change in consciousness," she writes: "I am looking out my window in an anxious and resentful state of mind, oblivious to my surroundings, brooding perhaps on some damage done to my prestige. Then suddenly I observe a hovering kestrel. In a moment everything is altered. The brooding self with its hurt vanity has disappeared. There is nothing now but kestrel. And when I return to thinking of the other matter it seems less important."[20]

There is here a shift in energy and affect whereby we are swept up in a "self-forgetful pleasure in the sheer alien pointless independent existence of animals, birds, stones, and trees. 'Not how the world is, but that it is, is the mystical.'" In writing of this experience of the "sheer alien pointless independent existence," Murdoch is not devaluing such beings as somehow not good in themselves. Rather, she is gesturing to our elemental experience of their value precisely in this selfless opening to the idea "that" they exist. Far beyond our accounts of "how" they have value, we are afforded, as in greatest art, "a pure delight in the independent existence of what is excellent"—the "spiritual thing which we love by instinct." Rejecting Kant's "self-directed" enjoyment of the beautiful, for Murdoch art (when it is not mere entertainment or consolation) "invigorates our best faculties and, to use Platonic language, inspires love in the highest part of the soul. It is able to do this partly by virtue of something which it shares with nature: a perfection of form which invites unpossessive contemplation and resists absorption into the selfish dream life of the consciousness."[21] Barry Lopez beautifully evokes this idea in a moment when he speculates that, even in the midst of the conquest, Cortés's soldiers must have gazed upon the flight paths of songbirds—"passing through sunshine and banking gracefully into a grove of trees"—and sensed for an instant something beyond the pursuit of destruction: "In neither a horizontal nor a vertical dimension do these pathways match the line and scale of human creation. . . . The corridors they travel are curved around some other universe. . . . It is the birds' independence from predictable patterns of human design that draws us to them. In the birds' separate but related universe we are able to sense hope for ourselves."[22]

Affording us potent experiences of magnetic attraction and energetic rearrangement of our being toward the excellence of independent beings, the beautiful is "the text written in larger letters. The concept of the Good itself is the much harder to discern but essentially similar text written in small letters."[23] When she claims that in beauty we find our most accessible experience of the invisible beyond the visible, Murdoch means that we enter into a relationship with something that exceeds the structures of purpose-related visibility through which the world is so often disclosed. We pay attention to, delight in, and love in relation to contingent particulars. It is both their alterity and our attentive joy in this facticity that manifest the spiritual.

Yet in such experiences we also witness the particular exceeding itself, and this is surely another sense in which we see the invisible beyond the visible—"a significance which is beyond themselves" yet not a product of our will. In such cases, Murdoch writes, the particular, rather than being absorbed in Hegelian fashion, connects with the larger world by "be[ing] allowed to glow with light" and "can image another." "The particular can figure the human individual and his rights; and we may say that non-human particulars have rights too. In a sense, everything about us asks for our attention. . . . The world of nature and of ordinary artifacts is full of potential points of light, of worlds within the world."[24] Just as metaphors shape perception, perception is profoundly metaphorical—each particular illuminates the world around it—just as, for Lopez, the flight of birds illuminates sunlight itself and a grove of trees, a "separate but related universe" and "hope for ourselves." In these ordinary moments of awareness, we undergo a sort of moral charge in which our cognition breaks free from the service of our will. Our sensual opening on the world becomes illuminated by things beyond us, which simultaneously illuminate things beyond themselves, such that we "experience a 'transcendence'"[25]—a sense of connection through the radical particularity of what is beyond us. There is an energetic rearrangement of our being that can happen in such "large letters" that we have an awareness of its happening as a moral shift in our being. "There is an ordinary mystical discipline which relies upon such insights."[26]

We are drawn by such insights to cultivate modes that enhance our hospitality toward these experiences; to make time for meditation and prayer more conducive to being opened by them; to practice attention and tending to the illuminative singularity of beings that discloses their connections with the world. We are even called to cultivate our hospitality in the form of duties like the "duty to fall out of love"—with techniques such as shifting our attention or our entire physical being away from people and things to whom we are drawn with such egocentric or other-centric intensity that these relationships block our ability to love rightly, as disclosed by the pluralizing fullness of our (extra)ordinary transcendent experiences. "This valuable exercise can occasion a rediscovery of the beauty of the world. Released we return to our friends, our work, our ordinary pleasures! . . . There is a better sunnier happiness when together with the beloved we are able to be aware of other things, other people, other joys, illumined by secure mutual love, when we can stand together and look at something else." "An unselfish person enlarges the space of the world"—and gains this very rebirth, energy, joy, and richness of experience from the world.[27]

But this ideal episodically born of experience is almost never easy or pure. Most often it is alloyed with varieties of self-deception and constitutes a work in progress: a discipline of selves and communities over time. Moreover, not infrequently the deception emerges from within the beautiful itself. We might even think here of a possible (or even likely) corruption that is latent within this transcendence. The beautiful that is the good "in larger letters" can mislead us by exaggerating the similarities in ways that conceal the generally much more difficult and sacrificial modes of being to which the good calls us: the "infinitely difficult task of apprehending a magnetic inexhaustible reality."[28] Assimilating the task of becoming better to the often much easier and more enjoyable experience of beauty gives birth to the illusions of Hegel's "beautiful soul"—and the consequent cynicism or rage such souls can muster when their deceptions encounter the recalcitrant flesh of human beings and power. The good often calls us to unselfing sacrifices that are not attractive. The detachments called for by the good are thus often "necessary" in a profoundly different sense: they are authoritative beyond beauty's "rewards of enjoyment," which are decidedly "out of place" in the contexts of the good—even if it too may have its pleasures.[29] If the light from the "larger letters" of the beautiful too strongly illuminates the good, Murdoch suggests, the former becomes a deceitful alphabet spelling us into a variety of consoling fantasies that readily lead us astray.

One central and related consoling fantasy that frequents such spellbound states is the idea that the pursuit of goodness should and can lead to various kinds of immortality (for ourselves, for the beloved—"yes" wants eternity). Yet this undermines our pursuit of the good by turning us away from the contingent mortal beings we are and the comportments required to tend to each other as such. It engenders a hubris bent on controlling History that sinks us more deeply into violence and undermines possibilities for emergence. For these reasons, Murdoch (paradoxically) argues that, to endure, the indispensable yet "tiny spark"[30] of insight in our experience of the beautiful must be "tied to an acceptance of death, chance, transience, and only on this background can we understand it. Acceptance of death is an automatic concern with what is not ourselves."[31] There is a "special link between goodness and death," without which we often morph goodness into plots that inscribe our own immortality as the driving ambition.[32] We are beings for whom efforts to care for the world must spring from an acknowledgment that our most certain fate is death.

Beyond the beautiful soul, beyond denials of death, when the beautiful comes to be overaccented in our aesthetic repertoire it conceals another aspect of the human condition, the acknowledgment of which is indispensable to our becoming less bad—or better. Here Murdoch has in mind the unbearable pervasiveness of murder, wanton and systematic destruction, evil—and the fact that in our age these threaten the globe itself. Any effort to sense and take stock of our world with a gravitas approaching what would be necessary in order to respond to the violence of our histories would have to come to terms with the proximity of the catastrophic: the absurd, the person "shot in the back of the head" by Nazis "on some unrecorded morning."[33] Without this sensibility we will likely fall victim to what Baldwin refers to as squeaky-clean pure-white narratives of goodness that are blind to the absurdities and catastrophes they harbor and that we must address if there is to be any emergence. Perhaps it is Benjamin who puts this most poignantly, when he writes of the ever-difficult, yet necessary, task of looking barbarism in the face if we are to tell a story—and thereby chart a new course—that avoids complicity with the "violence of the victors." He quotes Flaubert: "Few will be able to guess how sad one had to be in order to resuscitate Carthage." The work of emerging from barbarism involves "brushing history against the grain."[34] We establish our incapacity to do so when we flee in feigned innocence from the catastrophic patterns of this grain.

It is thus crucial, Murdoch enjoins, to juxtapose our deep experiences of the beautiful with the experience and work of the tragic sublime. Great tragedy is Murdoch's favored genre for putting us face-to-face with the catastrophic grains of our history. Yet tragedy is the most difficult aesthetic form because true catastrophe is beyond form—it is the breakdown of form, narrative, reason, coherence, sense, consolation. Tragedy works to record the morning, yet the morning was unrecorded. Thus tragedy always in some sense departs from the event. Indebted to Adorno, Murdoch argues that tragic philosophy and art must seek—impossibly—to give expression to catastrophe by pushing form and expression to the breaking point. This task is essential for reopening our ears to the violent grains of history in which we ourselves are implicated. Yet this is so difficult that she suspected there was perhaps only one genuine tragedian—Shakespeare—and perhaps only one genuine tragedy—*Lear*. I would nominate Euripides' *Trojan Women* as well.

In all of this, I suggest, we see Murdoch moving powerfully beyond the naive aestheticism that modernity has produced in endless forms: aestheticism that articulates innocent play, harmony, totality, immortality, sovereignty, heroism, a sense of superiority, transparent touchstone of truth, and so on. Murdoch's articulations of the beautiful and the tragic sublime endlessly spur us to realize the extent of our contingent finitude in the face of a world that exceeds us, the profundity of a tragic perspective on history in which no one is flattered—least of all ourselves. It calls our fantasies into question and impels us to pay careful attention to others and the world beyond us. In this sense Murdoch offers an aesthetic sensibility that greatly resists what many have seen as the ideological character of most aesthetic reflection.

* * *

As beauty is in important ways the good in "large letters," it could be said that Flagstaff, Arizona, is a place where beauty itself is found in large letters. We may witness the tragic sublime here in this way too. Moreover—and no less important—one finds emerging in Flagstaff practices that are inspired and informed by these experiences, as well as dedicated to shaping, sustaining, and enhancing them in ways that are beginning to make this emergence articulate.

I realize there are risks in leaping from broad theoretical reflections to a discussion of specific experiences and practices in a community to which I am very new. Yet I think the following tentative juxtapositions help illuminate and give flesh to ideas we have been examining in more abstract registers. What follows is less a "root" and more a "route" through this place: a reflective journey through aesthetic sensibilities, practices of tending, and expressive articulations that suggest possibilities proximate to Murdoch's vision. These possibilities are still in search of themselves. My articulations seek to lend them support, recognizing that articulation shifts foregrounds and backgrounds in ways that are by no means innocent. But "what good is innocence"?[35]

* * *

"The Peaks" rise dramatically from this small city of sixty thousand tucked at their base. Each evening as I pump my bike up the long hill to our new home, they spill across the horizon. Sometimes, beneath their upward sweep, I sense with ineffable fear and hope that they may swallow the sky. The shadows pool in the dips and valleys, and then they advance upon the deepening red light that still lingers on the higher ridges and tundra summits. Each time this happens I am overwhelmed, awed, and altered.

This place—which is so dramatic at every turn that it might best be called an event—has struck people with a sense of the holy for eons. Long before Christians arrived and renamed the peaks after Saint Francis, these mountains were sacred to thirteen tribes. For the Navajo the Peaks are the sacred mountain of the west, Doko'oo'sliid, "Shining on Top," a key boundary marker and a place where medicine men collect herbs for healing ceremonies. To the Hopi the Peaks are Nuvatukaovi, "The Place of Snow on the Very Top," home for half of the year to the ancestral kachina spirits who live among the clouds around the summit. When properly honored through song and ceremony, the kachinas bring gentle rains to thirsty corn plants. The peaks are one of the "sacred places where the earth brushes up against the unseen world," in the words of Yavapai-Apache chairman Vincent Randall. They are a place of profoundest offering and emergence.[36] When five thousand citizens of Flagstaff spent over a year in the mid-1990s deliberating in a variety of forums about their ideal vision for Flagstaff in 2020, here is what they had to say: "In 2020, greater Flagstaff residents share a common bond in their love of the environment. The natural beauty that surrounds and encompasses the community is more than just a backdrop; it is its soul and the essence of its values. Nature is precious to people who live here and they devote considerable energy and attention to enjoying, protecting and enhancing it."[37]

Yet as the shadows rise at dusk and light passes from the summits and into the "unseen world," it is often impossible not to be swept up in a sensuous crosscurrent where awesome beauty is awash and trembling with the tragic sublime. For as Al Gore's *Inconvenient Truth* and so many works on global warming declare, as the planet heats up, life on mountains around the world is ascending the slopes and disappearing from the earth like the sun's last rays. As Tim Flannery writes in his instant classic *The Weather Makers*, "Nothing in predictive climate science is more certain than the extinction of many of the world's mountain-dwelling species."[38] Hence, recalling Murdoch's words, as "metaphor and perception merge" so too do the beautiful and the tragic sublime—as last light speaks not just of death's radical contingency but of something akin to murder—or at least manslaughter—on a global scale. A few evenings each week I cycle up a steep, winding road that leads to the base of a ski area at 9,500 feet. I always linger there, bathed in the odor of moist spruce—as the sun sets over dozens of volcanoes protruding from a sea of ponderosa pine below. The beauty of orange twilit aspen trunks backdropped by a rapidly cooling cobalt sky finds itself haunted by ghosts-to-be: we humans are killing this place. There is a decades-long slaughter under way, and even the most valiant efforts to shift direction would halt only some of it. I love this place, so profoundly consoling (aspen trunk: "dry bones rattling") and unconsoling (aspen trunk: austerity of dead bones) as it draws my breath. "Grand Canyon": anemic name for a vast bottomless crack fracturing the earth to the northwest and filling with darkness.

The medicine men collecting herbs? The healing ceremonies? These are the liturgies of a remnant fleet—the particular practices through which communities have continued to worship the holy and perform freedoms, structures of care, and pedagogies in relation to it; these are among the ways that Hopi, Navaho, Havasupi, Apache, and so many others have struggled to emerge from under a centuries-long onslaught of white "civilization" enacting genocide in manifold forms. When the herbs flee from the mountaintops into the "invisible world," what will remain of those cultures that cultivate their spiritual heights gathering them? Will they follow?

Many Native Americans living, speaking, and writing in a state of emergency—like Baldwin, like Benjamin—are struggling to resist such a fate and make their damaged traditions and practiced modes of emergence articulate. Yet many of those who are most powerful in our region remain intensely occupied with maintaining a world in which these articulations would be inaudible. Exemplary here is the response of the majority opinion in the Ninth Circuit Court to an appeal by tribes and environmental groups contesting the development of a major reclaimed wastewater snowmaking operation because they say it would interfere with the holy practices that are integral to their traditions of becoming who they are called to be by protecting and celebrating the land. According to the court's majority opinion, there would be no effect whatever on the religious practices: "The sole effect of the artificial snow is on the Plaintiffs' subjective spiritual experience."[39] With this all-too-familiar move they detach spirit from the body practices of peoples and the land—the web of more than subjective relationships with the more than human; and as they do, they perpetuate a colonial framework in which the death of native peoples is as sure as that of the herbs moving up and off the slopes into the "invisible world." If there is any hope of making these traditions and these struggles for emergence articulate so as to resist this dominant order with alternative patterns of goodness, the epicenter of the struggle is right here: contesting the disarticulations (e.g., "subjective" versus "objective") of the quotidian practiced ways in which spirit and peoples give and take place. We must seek to dwell here in aesthetic modes that might once again make the truths of intertwinement apparent. Many Native Americans would likely say that it is precisely the way the court abstracts "subjective spiritual experience" from a network of practices of care for the land that enhances the probability of catastrophic relations with the earth to begin with.

To what extent will an awareness of these tragic revelations inform Flagstaff's "soul and the essence of its values"? To what extent will this sobering sublime apparition be eclipsed by the dangers of a beauty that casts the task of goodness in too easy and too victorious hues? To what extent may the experience of beauty in large letters itself slide so steeply toward the "pleasures of enjoyment" that the deep relation between beauty, contingency, and death is forgotten? To what extent will this lead to what my new friend, the prominent applied anthropologist Miguel Vasquez, worries could become a lifestyle enclave rather than a community deeply attentive and tending to the nonhuman world and the diverse human beings we are struggling to become? Will we lose sight of the deeply practiced and mediated character of what it takes to become better? Will we forget the way Murdoch says we must develop practices of loving rightly, practices of being still, practices of falling out of loving wrongly, as well as languages that would make these necessities less inarticulate? Will we fail to respond to the demand that the foremost difficult public work we must tend to is the work of becoming publics?[40] We are a work in progress, and it is impossible to say. Nevertheless, there are some hopeful practices emerging, and I seek to make them articulate in the context we have been exploring.

* * *

In relation to the aesthetic intensity of the land, Flagstaff is developing a rich emergent tradition of citizen action to protect and enhance common goods—including copious, widely used, and dearly loved parks and open spaces, dozens of miles of urban trails, a piazza downtown, and many other efforts too numerous to name concerning water, global climate, urban community gardens, expressive murals, sustainable economic development, greening the K-12 curriculum, bike lanes, mass transit, and the like. This relationship is one of responding to the land, as well as cultivating this responsiveness: teaching it, making times and spaces for it, celebrating it. There is a long way to go, and as in any city struggling to be a steward of place in the privatized culture of the United States, there are myriad common goods that are neglected and assaulted, a host of catastrophic inequities and modes of oblivion, and tremendous larger-scale barriers and counterforces to Flagstaff's efforts. Yet . . . Yet what is under way here remains impressive. The practices and policies regarding each common good have been the result of amplified citizen involvement—dispersed efforts in which grassroots responsive engagement itself is among the greatest emerging public goods: the goodness of becoming a public that is more receptive to the human and nonhuman world; the goodness of becoming a public that seeks to cultivate and tend to this receptivity itself.

To my mind, perhaps the most exemplary commons that the community has organized itself to preserve is the night sky. There have been many aspects of this ongoing effort. It began in 1958 with an ordinance that protected the work of astronomers at the Lowell Observatory from roving commercial advertising beams that polluted the sky. This eventually led to a broader restrictive lighting policy; then came a successful struggle against a proposed huge truck stop, to be perpetually illuminated. It has percolated into a widely supported citizen ethos that minimizes outdoor home lighting and turns out many hundreds to opening evenings of art exhibitions celebrating "Night Visions." All of this informs Flagstaff's reputation as the world's first "International Dark Sky City." For reasons that have both strategic and genuine merit, the citizens' Dark Skies Coalition often frames its (frequently successful and ongoing) efforts to reduce light pollution in terms of the economic values of the region's astronomical institutions, energy cost savings, carbon footprint reduction, tourism gains, and so forth. All of these are important.[41] Yet in view of the argument I am pursuing here, the issues go much deeper: they concern the shape of the community we are becoming, our character, and our ethos.

In a world that exerts intense pressure to frame public discourse in terms of the economic "bottom line," these emerging depths often remain inarticulate—or confined to the art exhibitions.[42] Yet in many small and not so small conversations they are very much at play in expressions regarding how and why people are coming to think more about the night sky commons. And you can hear them whispered in a variety of other public contexts. Take, for example, David S. F. Portree, who writes compellingly and often primarily in terms of economic benefits when discussing the development of the Dark Skies policies and practices in Flagstaff. In pauses between the dominant discourse in his texts you'll find energetic whispers of an emergent sensibility that is at the heart of a community seeking to become something better in relation to responsive care for this commons:

> A cynic might argue that astronomers battle light pollution to protect their jobs. Astronomers do not, however, become astronomers because astronomy is a wealthy industry; they become astronomers because the universe touches their souls. Battling light pollution is, deep down, an attempt to maintain contact with something bigger than humanity. Infinite space comes down to Earth at night unless stray, trivial light banishes it beyond our awareness.[43]

This contact with something bigger finds frequent expression in photos from the observatory that are so beautiful they can make you weep. Sometimes Portree carves out designated spaces in his articles—"Interludes," he calls them—where he tries to give voice to this "contact with something bigger":

> Andromeda is actually a spiral galaxy half again as massive as our Milky Way, and the farthest object one can readily observe without a telescope. Though divided by two million light-years of emptiness, the Milky Way and Andromeda feel a mutual attraction. Soon, as the universe reckons time, they will fall together. Their dark dust clouds will collide in a frenzy of star birth and their classic spiral forms will rupture, spilling their stars across intergalactic space. The collision might cast our Sun and Earth into the starless void for the rest of time.[44]

I can think of little that gives better expression to Murdoch's sense of the intimate connections between beauty, excellence, contingency, and death, and nothing that tends more powerfully to draw people beyond themselves to alter our sensibility. I have repeatedly heard people talk about how happening to look up at the night sky while taking out the garbage in Flagstaff can take your breath away and change your entire evening.

Even so, I am not most concerned here to wax on about these individual transformations. I want to pursue what it might mean for a community to come into being by gathering itself in the face of this event of the night sky commons, tentatively giving expression to it—naming the beautiful, the sublime—in specific words, paintings, photography, pottery, music, cloth. And even more: What might it mean to embark on paths of becoming a community precisely in the slow crafting of a way of life that takes practices of care for the night sky commons—as well as care for our capacities to experience this commons—to be an elemental aspect of our emergent being? What might it mean to devote ourselves to fashioning emerging traditions of understanding our selves, our community, our commons, precisely through myriad efforts to articulate—which is also to complicate—how and why we do so? How and why do we practice this care?

The dark sky itself dictates that there can be no simple answers to these questions. Yet we can make some guesses that might aid us in attending to our tending to what draws our attention—making this emergence articulate. Let me follow the gesture of poetic whispers that conclude a recent article by Verlyn Klinkenborg, "Our Vanishing Night," in *National Geographic*:

> Like most other creatures we do need darkness. Darkness is as essential to our biological welfare, to our internal clockwork, as light itself. The regular oscillation of waking and sleep in our lives—one of our circadian rhythms—is nothing less than a biological expression of the

regular oscillation of light on Earth. So fundamental are these rhythms to our being that altering them is like altering gravity. . . . In the end, humans are no less trapped by light pollution than the frogs in a pond near a brightly lit highway. Living in a glare of our own making, we have cut ourselves off from our evolutionary and cultural patrimony—the light of the stars and the rhythms of day and night. In a very real sense, light pollution causes us to lose sight of our true place in the universe, to forget the scale of our being, which is best measured against the dimensions of a deep night with the Milky Way—the edge of our galaxy—arching overhead.[45]

I want to suggest that in allowing the night sky to redraw our attention, in responding to this experience through community practices that both preserve the darkness and cultivate our sensuous relation to it, and in crafting narratives that place such practices at the heart of our community and speak to how and why this is so, we may engender an ethos of hyperenergetic modesty.[46] We may become animated and energized as the night reorients our being with a set of charges different from those that fuel egoistic fantasy. Many cultures have done so—many right here on the Colorado Plateau. We may become modest in the "sight of our true place in the universe," recalling the "scale of our being measured against the dimensions of a deep night." It may be here that we begin again to develop modes of becoming a community and reflective expressions that cultivate resources to energetically resist the apathy of civic privatism, while modestly resisting the hubris that frequents more than a few common expressions of activism. It may also be in this emergence that we find sources for articulating anew a differently emerging enlightenment. One of the principal weaknesses of many articulations of enlightenment—suggested metaphorically by Descartes' *Dioptrics* or Kant's emphasis on emerging into the light of maturity—is that there is no place for the energies and relaxations of darkness; no place for what Klinkenborg refers to as "our evolutionary and cultural patrimony," in which lies the vitality of the rhythms of day and night, waking and sleep, for cultivating lives and intelligences that resist drowning in their own glare.

Derrida draws on Aristotle's *De anima* to make a similar point. Aristotle claims that bees have no capacity to reason because they are unblinking beings; beings whose eyes and minds are perpetually wide open or, better, wide shut. Following this insight, Derrida argues for an enlightenment that blinks, that cultivates intelligence in the rhythms between light and dark through which we might become more receptive to what lies beyond each exposure of the opening eye; might relax the tractor beam of what easily becomes a stare; might, in the moment of blinking or in the darkness of a night not saturated with the fears of glare-habituated beings, become sensitive to the presence of what he calls "headings" (or directions) other than our own and those we have imposed. Derrida calls us to become communities that blink as the best hope for learning how to live better amid the heterogeneity of the world and our legacies of violence—less fixed by stare and glare, cultivating a greater readiness for reception.[47]

Murdoch was no fan of Derrida. Moreover, as her engagement with Martin Buber makes particularly plain, vision and light are indispensable and central to her understanding of how we should figure our pursuit of the good. Yet she repeatedly writes of how we are "blinded" by the self, even blinded by the other, suggesting that the energetic sources of light can be a profound problem as well as our highest hope. She calls us to turn away from—fall out of love with—these blinding lights and turn toward the reception of multifarious existences beyond our own or a single other's being. Something like the night sky comes to mind, as an awe-inspiring perception metaphor for our emerging sense of the manyness beyond us that is an integral aspect of her notion of goodness. And perhaps the night sky also evokes something elemental about her attraction to Weil's notion of "void" (not to mention strands of negative theology), in the presence of which we listen, wait, and offer our attention in silence. Or so I guess in wonderment. Finally, everything hinges on how we practice our care and how, in narratives such as this, we might care for our practice—hoping for an emergence in which Christians, Hopi, Navaho, Apache, and "undocumented aliens," among so many others, might learn to meet beyond war in the face of that "edge of our galaxy."

* * *

The night won't do this for us. The night won't make us any better than the day. Again, everything about whether and how we might become better hinges on how we practice our tending and tend to our practices in response to a possibility twinkling in the darkness. So much depends on how we make this emergence articulate. And so much depends on how our nights might infuse our days.

Dark skies might inform and inspire, but they cannot stand alone. They could easily become folkloric consolation, a bit of entertaining relief as we otherwise stare our way through our days, blinded by myopic purposes both to the damages we enact and to the gifts we might witness and bring to others and the surrounding world. Or dark skies could themselves become a new spell—a beauty that itself blinds us to the heterogeneous riches and damages of the world. Yes, we are beings prone to fantasy.

All of this suggests how crucial it is to develop languages and pedagogies for receiving the night that help guide us away from these pitfalls. Murdoch can be of some help here, as we gather in specific communities before the awesome beauties and terrifying sublimities of our places and strive to give expression to these aesthetic experiences in ways that inform our understanding of what it might mean to become better—or at least less bad. She may also help us find ways to cultivate our sense of the ineffable.

Even more paradoxically, she may suggest to us ways it may be desirable episodically to fall out of love with the dark sky—to prevent it from becoming an all-absorbing fetish that blinds us to the broader senses of what it might mean to strive to become better—or at least less bad. Just as night ought to rhythmically follow our days, so too perhaps our experience of night must be allowed to emerge from itself. Perhaps night too needs to rest in order that we might articulate its senses for our lives.

And not just in words. To begin to make this emergence articulate is to discover or invent ways myriad practices and perceptions throughout our lives might be informed by and inform our caring for the dark skies. Articulating emergence is about how we live, because articulation happens in the ways we fashion the interconnections of our lives: how we welcome the stranger; how we work together; how we harvest rain and sun; how we work to heal the wounds of history that saturate the soils of this arid land; how we learn to forgive what cannot be healed; how we cut each other some slack; how we learn to "know not to know too well."

How?

I have suggested, following Murdoch, that there is much to be learned about goodness, as well as a tremendous source of energy, in our aesthetic relationship with the beautiful and the sublime—if we cultivate these possibilities and teach them well. I have further argued that we can similarly learn a great deal about becoming communities beyond violence and injustice from the ways we come together and tend to such common goods. Finally, I have ventured that giving these practices reflective expression can aid the processes through which we discern how the depths we experience and practice around particular goods can find transformative expression in very different registers, regions, and purposes of our lives. None of this is to suggest that, in these ways, becoming less bad or better will be easier or even more coherent. Nevertheless, it might offer something in regard to the energies, textures, and shapes of good work.

Such work—as Baldwin, Benjamin, and the Hopi know—is almost always cross-grained in relation to the dominant powers of our day, and we forget this at our own peril.

To shift to aquatic metaphors, in Flagstaff I seek to articulate the cross-current rivulets and back eddies in order to advance possibilities for undomesticated (yet not undisciplined) flows of more generous and receptive practice beyond the canalized mainstreams. Yet the canals or such mainstreams are deep and damaging, here as elsewhere. The vast discrepancy between what most people earn in this town and the price of housing is summarized in the phrase "poverty with a view." Your odds in this game are much worse here—as in most places—if you are brown or red. We have our corridors of careless concrete and disposable ugly corporate boxes in which many work for unlivable wages and no benefits. Most of us live utterly oblivious (or worse) to the immigrants who flee political and economic catastrophes in which we have had a hand, do the most menial labor for very little return, and are victims of nighttime deportation raids of the Immigration and Customs Enforcement squads. We are oblivious to the children who leave trails of tears in our schools the following days. We drive vehicles that will surely destroy the globe. Many are deaf to living legacies of colonialism on the Northern Colorado Plateau. The state of emergency is not the exception but the rule, and this truth rings here too.

Yet everywhere so much more is teeming and under way. In gratitude and hope—and amid long lineages of struggling strangers—we thus seek to make this emergence articulate.

NOTES

1. James Baldwin, "Many Thousands Gone," in *Price of the Ticket: Collected Nonfiction, 1948–1985* (New York: St. Martins, 1985), 65–78. My reading of Baldwin is greatly indebted to the incomparable interpretation that George Shulman has developed over the past dozen years, the consummate expression of which is found in *American Prophecy: Race and Redemption in American Political Culture* (Minneapolis: University of Minnesota Press, 2008).
2. Ibid.
3. Walter Benjamin, "Theses on the Philosophy of History," in *Illuminations: Essays and Reflections*, ed. H. Arendt, trans. H. Zohn (New York: Schocken Books, 1968), 257.
4. James Baldwin, "Stranger in the Village," in *Price of the Ticket*, 89.
5. James Baldwin, "White Man's Guilt," in *Price of the Ticket*, 410.
6. James Baldwin, "In Search of a Majority," in *Price of the Ticket*, 234.
7. Iris Murdoch, "Against Dryness," in *Existentialists and Mystics: Writings on Philosophy and Literature*, ed. P. Conradi (New York: Penguin, 1997), 293.

8. Iris Murdoch, "The Idea of Perfection," in *Existentialists and Mystics*, 331.

9. Ibid., 330.

10. Iris Murdoch, "The Sovereignty of Good," in *Existentialists and Mystics*, 376.

11. Murdoch, "Idea of Perfection," 335.

12. Iris Murdoch, "Imagination," in *Metaphysics as a Guide to Morals* (New York: Penguin, 1992), 328.

13. Murdoch, "Sovereignty of Good," 363.

14. Murdoch, "Idea of Perfection," 326 and 325.

15. Ibid., 299.

16. Murdoch, "Sovereignty of Good," 373.

17. Iris Murdoch, "Morals and Politics," in *Metaphysics as a Guide to Morals*, 355.

18. Ibid., 377.

19. Murdoch, "Idea of Perfection," 332.

20. Murdoch, "Sovereignty of Good," 369.

21. Ibid., 369-70.

22. Barry Lopez, *Crossing Open Ground* (New York: Vintage, 1989), 208.

23. Murdoch, "Sovereignty of Good," 374.

24. Murdoch, "Imagination," 339.

25. Ibid., 340.

26. Ibid., 339.

27. Quotations in this paragraph are from Murdoch, "Imagination," 345-47.

28. Murdoch, "Idea of Perfection," 333 (my emphasis).

29. Iris Murdoch, "On 'God' and 'Good,'" in *Existentialists and Mystics*, 353.

30. Ibid., 360.

31. Murdoch, "Sovereignty of Good," 385.

32. Ibid., 377.

33. "Comic and Tragic," in *Metaphysics as a Guide to Morals*, 221.

34. Benjamin, "Theses on the Philosophy of History," 256-57.

35. Apologies to Peter Euben.

36. http://www.savethepeaks.org/background.html.

37. *A Vision for Our Community: Flagstaff 2020* (Flagstaff, AZ: Grester Flagstaff, 1997), 16.

38. Tim Flannery, *The Weather Makers: How Man Is Changing the Climate and What It Means for Life on Earth* (New York: Atlantic Monthly Press, 2005), 172.

39. Ninth Circuit Court of Appeals, *Navaho Nation v. USFS*, August 8, 2008, 10041.

40. Stanley Hauerwas and I discuss this idea extensively in *Christianity, Democracy, and the Radical Ordinary: Conversation between a Christian and a Radical Democrat* (Eugene, OR: Wipf and Stock, 2008).

41. For example, it is estimated that Arizona would save $30 million annually if municipalities across the state adopted Flagstaff's Dark Skies ordinance.

42. Art exhibitions such as Flagstaff's "Night Visions," can be wonderful sites of provocative expression. The problem arises when the insights they explore are strongly inhibited from the "serious" talk in public conversations about public practice, power, and political-economic decision making.

43. http://altairvi.blogspot.com/2008/04/flagstaffs-battle-for-dark-skies.html.

44. http://altairvi.blogspot.com/2008/04/wes-lockwood-saves-universe.html.
45. *National Geographic*, November 2008, 109.
46. This is not identical to Foucault's "hyperactive pessimism," though it may be a friendly relative with whom he occasionally enjoys the night.
47. For an extended discussion of Derrida on these points, see Romand Coles, *Beyond Gated Politics: Reflections for the Possibility of Democracy* (Minneapolis: University of Minnesota Press, 2005), chap. 5, "Derrida and the Promise of Democracy."

SEVEN

The Tragedy of the Goods and the Pursuit of Happiness

THE QUESTION OF THE GOOD AND THE GOODS

Michael Allen Gillespie

The term good is used in a wide variety of ways. As an adjective it seems to mean that something is conducive to an end we consider pleasant, admirable, profitable, morally obligatory, divinely commanded, or in some other way suitable or choiceworthy. A thing or action or process, then, is "good" not in itself but because it leads to an end we consider to be good.[1] This definition is obviously circular, but it does allow us to pose an important question. We know that many different ends are good in their own way or according to their own kind, but is there something all these goods have in common that renders them good and allows us to compare them with one another? Is there one thing, in other words, that makes them all good? There is no question that we can and do recognize standards for specific kinds of goods. We can easily compare apples and distinguish a good apple from a bad one, for example, but can we compare a good apple and a good deed, or a good man and a good time? In what sense are all of these conducive to *a*, or indeed *the*, good? A moment's reflection reveals that the notion of such an all-embracing idea or essence of the good is problematic. Is there one quality by which all good things are called good, or are they called good in different senses? If the former, why do we have so much trouble imagining or defining it? And if the latter, how can the term good be meaningful at all?

This essay considers the consequences for ethics of displacing a notion of the good by a notion of multiple, disassociated, and potentially conflicting goods. It is impelled by the insight that in modernity we have seen a decisive shift away from a unitary notion of the good that was rooted in the Christian conception of the world as the creation of a single (supremely good) God. This shift had its roots in the nominalist-voluntarist revolution of the fourteenth century. It first became apparent in the later sixteenth century in the thought of skeptics such as Montaigne and Charron, and it was explicitly articulated in the seventeenth century by Descartes and Hobbes, who declared not only that there is no one quality by which all good things are good, but that there is not even a supreme good or summum bonum that can serve as the basis for ordering the various goods.[2] In their view the good is always only what is good for a particular individual, what satisfies his or her particular passions. The full meaning of this transformation in the understanding of the good, however, did not become evident until the end of the nineteenth century, with Nietzsche's observation that the Christian God was dead, and that as a result humanity had been catapulted "beyond good and evil" into a world of multiple disassociated and potentially conflicting goods (gods, standards, moral codes, ways of life, etc.) in which everything was permitted. The pressing question Nietzsche raises is how each of us can live with himself or herself and how all of us can live with one another in such a world. He believes there are only two possibilities—one that is essentially modern and another that harks back to antiquity. Let us examine these two more closely.

Since the early seventeenth century, humans have tried to find ways to live peacefully and prosperously with one another in the absence of a common notion of the good. This effort has been identified with liberalism, which has emphasized toleration, individual choice, and maximizing general utility through market mechanisms and government constraints. To this end, liberalism has treated all goods as effectively equal, interpreting them as merely the subjective preferences of individuals.[3] This move entails recognizing and admitting that no good is better than any other good. My preference for justice or a moral life is thus essentially no different from my preference for an apple, sex, or salvation. Thus no good (thing, process, activity, way of life, etc.) in itself is special, sacred, or necessary. In principle, then, there can be no rational (as opposed to affective) ground for preferring one good over another. All preferences are contingent and arbitrary. The things I prefer thus are lovable not in themselves but only accidentally, a fact I myself recognize even when I prefer them. As mere preferences they thus have no intrinsic value. In view of this transformation, Nietzsche believes modern human beings have lost any capacity to recognize something as higher or more important than their own preferences and have consequently lost the ability to love. In his view the world that contemporary humanity finds itself in is thus the world of his last man, who asks, "What is love? What is creation? What is longing? What is a star? . . . and blinks."[4] One possible outcome of the death of God and the subsequent recognition of multiple goods for Nietzsche is thus banality, which he identifies with the last man. He condemns this liberal democratic possibility and proposes in its place what he takes to be a nobler but also thoroughly tragic alternative.

This second possibility Nietzsche sees for the post-Christian world draws heavily on the heroic master morality he believes characterized the pre-Platonic, tragic age of the Greeks. These early Greeks, in his view, recognized a multiplicity of goods and conflicts among them, but their solution to this conflict was not equalization or homogenization but the constant struggle for the dominance of one's own good over that of all others. Nietzsche's hopes for founding a new tragic age are rooted in this vision. In such a world the goods are not merely subjective preferences but are real goods that overpower, possess, and command us. They are loved not contingently or merely because we choose to love them but because they assert themselves against all other goods. Indeed, we become the people we are only by being possessed by these goods (gods, ways of life, activities, etc.). In contrast to the liberal alternative, this view of the goods is rooted not in fear and greed but in hope and ambition, and it leads not to peace and prosperity but to war and a struggle for dominion. Nietzsche advocates this path because in his view it alone opens up the possibility for a new nobility.[5]

Setting aside Nietzsche's animosity toward liberalism, there are compelling reasons to consider his claim that the various goods are multiplicitous and at odds with one another. If goods are as he describes them, he believes there can be no rational means for comparing them with one another or developing a general notion of happiness or the good life. This claim is obviously not entirely new. As I mentioned above, Descartes and Hobbes, for example, believed that while there is no objective order among the goods, we are able to judge their relative value by a subjective calculus of pleasure and pain. We may not be guided by reason in these determinations (since, as Hobbes puts it, reason may be only the spy and scout of the passions), but we do sense or feel the relative value of these satisfactions on a hedonistic scale.[6] Nietzsche, however, pushes us to consider a more disturbing possibility. If one accepts the ontological and epistemological presuppositions of modernity, individuals not only have no objective standard for choice, they also have no subjective standard for choosing between the various goods. Indeed, he claims that we do not choose between them at all but are in fact ourselves captured or chosen by them. Or to put the matter in a slightly different way, using the phrase first coined by Pindar and later repeated by Nietzsche, you "become who you are" by being dominated by your ownmost passion.[7]

This insight has a number of important consequences. It suggests that our efforts to compare and maximize the satisfaction of individual passions can succeed only if we homogenize (or commodify) goods, converting them from real things, actions, or practices into mere preferences measured by their pleasure, cash, or social status value. This transformation of lovable things into preferable objects is not only a process by which man transforms the world, but also a process by which human beings transform themselves. As Hobbes concludes, "The value, or WORTH of a man is as of all other things, his price."[8] If Nietzsche is right, no matter how prosperous a world organized in this manner might be or become, it will never be a world in which humans can truly be happy. Indeed, those who live in such a world will remain, as Tocqueville put it, "restless in the midst of their prosperity," unable to settle on one good or one way of life as superior or preferable, vacillating between goods, unable to experience or dedicate themselves to any one above the others, unable, as Nietzsche puts it in his description of the last man, to truly love anything.[9]

But while Nietzsche may or may not be right about the banality of liberalism, is he correct that the only alternative is a return to tragedy? In what follows, I argue that he is not. I first examine the problem of the multiplicity of goods as it appears in the *Iliad*. My analysis suggests that Nietzsche's interpretation of the multiplicity of goods in the tragic age of the Greeks is essentially correct. I argue, however, that Nietzsche is wrong to assume that Greek philosophy from Plato on rejects this multiplicity in favor of a unitary idea of the good. Through an interpretation of Aristotle, I argue that there is another alternative to the problem of the goods that does not end in tragedy or banality. I thus believe Nietzsche is wrong in his conclusion that we must choose between a hedonistic liberalism and a new and violent tragic age, and I suggest that while a different view of the good/goods that builds on Aristotle will probably not replace the dominant liberal view of the goods, it might modify it in ways that would elevate liberalism and promote human thriving.

THE *ILIAD* AND THE TRAGEDY OF THE GOODS

The *Iliad* tells the story of a few days in the ninth year of the war between the Achaeans and the Trojans. As the poem begins, the Achaeans have captured the daughter of Apollo's priest Chryses and given her as a prize to Agamemnon. When her father seeks to ransom her and Agamemnon rejects the offer, the priest appeals to Apollo, who sends a plague against the Achaeans. At Achilles' initiative the Achaeans consult their own seer, Calchas, who tells them (after extracting a promise of protection from Achilles) that to end the plague they must restore the girl to her father. Agamemnon is furious, in part because he believes Achilles has orchestrated this event in order to usurp his power. To demonstrate his power and humiliate Achilles, Agamemnon takes Briseis, the young woman the Achaeans had given to

Achilles as a prize of war, to replace the girl he lost. Achilles perceives this as an effort to deny him the honor he is due for his superior performance in battle, and he wants to kill Agamemnon on the spot. However, he is restrained by Athena, who advises him instead to heap insults on Agamemnon. This leads to a quarrel, and Achilles vows in anger to withdraw from the fighting to demonstrate how supremely important he is to the Achaeans' cause and thereby extract from them the recognition and honor he deserves.

In counterpoint to Achilles' single-minded pursuit of glory stands the Trojan prince Hector, son of King Priam, a husband and father who is the chief defender of his city. With Achilles sulking in his tent (and Diomedes trying to make the best of this opportunity to demonstrate his own prowess as the principal Achaean warrior), Hector leads a series of successful counterattacks against the Achaeans, who are forced for the first time to build a fortified camp around their ships on the beach near Troy. The Achaeans appeal to Agamemnon to placate Achilles, and Agamemnon agrees, but when they send an embassy to deliver Agamemnon's offer, Achilles does not react as they anticipate. He is angered by Odysseus's speech making the offer and says he will leave immediately, in part because he does not trust Odysseus but also because the offer contains a provision that Achilles become Agamemnon's son-in-law and thus subject to his (patriarchal) authority. He also feels betrayed by Phoenix, who in a second speech urges him not to commit filial impiety (as he himself did). Achilles asserts that he will consider whether to depart the following day. In fact, the only one who is able to move him at all is Aias, who gruffly tells him that he does not care enough for his friends. In response to this assertion, Achilles says he will not leave, but he will return to the fighting only when the fire comes to the Achaean ships. The Achaeans are dismayed by his response and have no choice but to rejoin the battle without him.

The following day Zeus himself takes a hand in the battle on the side of the Trojans, and the Achaeans are broadly defeated. The best remaining Achaean fighters, including Odysseus and Diomedes, are wounded and forced to withdraw. With the Trojans on the brink of victory, Patroclus, Achilles' closest companion, persuades Achilles to lend him his armor and men so he can enter the battle in Achilles' place and stave off defeat. Achilles reluctantly agrees but warns Patroclus not to overreach himself. In the heat of battle, however, Patroclus does exactly that and is killed by Hector.

Achilles then recognizes the tragic consequences of his inability to digest his anger and has to face the horrifying consequences of his single-minded desire for glory, declaring himself a useless clod on the good earth because he did not come to the defense of his friends. He decides to return to the battle and slay Hector even though his mother, Thetis, tells him that if he does so he too must die shortly thereafter. After the god Hephaestus forges new armor for him, he returns to the battle, driving the Trojans back into their city and slaying Hector in single combat.

At the command of Zeus, Hector's father, King Priam, comes alone to Achilles in the middle of the night to ransom his son's body, and Achilles, though still angry, pities the aged and grieving man, seeing in him the father he will never return to, just as Priam sees in Achilles the son he has lost. The poem ends with the funeral of Hector.

As the poet tells us in the first line, the subject of the poem is wrath—that is, anger and conflict. The struggle of those few days in a distant war was thus not an arbitrary and contingent historical event worthy in itself of being remembered but having no further meaning or consequence. Rather, it epitomized for the Greeks the discord and struggle that they believed lay at the heart of the cosmos and underpinned their daily lives. From the Greek point of view the immediate cause of the war was, of course, the abduction of Helen, but they knew that this event was only the last in a long train of events that led to the conflict. To understand the primordial nature of this conflict, we need to examine their understanding of the many factors or causes that produced it.

Within the shared Greek mythology, the Trojan War is the culmination of a gripping drama that begins with the genesis of the cosmos out of chaos and the subsequent cycle of becoming driven by *eros* and *eris*, love and discord, which determine the generation and destruction of all things—the constant and repeated replacement of the old by the new, of fathers by sons, of the weaker by the stronger. Hesiod describes this process of becoming in powerful and terrifying detail in his *Theogony*, and these mythological images suffuse Greek culture, repeated and elaborated in various ways on their vases, on the friezes of their buildings, in their dramatic competitions, in their athletic festivals, in their historical works, and undoubtedly in their dreams and imaginations as well. The struggle appears at first as the wars among the gods or between different generations of gods. This terrifying *gigantomachia* that repeats itself over and over as one generation is forced to give way to the next is displaced from the cosmological realm into the world of men when Zeus establishes a lasting order by allying himself with Prometheus (whose name means "forethought"). Forethought gives him the capacity to disrupt and redirect (but not to stop) this process. This story is represented mythologically by Prometheus's knowledge of the secret of Thetis, that she is fated to give birth to a son who is stronger than his father.[10] Zeus agrees to release Prometheus from his punishment for stealing fire and giving it to men in return for this knowledge. With it he is able to secure his rule and the order of the natural world, marrying Thetis off to the human Peleus rather than taking her himself.

Zeus recognizes that this marriage presents a real danger to humanity, since it threatens to unleash among men the same discord that plagued the gods, and thus he orders the goddess of discord, Eris, not to attend the wedding of Thetis and Peleus. Eris obeys, but she is angered by his command and throws into the throng of guests at the wedding a golden apple inscribed "To the most beautiful." Hera, Athena, and Aphrodite each claim it. To decide which of them is the most beautiful, they choose as judge a shepherd, Paris (Alexandros), the son of Priam, king of Troy. Then they each offer him a bribe corresponding to their individual natures. Hera offers him great power, Athena undying fame, and Aphrodite the sexual pleasures of the most beautiful woman in the world. His choice produces the war that is the background of the *Iliad,* and the union of Thetis and Peleus produces Achilles, the central actor in that war.

This mythological story sees human conflict as rooted in the primordial antagonism at the heart of things. Conflict, as the early Greeks understood it, comes about not because of a struggle of good and evil that might someday be finally won and brought to an end, and not as a result of accidental conditions that might be otherwise, but because of an ineluctable competition between disassociated goods epitomized by the competition of the three goddesses. Humans are pulled in conflicting directions toward different goods, toward power, honor, and pleasure. Each of the three leading characters in the poem is a devotee of one of these three: Paris/Alexandros (and all the other children of Priam, who himself sired fifty sons and many daughters) longs for pleasure and above all for erotic pleasure; Agamemnon desires power; and Achilles pursues glory. It is no accident that the Trojans' patron goddess and defender is Aphrodite, that Agamemnon worships Hera, and that Achilles is devoted to and defended by Athena. The poem is an account of the inevitable conflict among these goods (gods, ways of life, etc.) and the necessarily tragic nature of a world in which there is no single or supreme human goal.

The *Iliad* begins as a conflict between the pleasure-loving Trojans and the power- and glory-loving Achaeans. However, already in the first book, the alliance between those who love power and those who love glory breaks down and the conflict becomes three-sided. Agamemnon believes Achilles challenges his power when Achilles is actually interested only in securing his glory, and Achilles perceives Agamemnon as seeking to diminish his glory when Agamemnon in fact wants only to secure his power. This problem arises not merely because human beings want power or wealth—that is, want to control the means to obtain what they desire—but because the goods they want are themselves in conflict with one another. The conflict among human beings thus lies not merely (or principally) in our inability to know others' intentions (as Hobbes was later to argue) but in the conflictual nature of existence itself, in humanity's different ways of being in the world.

The reasons for this conclusion are not as obvious as they might seem. It is clear that two people who want the same thing—for example, glory—may come into conflict over that good. Diomedes, for example, clearly is delighted to have Achilles out of the way because in Achilles' absence he has a chance to demonstrate his own prowess and win his own glory. But it is less clear why the man who longs for glory cannot live happily with the man who seeks pleasure. The action of the *Iliad* indicates how difficult it is to harmonize these different desires, because the objects of each desire cannot be neatly divided. It often happens, for example, that two people want the same thing for different reasons. To take the most obvious example, both Achilles and Agamemnon want Briseis, but Agamemnon wants her as a sign of his power while Achilles wants her as a sign of his glory. That she will provide sexual pleasure for both is also true, although in both cases this is clearly a subordinate use to which the parties are relatively indifferent.[11] In their case no solution is possible, and it is even impossible for them to understand one another because their entire view of the world is shaped by their dominant or dominating passion. They do not merely have preferences; they are driven or possessed by their desires.[12] The problem that drives the action of the *Iliad* is the difficulty men have living in community with those who desire different things than they do and whose visions of the good are shaped by their desire for those particular things they love.

On the surface this may seem to be an odd way to think about the sources of conflict, which we more typically imagine to be the result of a dispute over power or property, or a struggle between good and evil. What is important to see is that if power (or property) alone were in question, it would be possible to reach a modus vivendi, because everyone could agree about what they wanted and what ultimately had value, even if they disagreed about the amounts they should have. Insofar as human beings have different commanding passions or desires, it is impossible to know in any given situation what they actually want, and impossible to find a scale for comparing what they want with what others want. Thus it is impossible to develop a system that could justly or impartially give different people what they deserve, or even determine what desert could mean at any given moment. While Hobbes, for example, can imagine that all men pursue the same thing (power) and therefore that we can develop a political and legal system to eliminate conflict by empowering someone to hold all power and distribute it as he judges best, no such solution is possible in the context of the *Iliad*.[13] It is not merely that people love or value different things, it is that their notions of what is lovable or valuable are incommensurable.

The *Iliad* is a consideration of the three most important goods — pleasure, glory, and power. The pursuit of these goods is the source of the wrath or conflict at the center of the poem. It brings individuals into conflict with one another, and their conflict disrupts the communities they live in. Alexandros's unbridled sexual passion, for example, brings about the downfall of Troy.[14] When Antenor suggests they should give Helen back to save the city, no one argues that he is wrong, but Alexandros and his father refuse to do so, and it is clear from subsequent scenes in the *Iliad* that most of the other males in the city would also have refused to return her.[15] They understand, accept, and defend what they recognize is Alexandros's unjust possession of Helen because they share his particular love. Similarly, we see repeatedly how Agamemnon's love of power disrupts the fraternal relations of the princes and warriors in the *Iliad*, and we also know from allusions in the poem and from further elaborations of the myth by Aeschylus and others that his unbridled desire for power leads to the destruction of his family, beginning with Iphigenia and including his own death at the hands of his wife and her subsequent murder by Orestes.[16] The central example of such a tragic contradiction in the *Iliad* is, of course, Achilles, whose single-minded pursuit of glory leads to the destruction of his best friend and many of his other brothers-in-arms as well.

When Briseis, the sign of Achilles' glory, is unjustly taken from him by Agamemnon (with no other Achaean coming to his defense) he is overcome by rage (*mênin*).[17] That this occurs is no accident. Rage is a particular danger for him because his anger makes him what he is; it is the source of his greatness and magnificence.[18] Like Hector, one may learn to be courageous, but one cannot learn to be cruel, hard, or unrelenting without a natural ferocity. Hector thus can never equal Achilles. He loves his wife and child more than he loves glory.[19] His courage and willingness to fight are thus merely a means to what he really loves. With Achilles they are his dominating (and characterizing) passion, because what he really loves is fighting and winning glory.[20] He does not choose to be a ferocious warrior; he merely becomes what he is. It is the way he is "honored in Zeus's ordinance," as he himself puts it (9.608). Such ferocity, however, is a great danger because it can turn into rage against one's fellows. Indeed, in the *Iliad* his misdirected ferocity is the source of the disaster that shatters the community. It is precisely because he loves fighting and glory so deeply that he is such an irreplaceable force but also such a disruptive one.

The tragic consequences of his and others' dominating passions on the relations among members of the community and between the individuals in the community are obvious and cry out for a solution. One might imagine that an institutional solution of the sort that Hobbes (who translated the *Iliad*) proposes to reduce the number of collisions among passionate human beings could solve this problem, allowing them to pursue their own goals in coordination with others. This possibility is certainly depicted in the city at peace on the shield Hephaestus forges for Achilles. Within the action of the *Iliad*, however, such a view is untenable, because the conflict among the goods is not merely between individuals but within them. Achilles' unlimited love of glory is at odds not merely with Agamemnon's longing for power but also with his own love for Patroclus and his other friends. In pursuing his glory so single-mindedly, he thus disrupts not merely the community of which he is a part, but also his community with himself. No human being is the personification of merely one passion (in the way some of the gods are). Everyone desires multiple things—we are compound beings, to use Aristotle's term. Pursuing any one thing so single-mindedly may lead to greatness, but it also means sacrificing something else that one loves (and in most cases *everything* else one loves). All of the goods we desire are thus potentially at odds with one another, and the choice of any one thus involves loss. Achilles' choice of glory is different only in its intensity and heedless disregard of everything else.

Confronting the fact that his single-minded pursuit of glory has destroyed his friend, Achilles' terrible anger is redirected not merely against Hector but at himself. When he learns of Patroclus's death he wishes that conflict (*eris*) would disappear from the world, but this is at its core the wish that he himself, the foremost embodiment of conflict, should disappear. This desire for self-destruction is also reflected in his final struggle with Hector. Hector appears for the battle wearing Achilles' armor, which he stripped from Patroclus. The remorseful and self-despising Achilles thus sees before him not only Hector but also the naively reckless Achilles who failed to protect his friends. He desires not merely revenge in the narrow sense but also and perhaps preeminently self-destruction. This is reemphasized by his inability to find satisfaction in Hector's death and his repeated (but unsuccessful) efforts to desecrate Hector's body. Killing Hector cannot assuage his pain because it was not Hector but he himself who was principally responsibly for Patroclus's death. Finally, he knows that slaying Hector is a form of suicide, since his mother has warned him that he is fated to die shortly after Hector. It is thus hard to escape the conclusion that he chooses to slay Hector not merely in spite of but also because of his mother's warning. The tragedy of the goods that manifests itself in Achilles thus strikes not merely at the community as a whole but at the internal psychic unity of the individual as well.

How can this problem be solved? For human beings within the world reflected in the *Iliad*, there is no solution; there is only a kind of tragic reconciliation in the face of death that we see depicted in the meeting of Achilles and Priam near the end of the poem. On the verge of death, there is a moment of solace. The cycle of the generations that lies at the heart of the agonistic Greek cosmos is not broken, but its victims are able to share their common agony. Symbolically, fathers and sons comfort one another in the face of death. The moment has a tremendous tragic pathos and grandeur, but it remains only a moment and is thoroughly tragic.

The *Iliad* does point toward a possible solution to the contradiction of the goods in its depiction of the rule of Zeus. All of the Achaeans and Trojans (and in fact all the other gods) in the *Iliad* are blind to anything other than the immediate good they desire. They recognize repeatedly that they have made errors, but they typically assert, often with considerable justification, that they were blinded by delusion, jealousy, hatred, or some other passion, since their loves or impulses are not chosen but forced on them. They are quite literally possessed. What matters is only what is in front of them. Achilles does eventually recognize and lament his fate, but his knowledge is entirely retrospective, a form of afterthought (*epimetheus*). The failure of the human characters to resolve their contradictions is thus due to the lack of foresight (*prometheus*).

Zeus rules not just by force but also because he can foresee the future. This does not allow him to eliminate the conflict among the gods or the goods, but it does allow him to balance conflicting passions against one another, to achieve an equilibrium of forces. No one in the *Iliad*, however, imagines that this kind of wisdom is available to human beings (or even to the other gods). The older and wiser characters such as Nestor and Antenor draw on their experience, but they see only what has been. Knowledge of the future is available only to the divinely inspired prophets, who are generally either hated (Calchas) or disbelieved (Cassandra). Even Odysseus, who is the best at manipulating events, does not depend on foresight but improvises using guile and deception.[21] Moreover, even he is overpowered by his anger with the suitors in the *Odyssey* and acts contrary to his own long-term interests. The world imagined in the *Iliad* (and the *Odyssey*) is thus inevitably tragic because humans do not have foresight and are repeatedly overpowered by their passions. In this respect they remain rooted in the moment.

Nietzsche believed that later Greek thought from Plato on abandoned the tragic notion of a multiplicity of contradictory goods in favor of a unitary idea of the good, and that this unitary notion was at the heart of the Christian notion of God. In his view the death of the Christian God and the advent of nihilism thus presented humanity with a choice between the more or less peaceful coexistence of disassociated goods within a liberal market economy and a rebirth of a tragic culture akin to that of the pre-Platonic Greeks. The death of God in Nietzsche's view thus poses a stark choice for us in our confrontation with the multiplicity of goods—either a banal hedonism or a tragic heroism. Nietzsche himself aims to persuade us to prefer the latter. But should we be convinced that these are the only two alternatives? His argument rests on the assumption that Plato and his philosophical successors were all wedded to a unitary notion of the good, which inevitably led to the univocal notion of good and evil that characterized Christianity. But is this true? Were Plato and his successors wedded to such a notion?

PLATO AND THE STRUCTURAL HARMONY OF THE GOODS

It is certainly true that Plato attempts to find a solution to the conflict of goods in his *Republic*. The solution he develops there is based on a series of radical social and pedagogical innovations, all of which depend on having a human being with quasi-divine wisdom and foresight exercising power in the city. *The Republic* thus raises the possibility that if a Zeuslike individual should exist and be able to rule, political life could be organized in a way that would avoid the conflicts that erupted so disastrously in the *Iliad*. Plato's Socrates insists in the dialogue that such a person could exist and could come to rule, although he admits that both possibilities are highly unlikely. Let us examine the argument more carefully.

Plato's Socrates argues in the context of the dialogue that human beings are motivated by different passions that draw them to particular goods, and that neither the individual nor the city can be happy unless all pursuits are organized to avoid the conflicts between the different goods. According to this view, the best or most beautiful city (literally, the *kallipolis*) is that city in which those who desire pleasure obtain pleasure, those who desire money obtain money, those who want honor obtain honor, and those who want wisdom are allowed to pursue it at their leisure (at least after they have served for a time as chief magistrate of the city). This familiar image with its clearly articulated and structurally separated classes, rooted in natural distinctions that are reinforced by the noble lie and cemented by an elaborate system of education and censorship, describes the prerequisites of a solution to the conflict of the goods, but on their own they are not enough. Crucial to such a city is the philosopher king who has the requisite knowledge and particularly the foresight that enables him (or her) to determine who should mate with whom and which children naturally belong in which classes.[22] In fact, the philosopher king will be even more effective than Zeus at maintaining stability and order, because his knowledge is not merely the foreknowledge of what will occur but the knowledge of what is everywhere and always the case. He knows the truth of things and the measure by which the value of all things is determined. This supreme knowledge, according to Plato's Socrates, is the knowledge of the idea of the good, and it is this knowledge that allows the philosopher king to assign every individual to the place in the social order that he is best suited for and that will give him the greatest access to the good he most desires, thus avoiding conflict with other individuals. The knowledge of the idea of *the* good thus makes it possible to harmonize the goods both in the individual and in the city.[23]

In developing this argument Plato's Socrates portrays the city as best not merely because it has no internal strife and gives each person what is peculiarly good for him or her, but also because it orders the goods according to the quality of the pleasure they afford. On this basis he argues that the supreme pleasure belongs to those who pursue wisdom, the second best to those who pursue honor, the third to those who pursue money, and the least to those who pursue bodily pleasure. Crucial to this distinction, however, is the previously mentioned idea of the good.

Nietzsche believes that Plato seriously put forth a theory of the forms with a unitary notion of the divine and the good at its peak. It is this notion of a unitary idea of the good that Nietzsche sees as essential to the development of the Christian notion of a unitary God and thus a binary notion of good and evil. Whether this conclusion is justified is a difficult question. It is certainly true that Platonism or at least neo-Platonism played an important role in shaping early Christianity, especially in first- and second-century Alexandria. Moreover, no one disputes the fact that Platonism also had a very important influence on the fathers of the church and in particular on Augustine, whose influence on Christianity was inferior only to that of Christ and Paul. Nietzsche's characterization of Christianity as Platonism for the people thus may exaggerate Plato's importance, but it also correctly captures a central element of Christian theology.[24] That Christianity made use of Platonism, however, does not prove that Christianity was an inevitable consequence of Platonism or that Platonism was proto-Christian. Moreover, while Plato's Socrates does suggest in *The Republic* that there is a univocal "idea of the good," there are good reasons to doubt that this notion reflected Plato's actual position on the relation of the good and the goods. However, it goes beyond the scope of this chapter to consider this argument.[25]

Even without such a defense of Plato against Nietzsche's charges, however, it is reasonably clear that not all of Plato's successors accepted such a univocal notion of the good. In fact, Plato's most famous student, Aristotle, explicitly rejected this notion. He sees the goods instead as multiplicitous, disassociated, and potentially in contradiction with one another, but he does not believe that this potential conflict has to end in tragedy. In his view the appetites we have for the goods can be moderated and harmonized by a system of education and training that transforms the passions into virtues. For Aristotle, reason does not rule the world as the Enlightenment later suggested, but it does make it possible for us to act practically in the world to reshape or retune our natures in small but still decisive ways that open up the possibility of nobility in place of tragedy and happiness in place of suffering.

ARISTOTLE AND THE PURSUIT OF HAPPINESS

Aristotle famously asserts at the beginning of the *Nichomachean Ethics* that "all art and all method, and likewise all praxis and deliberation, seem to aim at some good; thus it has been well said that the good is that at which all aims" (1094a). While this initial assertion seems to suggest that there is one single good at which all things aim, Aristotle notes in the following two sentences that as the arts and sciences are many, so are their ends—that is, that it is not obvious that there is a single end uniting the many things that are good. That Aristotle recognizes this difficulty is clear from his following assertion that if among the many ends we pursue, one is pursued for its own sake and not for the sake of something else, it will be the supreme good. He then suggests that happiness or well-being (*eudaimonia*) is thought to be such a good and thus conceived to be the ultimate end of all human striving.[26] However, this is not quite as definitive an answer as one might like, and as the argument develops Aristotle shows that it is difficult to define happiness as anything other than the pursuit and acquisition (in the right amounts and at the right time) of the set of things that make us happy— pleasure, honor, wealth, wisdom, health, and friends. In one sense we thus do always aim at happiness, and that does then in fact constitute the highest good. But typically we actually pursue not the general thing "happiness" but the particular things that are good for us in different ways (1096b). Happiness or well-being, understood as the highest good, thus seems to be nothing other than the name for the activity we engage in when we do the things that are good for us. To complicate matters further, in the course of Aristotle's argument it becomes clear that the various goods that make up happiness or well-being are not naturally harmonious or compatible with one another. As a result, the realization of happiness (and thus the good for man) crucially depends on practical reason and an elaborate system of education and training as well as sound laws and a great deal of good luck. This luck includes external goods, such as slaves, wealth, and power, that create the conditions for the life of leisure essential to the harmonious enjoyment of the primary goods. Thus, while the idea of the good, which Plato first articulated, seems at first glance to be the presupposition of Aristotle's argument, it soon becomes evident that Aristotle does not believe there is such a unitary good and rejects Plato's purported solution to the problem of multiple, disassociated goods (1096b).[27] To understand Aristotle's critique of Plato and his own solution to the problem, we need to examine his argument more carefully.

Aristotle asserts that there are four views of what constitutes happiness or well-being. Some think it is pleasure, others honor, a few contemplation, and many others moneymaking. Aristotle argues that moneymaking cannot qualify as happiness or well-being because it is merely a *means* and not an *end*, but he admits that the other three are ends that all or almost all humans pursue to a greater or lesser extent, and that nearly everyone needs (and in many cases pursues) money or wealth in order to have the other three.[28] His goal in the *Ethics* is to determine which mixture of goods is most conducive to human happiness.

To understand what is good for human beings, we first need to understand human nature. For Aristotle, humans are living beings and like all other living things are animate, or ensouled. By this he means that they have something in them that is self-moving and not just pushed or pulled in the manner of inanimate matter. He calls this thing a psyche or soul. The human psyche in his view consists of two overlapping parts, one nonrational (literally, without speech) and the other rational (1102a–b). The part that is bereft of speech governs autonomic processes such as digestion, growth, and respiration. Aristotle recognizes that these processes are essential to all life and are not unique to humans. Whatever we ultimately regard as the peculiarly human good, it must also support these processes, although for the most part (at least when we are healthy) we take them for granted.

More central to human happiness are the appetites or passions, which we share with the animals. Appetites are closely connected to our capacity for locomotion. Like animals and in contrast to plants, we are able to pursue things in space. The appetites propel us toward objects that we both need and want. Though they are nonrational, they can be guided and shaped by reason and hence occupy a middle part of the psyche that has both a rational and a nonrational component.

To say that the appetites can be guided by reason, however, does not mean they can be moved directly by argument or persuasion. Rather, they are guided indirectly by the promise of pleasure or the threat of pain, typically in the form of praise and blame. In the case of children, praise and blame come from parents and other adults who typically act according to the prevailing moral opinions in their cities. In this way, public opinion sets the standards of what constitutes the proper mixture of goods for its citizens. As children get older, they internalize these opinions and are able to rule their own appetites with little effort because the appetites themselves have been shaped to want what is right and the individual has the proper opinion about what is excellent and what is reprehensible. In this way the child becomes virtuous.

Aristotle's initial answer to the problem that the multiplicity of goods poses for human life is this notion of virtue, which makes possible the more or less harmonious enjoyment of the goods both by the individual and among members of society.[29] The importance of moderating and harmonizing the particular goods is evident in Aristotle's account of the specific virtues. There he discusses the habituation of the passions that correspond to all of the particular goods. This discussion is divided into two parts. Aristotle first discusses the virtues of individuals taken in themselves, and then the virtues of individuals in interaction with others. The former include those concerned with *pain and pleasure*, that is, courage and moderation (1115a–19b); those concerned with *money*, that is, generosity and magnificence (1119b–23b); and those concerned with *honor*, that is, ambition and great-souledness (1123b–25b). The interactive virtues also are portrayed as corresponding to the specific goods. They include receiving and dispensing *pain* and *pleasure* in social interactions (1125b–28b); receiving social *dishonors*, that is, disgrace (1128b); and maintaining a fair (and therefore peaceful) public system for the distribution and allocation of *wealth* and *honor*, that is, justice (1128b–38b). Aristotle notes that justice is also identified with law (written and unwritten), and thus in one sense seems to include all the other virtues and to be the foundation of the communal life of the polis.[30]

The moral virtues are famously described as the mean between the excess and deficiency of a particular passion, which is to say the excess or deficiency in the desire felt for a particular good. The character of that mean and thus of the acceptable love for particular goods both in themselves and in comparison with other goods is not given by nature but is determined by the prevailing view in each city of the proper amount of enjoyment the citizens should have of the particular goods. This view is embodied in the norms of the society and serves as the basis for training and habituating the appetites that prevent (or at least guard against) the extreme passions that generate tragedy in the *Iliad*.

The city is necessary to virtue because by nature these goods—pleasure (and/or absence of pain), honor, and wealth—conflict with one another. Moral virtue as a whole is thus possible only when the pursuit of these various goods can be limited and harmonized. That means that the single-minded passions that dominated Achilles, Alexandros, and Agamemnon must be moderated and put in their place beside the other goods. Aristotle is convinced, however, that the passions for these goods can be moderated only if the city or the parents or both put in place a coherent and continuous system of training that begins in childhood. From their earliest days children must learn to enjoy these goods only in the right amounts.

What constitutes the right amount, however, is not merely dependent on reason. There is no single form of political life that is preferable to all others. Indeed, in Aristotle's view there seem to be many possible ways to reconcile the goods with one another. Aristotle thus recognizes that what is proper will vary from place to place depending on a variety of factors including the external goods or resources available, the traditions of the people, the geopolitical character of the state (e.g., whether it is maritime or land-based), and so on. Virtue is thus rooted in human nature, but the particular form it takes is not natural but conventional. Whether a city is able to foster a successful regime of virtue thus depends on a wide variety of factors, but especially on good laws and the proper shared opinions about what is praiseworthy and what is blameworthy.

Some cities will not be able to foster or sustain virtue. In the *Politics*, Aristotle points to Thurii as an example of a city that initially gave too much power to the wealthy and was never able to achieve a proper balance of the goods (1307a–b).[31] In fact, Aristotle claims that only Sparta has consciously put in place a system of education that aims at virtue (1180a). He believes the likelihood that such a code of laws will be instituted is slight. In the second half of the *Ethics* he thus lays out a broader basis for ethical life that enables even those who live in corrupt cities or who have not been properly trained and habituated by their parents to attain some degree of happiness.

This account begins with a reexamination of the nature of the psyche (1135b). Aristotle asserts here that the original division of the psyche into two overlapping parts was inadequate. A closer examination reveals that the middle is actually composed of two parts, an appetitive or passionate element and a deliberative or calculative one, which must be attuned for virtuous action (1139a). This recognition of the need for the harmony of practical reason and desire reveals that they may be and in fact often are at odds with one another. Aristotle also reexamines the rational part of the psyche and concludes that it consists of a contemplative element that considers only things that do not change and a calculative element that considers things that do change. This division of the psyche suggests there are eight possible forms of human ethical activity:

1. The contemplation of the unchanging. In Aristotle's view this is a purely theoretical rather than practical activity. It is an end in itself. It is thus not a source of human action and is not a concern of ethics. It does, however, involve the enjoyment of one of the principal goods, wisdom (*sophia*).

2. True practical reason (*phronêsis*) with no opposing passion or desire. Aristotle characterizes this as godlike or superhuman virtue and holds up Socrates as an example.

3. True practical reason commanding improperly habituated passion. This is what Aristotle calls self-command.

4. True practical reason in harmony with properly habituated passion or appetite. This is virtue.

5. Improperly habituated passion or desire commanding right practical reason. This is what Aristotle calls unrestraint or moral weakness.

6. False practical reason in harmony with improperly habituated passion or appetite. This is Aristotle's definition of vice.

7. Unhabituated or improperly habituated desire with no practical reason. This is what Aristotle identifies as bestiality.

8. Growth, nutrition, and other similar nonrational processes. These correspond to the autonomic element discussed above, and while these processes are forms of motion, their motion is completely involuntary and thus does not fall in the realm of ethics. Like contemplation, they thus originate no action.[32]

In the first half of the *Ethics* the polis plays the crucial role in fostering moral virtue and reconciling the goods with one another. In the second half of the work Aristotle broadens his point of view not merely with respect to the character of the psyche and the variety of human ethical possibilities, but also with respect to the nature of the human community that makes a reconciliation of the goods possible. Whereas the first half of the *Ethics* ended with a discussion of justice as the foundation of ethical life in the polis, the second half turns to a consideration of friendship, the natural love that human beings have for one another as the bond of communal life. The polis, as Aristotle understands it, is the preeminent form of friendship, but it is not the only one. Indeed, all of our social relations, including the family, economic life, and voluntary associations, are forms of friendship broadly conceived, and in the absence of good laws all of them can help to foster ethical behavior that helps us harmonize the goods with one another. Aristotle believes that the love we feel for friends and our desire to emulate and please them gives us a powerful incentive to moderate our other passions. We want to be loved by and be like those we love, and thus by surrounding ourselves with good people we can become good ourselves. Or to put it another way, by choosing good people as our friends, we will come to love the goods in the same way they do.

While friendship aids us in our continuing pursuit of happiness, it does not direct us to one good (or one particular constellation of goods) rather than another. In fact, we seem at least in part to pick our friends because we love the same things and activities as they do. As Aristotle puts it, "Whatever pursuit it is that constitutes existence for a man or that makes his life worth living, he desires to share that pursuit with his friends. Hence some friends drink or dice together, others practice athletic sports and hunt, or study philosophy, in each other's company" (1171b).[33] Friendship thus promotes emulation but does not tell us what we ought to emulate, and it does not tell us how to avoid tragedy. Patroclus loves Achilles and desires to emulate him, but it is precisely this love that leads to his death and the death of Achilles. Friendship is thus as likely to produce extreme, single-minded behavior as moderation.

As a result, neither the laws of the city nor the opinions of our friends can tell us definitively which good or which mix of goods is most conducive to happiness or well-being. To understand which goods (and thus which friends and which cities) are preferable and how to balance the pursuit of different goods in the context of a whole life, we need to be able to compare the goods with one another. Following Plato, Aristotle argues that we can measure the value of the goods in terms of the pleasure or happiness they give us not by means of our subjective impressions and preferences, but by a concrete analysis of how conducive they are to human thriving.

On the surface, this turn in the argument seems to have much in common with the homogenization of the goods under the utilitarian rubric of preference, which I discussed above. Aristotle, however, does not seek to reduce all goods to quanta of pleasure but seeks to evaluate them in terms of the sorts of pleasure that accompany them and the conduciveness of these activities and their accompanying pleasures to happiness or well-being. The utilitarian calculus that liberalism employs in distinguishing the relative value of goods, whether expressed in individual preferences or in market valuations, is thus foreign to Aristotle. In his view the term pleasure has generally been too narrowly identified with the bodily pleasures. This mis-identification is the result of the fact that such pleasures are universal and are the only ones available to most human beings, since they are incapable of experiencing higher pleasures (1154a). Thus the pleasures we derive from food, sex, and drink have wrongly been taken as emblematic of pleasure as a whole. While a life without such pleasures could hardly be a happy one, in Aristotle's view a life devoted simply to these pleasures would certainly be unhappy (or at least less happy). As he puts it, everyone enjoys savory food, wine, and sexual pleasure to a degree, though not everyone to the right degree (1154a). For Aristotle bodily pleasure is not *the* good, and not every pleasure is even desirable, although some are desirable in themselves (1174a). What is crucial is thus to discover which are indeed desirable in themselves and not merely as a means to something else.

Although Aristotle is convinced that no one thing can continuously give us pleasure because we are compound beings (1154b), he believes there are crucial differences between the pleasures that derive from the nature of the activities they are associated with. Bodily pleasures, for example, are limited in several ways. They arise out of the need to restore a natural bal-ance and are thus always associated with pain. We eat or drink because we are thirsty or hungry, that is, because we feel pain or discomfort and know that eating or drinking will alleviate it. We feel pleasure in returning to our natural equilibrium, and if we eat, drink, or have sex excessively we feel diminishing pleasure and ultimately pain. There are thus natural limits that govern bodily pleasures. But this is not true for other forms of pleasure.

In particular Aristotle discusses the pleasures associated with the other two primary goods, honor (or glory) and wisdom. There is no bodily limit, for example, to honor. We do not seek it because we need it to survive, and having too much is not painful. However, as the case of Achilles makes clear, honor depends on others and can be justly or unjustly bestowed or de-nied. The pleasure associated with living a life filled with honor is thus not in the individual's control. While honor is generally a component of hap-piness or well-being, it is always contingent and insecure. Thus Aristotle argues that anyone who seeks to be truly happy should seek not honor but excellence, by which he means the knowledge that we are worthy (or honorable) whether or not others recognize this and actually honor us.[34] Such a life certainly characterizes the great-souled man, who has all the particular virtues and has achieved all that humans can attain in the practical sphere. He takes great pride in his own accomplishments, and in the good city he is universally admired and emulated by the younger generation. His life, however, is not perfect because he must involve himself in politics and seek power. He thus lacks leisure, and he is always dependent on circumstances for his ultimate success (1177b). Moreover, like Achilles, he is always also dependent on the opinions of others.

The supremely happy life for Aristotle is the life of the philosopher or sage who contemplates unchanging things. His activity is complete and pleasurable in itself. It is never a means to something else. In contrast to the glorious deeds of the great-souled man, the philosopher's activity is quiet and reserved, invisible to most human beings. Insofar as he seeks to contemplate, he is always entirely independent and self-sufficient or, in Aristotle's language, autarkic. Contemplation in Aristotle's view is the only activity that is loved for itself and not for what is can give us (1177b). While such a life is naturally best, it occurs only incidentally within the political realm and is fundamentally apolitical, for contemplation originates no action and draws the philosopher away from the common life of his fellow citizens. In fact, "such a life as this . . . will be higher than the human level" (1177b).

Despite the quasi-divine character of his activity, the philosopher remains a mortal being and lives in a society he must come to terms with. To be happy he needs external goods (moderate wealth and slaves) to provide him with leisure and with the modicum of physical pleasure that all humans need and desire (1179a). In contrast to the great-souled man, he does not need honor, although it is hard to believe he would not want to be worthy of being honored, even if like Socrates he is unjustly thought not to be so. Moreover, while the philosopher is more independent than anyone else, he still needs friends in order to philosophize more continuously.[35]

The life of moral virtue based on honor is the second happiest life. The life of self-command may transcend that of moral virtue in excellence, but because it is fundamentally discordant, it is painful. The lives of most men, however, are the least happy, for they live by unmoderated passion and pursue pleasure according to their nature, without any knowledge of nobility or true pleasure (1179b; see also 1154b).[36]

While Aristotle recognizes that some activities and pleasures are superior to others, he does not deny that the lesser activities and pleasures contribute to happiness. Moreover, he clearly recognizes that all kinds of human beings live (and as political animals, must live) together in cities.

In contrast to the image Plato presents in *The Republic*, Aristotle is doubtful that there is one best or perfect model that will give all human beings the particular mix of goods that is best for them. In Aristotle's view many solutions are thus possible to the conflicts among the goods and the different views about the potential mixtures of the goods. He does not believe, however, that these possibilities can be rationally deduced. The determination of the best structure for achieving harmony is always a practical question that can be answered only by the use of practical wisdom in the moment. Such knowledge, however, is not always present, and even when it is, it is not always successful, since the nature of the particular form of the regime is typically answered through political competition and the triumph of one party over another. That does not mean, however, that one cannot determine which set of institutions is most likely to be best in any given situation. Indeed, making such a determination is the task of the political philosopher, that is, the philosopher who studies constitutions and politics (1180b). As Aristotle puts it, "It is the business of the political philosopher to examine the nature of pleasure and pain; for he is the architect of the end by which we say things are bad or good in the absolute sense" (1152a).

But who is this strange being? He is related to the great-souled man who is the supreme example of the *vita activa*, and to the philosopher who is the supreme example of the *vita contemplativa*, but he is distinct from both. He is clearly not involved in politics and not lost in contemplation. In his study of the constitutions or the political histories of cities, he seeks to improve his prudence or practical wisdom (*phronêsis*), while in constructing laws and building the state he also seems to employ a kind of technical knowledge (*technê*). According to the account given in book 6 of the *Ethics*, he is thus concerned not so much with science (*epistêmê*) as with praxis. His goal, if the *Politics* is any example, is the production of the good life that is the end of politics. The good life, not the best life. In contrast to his teacher, Aristotle is realistic about the possibilities of finding a suitable mixture of the goods for any given city and recognizes that the continued success of such a city will depend on the continued action of practically wise and philosophically trained individuals in maintaining the balance necessary for a successful common life. A great deal of the *Politics* is thus devoted to advice on how to sustain different kinds of regimes.

Aristotle's notion that the proper end of human life is happiness is thus radically different from the pursuit of happiness that modern liberalism proclaims to be the end of human striving. Liberalism imagines that each man is the best judge of what is good for him, because the good is what feels good, and the knowledge of our feelings is available to us only subjectively.

The goods in this way become mere preferences. Aristotle, in a manner surprisingly akin to many modern biologists, believes that the good for man is not a choice but a consequence of our biological nature and the way we exist in the world with other beings, including other human beings. This does not mean we are powerless or that all our actions are involuntary. For Aristotle happiness depends in the end on finding a balance among the goods that frees us from the domination of our passions without reducing the objects of our loves to mere commodities.

CONCLUSION

In the aftermath of what he perceived as the death of God and the inevitable collapse of a moral system based on this God, Nietzsche believed that European humanity would be catapulted beyond good and evil into a world of multiple goods (and multiple bads). In this world he feared that humans would degenerate into merely pleasure-loving beings who were drawn first one way and then another toward whichever good presented itself. He identified this possibility with democratic liberalism and saw it as the lowest human possibility. He was convinced that such a path was incompatible not merely with human thriving but with human existence, and he feared widespread suicide if it should be triumphant.

He believed the only possible alternative to such decadence was the rebirth of a tragic age akin to that of the pre-Socratic Greeks. While he recognized that the costs of pursuing such an option would be horrific, producing wars greater than anything humanity had ever seen, he believed it was the only option that could promote human excellence and thriving.[37] His work from beginning to end thus sought to advance this alternative. I have argued in this essay that he was mistaken about the choice he saw for humanity and did not recognize more desirable alternatives. This was principally because he wrongly interpreted almost all other forms of European thought after Socrates as Platonist and proto-Christian. He thus believed they all were based on a unitary notion of the good that had become unbelievable with the death of God and were thus unbelievable in our post-Christian world. Such an undifferentiated account of European thought clearly distorts the actual positions on the nature of the good/goods of a number of European thinkers. I have tried to show in particular that Aristotle did not accept such a view of the good/goods and in fact laid out another way human beings can live harmoniously in a world of multiple, disassociated, and conflicting goods. Nietzsche's unwillingness to seriously consider this possibility as it appears in the work of Aristotle and similar virtue theorists certainly weakens and arguably totally undermines his strong claim that the only solution to the decadence of liberal democratic society is tragedy.[38] The success of this Aristotelian alternative, however, depends on paying a great deal of attention to political philosophy, to the structure of the regime, to party conflict, to ameliorating the distinctions of rich and poor, and to forming the character of the citizens, factors of human life that Nietzsche with his grandiose and apocalyptic vision of the superhuman had little time for.

Nietzsche and his successors believe that liberalism is a form of decadence and that only a turn to a tragic agonism offers any hope for the future. Rather than simply rejecting liberalism in pursuit of a superhuman or postmodern alternative, however, we might do better to consider ways of drawing on Aristotle and other thinkers who have been deeply concerned with virtue, character, and politics in order to elevate and perhaps even ennoble our liberal aspirations.

NOTES

1. One might ask whether the term describes the way something is done regardless of the outcome. For example, we might characterize a meeting as good even though we did not get what we wanted, because we thought the procedures for reaching a decision were fair, just, or right. The fair, the just, and the right, however, are good only because they produce an end that we consider good—for example, peace, harmony, justice. If decision-making procedures were fair and just but consistently produced bad results, we would inevitably conclude that the meetings were not going well—that they were not good—and change our procedures.

2. This rejection of a summum bonum was connected to the horrifying Wars of Religion that arose out of the Reformation. While Hobbes, for example, argues that there is no summum bonum, he does regard violent death as a summum malum that must be avoided at all costs. Thomas Hobbes, *Leviathan*, ed. Edwin Curley (Indianapolis, IN: Hackett, 1994), 57.

3. This assertion may seem to identify liberalism too readily as either purely emotivist or radically libertarian. I recognize that any number of liberal thinkers seek to differentiate the pleasures in order to sustain a doctrine that promotes human dignity and virtue rather than decadence and license. I just do not believe that there are ontological resources within liberalism for such distinctions and that such distinctions thus typically rest on moral or religious feelings or imported notions of virtue ontologically incompatible with liberalism. I take it to be Nietzsche's point that the demand for consistency inevitably drives liberalism into the sheer hedonism that characterizes the last man. Whether he is right about this is another matter. Many people (and Americans in particular) often live according to contradictory doctrines for long periods. For an alternative account that sees a greater possibility for liberal virtue, see Peter Berkowitz, *Virtue and the Making of Modern Liberalism* (Princeton,

NJ: Princeton University Press, 1999), and William Galston, *Liberal Purposes: Goods, Virtues, and Diversity in the Liberal State* (New York: Cambridge University Press, 1991).

4. Friedrich Nietzsche, *Thus Spoke Zarathustra*, prologue, 5, in *Werke: Kritische Gesamtausgabe*, ed. G. Colli and M. Montinari (Berlin: De Gruyter, 1967–), (hereafter cited by section, volume, and page number as *KGW*), VI 1:13.

5. Nietzsche's argument in some measure is a reflection of the moral debate in Germany in the latter half of the nineteenth century. Nietzsche clearly believed that the attenuated Christian theology of his time was unable to sustain the faith and dedication necessary to maintain order. In place of this fading Christian religiosity he saw two possibilities for Germany: the adoption of Anglo-American liberalism or a renewed and intensified Hellenism. In a post-Christian world, in other words, one had to chose between the ancients and the moderns, between aristocracy and democracy, and ultimately between tragedy and comedy.

6. Hobbes, *Leviathan*, 41.

7. Pindar, *Second Pythian Ode*. Nietzsche's Zarathustra goes so far as to describe this dominant passion as one's "virtue." *KGW*, VI 1:13.

8. Hobbes, *Leviathan*, 51.

9. Alexis de Tocqueville, *Democracy in America*, 2 vols. (New York: Alfred A. Knopf, 1945), 2:136–39.

10. See Aeschylus, *Prometheus Bound*, 947–48. See also Laura M. Slatkin, *The Power of Thetis: Allusion and Interpretation in the Iliad* (Berkeley: University of California Press, 1992).

11. In the analogous case of Helen, of course, sexual pleasure is the motivating cause for Paris/Alexandros, and he is unwilling to give her back even though it could save his city, increase his power, and enhance his glory.

12. This is indicated by the Greek characterization of the desires or passions as divine powers that humans not only cannot control but are largely defenseless before.

13. Agamemnon seeks to persuade Achilles to come back by offering him money, his daughter in marriage, and power over several cities if he will submit. None of these can satisfy Achilles, though, because they are not goods he wants. The second problem that scarcely appears in the *Iliad* but that becomes increasingly visible in later Greek thought is the conflict engendered by those who seek supreme power not to satisfy their characteristic love or longing but to have all good things whatever, that is, everything that gives them power, honor, or pleasure. For the Greeks this was the problem of tyranny, which they saw as both a psychic and a political disorder. To want multiple disassociated goods is to be dominated by disassociated passions and thus to cease to be a coherent being.

14. The source of his love and of such passions generally is made clear when Helen complains to Aphrodite that she doesn't want to love Alexandros, and Aphrodite tells her to shut up because she doesn't have any choice in the matter, since the attraction is entirely due to Aphrodite herself. *Iliad* 3.390–417. Numerous examples from Greek drama emphasize the fact that passions are not chosen but are forms of divine possession.

15. Even the wisest of the Trojan elders recognize how appealing Helen is, although they recognize the danger she poses to the city not merely as the cause of the war with the Achaeans but also as a source of contention among Trojan males as well (3.146–60)

16. Agamemnon perhaps inherits his unrestrained love of power from his ancestors, who involve themselves in incest, murder, cannibalism, and any number of other crimes in pursuit of power.

17. The importance of rage in Homer's account is perhaps indicated by the fact that the first word in the *Iliad* is *mênin*.

18. In contrast to modern tragic characters, he is thus destroyed not by a tragic flaw but by a tragic virtue. What makes him great is also what destroys him. Or to put the matter in somewhat different terms, he honors only a single god and thus offends the others, who in turn destroy him. In a world governed by a single omnipotent and infinitely good God, tragedy is possible only based on some defect arising out of human sinfulness. It cannot be the necessary consequence of a virtue or strength, for then the responsibility for the tragedy would lie with God and not with man.

19. Thus when he explains why he fights, he refers to the fact that he *learned* to be courageous and fight for his father's honor before the Trojan women of the long flowing robes (6.440–46).

20. At the beginning of the *Iliad*, Agamemnon correctly describes Achilles as an *eris* lover (1.117).

21. Even when he knows the future, he is unable to master it, as we see from his inability to prevent his men from eating the cattle of the sun, even though he knows that if they do so they will be destroyed. *Odyssey* 12.922–24.

22. This knowledge was, of course, precisely what Zeus gained from Prometheus. The stability of the regime in *The Republic*, like Zeus's rule on Olympus, crucially depends on the younger generation's obeying their elders and not overthrowing them. The decline of the regime in *The Republic* thus begins with the inability to understand the nuptial number, the disagreement among the parents about what is good, and the child's rejection of his father's idea of the good.

23. What this knowledge is, however, is never explained, and it is clearly possible that Plato does not seriously believe such knowledge exists.

24. Nietzsche seems to have concluded in his later thought, and particularly in *The Antichrist*, that Paul was more important than Plato in the development of Christianity.

25. It is hard, for example, to see how Plato could maintain the notion of the idea of the good in the face of the argument he deploys in the *Parmenides*.

26. The term *eudaimonia*, usually translated as "happiness," actually means being well-spirited, in the sense of having a good spirit associated with one's being or watching over one. Happiness for Aristotle is thus not a feeling or state but an activity, and the word thus might be more accurately translated as "well-doing" or "well-being."

27. Aristotle's treatment of the unity or multiplicity of goods thus parallels his treatment of the unity and multiplicity of being in the *Metaphysics* (998a–1001b).

28. What is surprisingly missing from this list, especially from the perspective of the *Iliad* and *The Republic*, is power. But presumably Aristotle would identify power,

like money, as a mere means and therefore reject it as a plausible component of happiness. Indeed, he asserts that virtue, which he believes is a key component of happiness, does not require power (1176a).

29. Except, of course, the slaves, who Aristotle believes are necessary so that others have the leisure to be virtuous. He does remark in the *Politics* that leisure would be possible without slavery if "each inanimate machine could do its own work, at the word of command or by intelligent anticipation" (1253b).

30. As we will see, he expands this notion in the second half of the *Ethics*, where he asserts that friendship is the primordial basis of political life.

31. Of course the account of the corrupt regimes in the *Ethics* describes regimes that are unable to find the proper balance or distribution of the goods (1060b–61a).

32. Obviously there are other forms of human activity that in Aristotle's view do not fall into the realm of ethics. Probably the most important of these is everything that involves technê, that is, making things. Presumably technical activity is not ethical or unethical, because it involves working on things rather than persons. It is hard to see, however, how one would then classify the activity of a doctor.

33. Thus Aristotle recognizes that "each man thinks that activity most desirable which suits his particular disposition"; he just does not believe that each of them is correct (1176b).

34. This is certainly what Achilles means when he says he is "honored in Zeus's ordinance," but he is unfortunately unable to live without his fellow warriors' recognizing his excellence. It is obvious that there is often a disproportion between honor and excellence. Some receive more honor than they deserve, triggering outrage among their competitors, while the excellence of others, such as Socrates, may consistently be undervalued. Finding a solution for the proper distribution of honor is particularly important for sustaining peace in a warrior society.

35. That said, in his critique of Plato, Aristotle does assert that the philosopher must love truth more than friends (1096a).

36. This is of course precisely the life of the last man that Nietzsche finds so despicable.

37. On the coming wars, see *Ecce Homo, KGW*, VI 3:364. Also see Elisabeth Kuhn, *Friedrich Nietzsches Philosophie des europäischen Nihilismus* (Berlin: Walter de Gruyter, 1991), 213–14. Nietzsche longed for this transformation: "I am glad about the military development of Europe; also of the internal states of anarchy: the time of repose and Chinese ossification, which Galiani predicted for this century, is over. . . . The barbarian in each of us is affirmed; also the wild beast. Precisely for that reason philosophers have a future." *Nachlass, KGW*, VII 2:261. He is quite clear that these wars are not just spiritual: "The consequences of my teaching must rage furiously: but on its account uncountably many shall die." *Nachlass, KGW*, VII 2:84.

38. Nietzsche recognized that some later thinkers such as Plutarch were throwbacks to an earlier tragic era, but he was convinced that these were rare exceptions. *Untimely Meditations, KGW*, III 1:291. He was certain from early on that Aristotle was essentially Platonic. He is particularly clear that Aristotle accepted and shared the Platonic notion of a unitary good. *The Dawn, KGW*, V 1:324.

EIGHT

The Goodness of Searching

GOOD AS WHAT? GOOD FOR WHAT?
GOOD FOR WHOM?

Amelie Oksenberg Rorty

If—as the title of our volume suggests—we are in search of "goodness," we'd best have some idea of where to look for it. Since I am skeptical that there is such a thing as "goodness," *überhaupt*, as such, I have turned to Plato—who introduced us to the Idea of the Good—in hopes of finding enlightenment.[1] As is often the case, I have found him a rich source of cogent and profound problems. In this essay, I have attempted to formulate some of the problems—and convictions—that we've inherited from Plato's Idea of the Good . . . and to summarize what remains of that inheritance. Although they are far from the grandeur of Plato's Idea of the Good, the modest recommendations of Epicurus and Epictetus about leading a good enough human life carry some unexpected Socratic echoes.

REMINDERS AND TESTIMONIALS

First, some anti-Platonic testimonials:

From Aristotle: "Every art or techne and every systematic investigation and every action and choice seem to aim at some good. . . . The [word] 'good' is used in as many senses as [the word] 'is'" (*Nicomachean Ethics*, 1096a, 23–25).

From Spinoza: "Perfection and imperfections . . . are only modes of thinking, notions we are accustomed to feign because we compare individuals of the same species or genus to one another. . . . As far as good and evil are concerned, they also indicate nothing positive in things, considered in themselves, nor are they anything other than modes of thinking, or notions we form because we compare one thing to another. For one and the same thing can, at the same time, be good and bad, and also indifferent" (*Ethics* IV, preface, II.107–8). "By 'good' I understand every kind of joy/elation (*laetitia*) and whatever leads to it" (*Ethics* IV.d1). "By 'joy'/elation (*laetitia*) I mean every sense of increase in one's power" (*Ethics* III.d2).

From C. K. Ogden and I. A. Richards: "The word "good" has a purely emotive use. . . . [T]he word stands for nothing. . . . [W]hen we use the sentence, 'This [object] is good,' ['good'] serves only as an emotive sign expressing our attitude to this [object], and perhaps evoking similar attitudes in other persons, or inciting them to actions of one kind or another" (*The Meaning of Meaning* [London: Kegan Paul, 1923],) 125).

From Judith Thomson: "There is no such thing as goodness [as such]; all goodness is goodness in a way" (Judith Thomson, *Goodness and Advice* [Princeton, NJ: Princeton University Press, 2001], 19).

From just folks: "Good job," the doting father says to a child who has just pooped in the pot. "Good for you," we say to an employee who has, at some risk to herself, blown the whistle on her devious employer. "That's a good knife for carving a duck; don't try using it to slice onions," says the chef to her apprentice. From a letter to the promotions review committee: "He's a good Kant scholar, but don't trust him on Hume." From Mae West: "Goodness had nothing to do with it."

These testimonials remind us that uses of the word good are not always meant to be descriptive: they also occur in a variety of alluring rhetorical and persuasive scripts. We sometimes say "Good!" to express approval or to give advice without indicating its intentional focus. In current usage, such approvals have the weight of "That's great!" and "Cool!" They express more about the speaker's endorsement than about the specific merits of their objects.

THERE IS NO "GOODNESS AS SUCH"

Agathos, "good," and their equivalents in other languages are adjectival evaluative terms; their use is elliptical; their meaning is fixed by a shared implicit understanding of the aims and standards for evaluating the "object" they are attributed to in a specific context, for specific purposes. The "object" may be an event, an idea, a state of affairs, or the attribute of an object or whatever.[2] What is it that we know when we know that something (a chain saw, a steak knife, a tax policy, a flu shot, an . . .) is good? It's an odd locution to begin with. The criterion by which we typically evaluate the value—the goodness—of an artifact is fixed by how well it serves our interests. The evaluation of "natural" objects (plants and planets, animals and avalanches) is more complex. By and large, anthropocentric as we are, we evaluate these things by how well they serve our interests. (To a farmer, "That's a good variety of pea" suggests that the variety is sturdy under difficult soil or climatic conditions, or that it reliably produces peas that are readily marketable. To a biologist, "Now that's a really good [example of] Apicotermitinae" suggests that this variety of termite is a useful sample for research in termite reproduction.)

There may be things—late Beethoven quartets and Bach Passions—that are intrinsically good, good in themselves, without reference to their functions or their serving our interests. They are admired, judged good independent of whatever desirable consequences they may also have. In this sense there may be many intrinsic goods: certain kinds of experiences and states of affairs (pleasures, friendships, and Bach cantatas, for example). But there is no reason to think that all intrinsic goods have something in common, "the good in itself."

To be sure, grading standards for both instrumental and intrinsic goods are contestable. We often have reason to question whether the cultural standards for a good shoe (a good mother, a good literary critic, a good mortgage-lending policy, a good death, a good war, a good peace treaty, a good run/a good Olympic run, a good discussion) are appropriate, whether they are, other things being equal, useful or appropriate standards of evaluation for us to adopt. If we persist in asking whether utility is a proper mark of "the good," we would do well to turn to G. E. Moore's dictum that "good is good and that is the end of the matter." As he puts it, "If I am asked 'How is good to be defined?' my answer is that it cannot be defined, and that is all I have to say about it. But disappointing as these answers may appear, they are of [very great] importance. . . . Their importance. . . . amounts to this: nobody can foist upon us such an axiom as that 'Pleasure is the only good' or that 'The good is the desired' on the pretence that this is 'the very meaning of the word.'"[3] But if good (as such) cannot be defined, it does not follow that it always refers to the same indefinable property, let alone the same indefinable ultra substance. We might ask, What good would such an indefinable "Good"—taken either as a noun or as an adjective—be? An indefinable singular property or entity could not provide criteria for evaluating anything in particular; and it certainly could not provide guidance for making something valuable (a portrait of Moore, a quiche to serve at a brunch for Quine, an article on the reproductive system of the Apicotermitinae).

With Aristotle and Spinoza, we might instead conclude that there is no sensible use of the word—there is no workable concept—of "good" or "goodness" as such, *überhaupt*, beyond criteria for evaluating specific types or kinds of "objects." This modest limitation on the concepts of "good" and "goodness" also applies to determining whether a particular criterion of goodness evaluation is useful, appropriate, or proper. It even applies to questions and controversies about whether it is good/appropriate to construe a specific cultural "kind"—quiches, termites, academic departments—as working categories. (For instance: Might political theorists be well served by dropping the category of *nations?* Might it be better (i.e., good) to use a whole different category to understand contemporary geopolitics?) Elliptically, we might say that the attribution of "good" to a particular object (event, organization, criterion for evaluation, etc.) presupposes a conception of "best of its kind"/"best you can wisely hope for"/"best for your purposes as a measure or standard for its presumed object-type." There is no overarching conception of goodness as univocally applied to all possible objects or kinds.

And shouldn't we be glad, shouldn't we celebrate the vast variety of reasons we have to admire and to prize the things of this world? Think how impoverished we would be if the wonderful diversity of modes of excellence—the many forms of grace and beauty, the value and benefit of objects, the sources of awe and admiration—all came to one and the same thing, if it really were the case that "'Beauty is truth, truth beauty,'—that is all / Ye know on earth, and all ye need to know"?[4]

ON THE OTHER HAND, PLATO THINKS OTHERWISE

But many, notoriously Plato, appear to have claimed otherwise. "What gives truth to the things known and the power to know to the knower is the Form [*idea/eidos*] of the good [*agathos*]. As the cause of knowledge and truth, you must think of it as an object of knowledge. . . . The objects of knowledge . . . owe their existence [*to einai*] and being [*ousia*] . . . to the good, even though it is not Being, but something yet beyond Being, superior in rank and power [*dunamis*]" (*Republic* 508e1–509b8; see also 517c).

Let's trace Plato's arguments and see what good, if any, his claims brought him. The rationale for the primacy—the power—of the Good really begins and emerges with arguments for the existence of the Forms (*eide*). Crudely reconstructed, there seem to be three types of schematic arguments for the "priority/superiority" of the Forms to particular objects, classes of objects, events.

1. The pedagogical arguments: Learning to identify and classify individual "objects" presupposes a grasp of stable conventional and natural Kinds or Types (*eide* and *ideai*). For instance, the content of certain kinds of ideas—of equality, triangles, justice, polis—cannot be acquired or projected from the "objects" that only imperfectly exemplify them. Like the objects of mathematics, moral and political ideals are abstract without being abstractions: we do not acquire ideas of justice, courage, or wisdom from experience. No

courageous person, as we might know her, exemplifies our idea of courage as such; rather, we call an individual "courageous," a polity "just" by reference to an ideal type. The content of such ideas cannot be derived by abstracting or projecting them from regularities among (alleged) examples. Indeed, the very process of identifying or recognizing examples of such "objects" presupposes the idea of an exemplar or a norm.

2. The pedagogical argument rests on more fundamental epistemological premises: Both natural and conventional or artificial objects are (ultimately) identified and distinguished by reference to stable kinds that they instantiate or exemplify. A merely postulated conventional definition of such objects would not do the explanatory work we need from definitions. The characteristics and behavior of individual objects are explained by reference to their increasingly formal reified properties and relational laws. The behavior of material objects—the evaporation of liquids, the behavior of falling bodies, the rotation of the moon—are explained by the law of gravity, the theorems of mathematics, the combinatorial laws of chemistry. These "abstract" formal laws and properties are metaphysically independent of human conventions or idealized projections. Although some "objects" like grammatical or linguistic categories are conventional, others—like the structures of ideal types of political systems—are both natural and conventional. The properties, relations, and activities of such individual "objects" are explained and rationalized by reference to the ideal types of their kind.

3. The epistemological argument echoes premises from an even more basic metaphysical argument: The fundamental explanatory *ideai/eide* are eternal and immutable, more "real" than contingent things that change and perish. "Equal sticks and stones appear equal to one person and not to another; but equals themselves [*auta ta isa*] have never appeared unequal, nor [the Form] Equality [*isotes*] inequality" (*Phaedo* 74b–c) What is unchanging, self-sufficient, invulnerable, necessary is nobler, better, more beautiful (*kalon*) than transient things that can change and decay, that can be affected by external contingencies. "Things that appear both to be and not to be . . . lie between what fully *is* and what absolutely *is not* (i.e., things that change with context and perspective); they cannot be correlated with knowledge nor ignorance" (*Republic* 478d). The implicit premise is that what is subject to external power—whatever can be diminished, changed or extinguished—is less real than what is impervious to such exogenous alteration, and as such it cannot serve as the basis for scientific knowledge. As Nicholas White put it, a form *F*—equal, beautiful, just, square—exists as what it is, independent of any temporal or physical circumstances or perspectives.[5] Or as Butler might have put it, "A Platonic Form is what it is, and

not another thing."[6] Degrees of explanatory power demarcate degrees of self-sufficiency that in turn indicate degrees of reality. Because the cosmos is an organized whole, hierarchically unified by a single principle, inquiry most profitably moves toward a systematic integration of knowledge claims that are fundamentally supported by a metaphysically grounded formal system. The Divided Line describes stages in such progressively abstract and systematic inquiry: starting with images (shadows, reflections), it moves to opinions about physical objects (chambered nautilus shells, falling bodies) and on to the formulae that explain the behavior of objects (Fibonaccio ratios, the laws of gravitation) and finally to the basic ideas of mathematics (*eide*) that are presupposed by these formulae (*Republic* 509d–511e)

As going beyond his postulate of the Forms, Plato's arguments for the objective existence of the Idea of the Good arise from the relations among the levels of the Divided Line.[7] The formal laws of physics and chemistry explain the Fibonaccio patterns in the growth of the chambered nautilus, the parabola of falling bodies, the structured composition of elements to form compounds. The formulation of such laws presupposes a set of assumptions and definitions of stable, unchanging mathematical Forms (*eide*): equality, curve, angle, straight line. Now imagine a world that is composed just of individual Forms, the most basic principles (*arche*) of the world, taken individually. Until we have some idea of the principle of their organization, their structured interrelation, we do not have an ordered *cosmos*.[8] We would then have eternal immutable objects, but no understanding of the relations among them, or the principles by which they cohere to form a well-organized system. The Good is introduced to give an idea of a structured, unified cosmos. If there were only individual Forms, organized haphazardly if at all, the world of eternal being would be as chaotic as the world of becoming. The Forms must therefore themselves form a system, organized by a unifying principle of Order, the regulative *Idea* of the cosmos as a *cosmos*, that is, a well-ordered, unified whole. Plato calls this principle the Idea of the Good (*Idea tou agathou*). At this stage, the unifying principle of the cosmos might as well be called "The One," "The System," "My Grandmother's Chicken Soup," or "the X factor." Nothing is established about its being a generative force or cause of existence or the possibility of knowledge, or the ground of objective value.

To connect the conditions for knowledge with the conditions for morality, Plato introduces two further considerations to give the Forms drawing power: besides being the sources of existence and knowledge, they are the causes (*arche*) of the *desire* for knowledge and for (what is perceived as) good. Besides being valuable, they are sources of value and the activity of valuing.

4. The value and motivational argument: Actions, institutions and persons are evaluated by reference to an ideal, whose content underlies and explains but cannot be derived from the characteristics or activities of standard-issue human beings. The properties, relations, and activities of individual "objects" are not only explained but also evaluated by reference to their fulfilling the function (*ergon*) of the ideal of their kind. As Plato puts it, The function of a thing is that which only it can do and which it does best. What a thing is—its ideal Form—defines its best functioning (*Republic* 353a). Postulating these ideals—the Forms of things—also explains the directions and motives of human striving. Whatever we may take the objects of our desires to be—a bauble or a book, the opportunity to teach better students or an all-expenses-paid trip to Marrakech—the obscure but real object of those desires is the Good they represent. There are several strands in this argument. To begin with, it is not we who give value to the objects of our desire. It is somehow they—and their relation to us—that draw us to them. We are moved by the objective features of the ultimate objects of our desires. But tracing the origins and real objects of desire ("Why do you want *that*?"), Plato thinks that the Good is the ultimate aim of our desires. "The Good is the end of all endeavor, the object to which every heart is set, whose existence it divines, though it finds it difficult to grasp just what it is" (505e). In a deft turn, he argues that the Good must not only ensure the direction and energy of our desires but also, in, the nature of the case, guarantee that it is also beneficial to us, constituted as we are. The objective aim of a desire and its ultimate subjective cause are presumed to be identical. However partially and shortsightedly we construe our desires and their imagined satisfactions, however benighted we may be about ourselves, we really aim at the Good. Moreover, it is this very Good that prompts and draws all possible desires, however much individual desires may seem to differ from one another. The ultimate objects of a desire for a good nap and for a good map are the same: both desires are ultimately, *au fond*, desires for (what is) Good. And further, the Good that is the ultimate object of all desire is identical with the "entity" that constitutes and ensures the unity of the cosmos. Some Plato scholars think we finite and shortsighted humans need to go through all the steps of dialectical inquiry (first desiring a good library, then desiring the good that is instantiated in that library, then desiring the good of understanding Plato's dialogues, then understanding the good of doing philosophy, then . . .) to realize that the unchanging eternal Good is the only thing that would give us real and lasting satisfaction. Others hold that we could bypass the long train of intermediate desires and realize that we can somehow—perhaps by virtue of having read Plato—make the Idea of the Good the direct object of our desires.

There is, finally, yet a further argument for the ruling power of the of the Good.

5. The crafts argument: Although some scholars argue that there are no tonic forms of artifacts, both the crafts (*technai*) and the arts (*poeseis*) presuppose an idealized norm of their objects.[9] The exercise of the skills of the shoemaker, the tragedian, the sculptor, the carpenter, and the cook are guided by their ideas of an ideal model of their products. But the ideal bed, shoe, soufflé, or eulogy does not exist as a material object. Even an architect's physical model of a temple is constructed according to an idealized formal and mathematized model. While a pediment may not be proper *eide*, presumably its components—a cube, an equilateral triangle, a sphere—ultimately refer to ideal types. We make and evaluate objects (shoes, tragedies, political systems) by reference to an ideal model of their paradigmatic functional type. Plato is of course acutely aware of cultural and political differences in the ideals and norms of the crafts. His point is that there are objective norms by reference to which we can and should evaluate the existing aims, models, and forms of the crafts. The individual or cultural ideals that guide them can themselves be critically evaluated by whether they truthfully represent reality and whether they direct the soul toward the Good. "The only poetry that should be allowed in a state is hymns to the gods and paeans in praise of good men; once you go beyond that and admit sweet lyrics, pleasure and pain become your rulers instead of law and the rational principles [that express the truth]" (*Republic* 607a).

DOUBTS ABOUT WHAT PLATONIC ARGUMENTS SHOW

Let's start with Aristotle's friendly critique of the ethical argument for the Good. Having proclaimed that all activity and action, including scientific knowledge (*episteme*), aims at some good, Aristotle notoriously proceeds to deny that there is a Good at which all things aim. "Every art or *techne* and every systematic investigation and every action and choice seems to aim at some good. . . . The [word] 'good' is used in as many senses as [the word] 'is'" (*Nicomachean Ethics*, 1096a, 23–25). With this proclamation in hand, Aristotle nevertheless proceeds to argue that all choices and actions—even those directed at pleasure or glory—ultimately aim at a more fundamental and comprehensive end, *eudaimonia* (human flourishing, thriving). But *eudaimonia* is notoriously a placeholder. There are at least two varieties of a self-sufficient *eudaimon* life, a life devoted to contemplation of the eternal, and a well-ordered comprehensive practical life. Furthermore, although *eudaimonia* is an activity (*energeia*) of the soul in conformity with human excellence (*arete*) (1098a, 15), there are distinctive ways such a life can be realized, since political systems differ. Although virtue is expressed in practical wisdom (*phronesis*), it is a mark of such wisdom to be able to discern the right and appropriate action and emotion as circumstances vary. No general conception of the good as such, no single principle or criterion or measure, serves to determine how human excellence is to be realized in different contexts.

Less friendly critics of Plato's Idea of the Good are exasperated by its metaphorical and schematic characterization. In *The Republic*, it figures as an analogue to the sun, as the true but obscure object of all desire, and as the self-referential limiting end of all inquiry. Plato himself represents Socrates as elusive when pressed for a more detailed and precise account. When Glaucon asks Socrates to "give an account of the Good similar to that of justice and moderation," Socrates replies, "I am afraid it's beyond me, and if I try I shall only make a fool of myself and be laughed at. So please give up asking for the present what the Good is in itself. I'm afraid that to reach what would be a satisfactory answer is beyond our inquiry" (*Republic*, 506d–e)

If Socrates had allowed Glaucon to press on for a characterization of the Good, he would have been obliged to address an array of difficult questions. The epistemological, metaphysical, and value arguments for the existence of the Good are all intended to point to the same postulate, the same entity, the one and only (*Idea*) of the Good. Yet they appear to characterize "its" function in radically different ways. Are they arguments for the same entity? Although the argumentative routes directing the postulate of the Idea of the Good are distinct from one another, they are meant to converge in one entity. To serve the many functions that Plato assigns to it as the cause of existence and of truth, as the object of inquiry, and as ensuring the power of the mind to know, as well as the aim and object of all desire, the Good must provide its own self-authenticating unity, as if it were capable of serving as the self-certifying security of its own loans. What justifies the claim that all these functions are served by the same entity? Further premises are needed to resolve an incipient regressive Third Good Argument: Having established the metaphysical Good as the unity and harmony of a cosmos, Plato seems to need to postulate yet another Idea of the Good to ensure that the metaphysical Good is identical with the Good that is the ultimate objective aim of desires. What is required to show that the Good(s) postulated by each of these arguments are identical with one another? Not even Kant was able to provide that missing premise: the best he could do was to postulate a self-authenticating regulative Idea that presumptively underwrites the attempt to treat the conditions for the possibility of knowledge as identical to those for ensuring the possibility of morality. As things stand, Plato needs many more premises to connect the Good as the unity of the cosmos with the Good as the source and realization of value and motivation.

But a host of problems remain. Suppose we let Plato have the *Idea* of the Good, parsed simply as a claim that although individual physical objects come into being and perish, the order of the cosmos, considered as a whole, remains stable, unchanged. So construed as the unchanging cosmic order, the nature of the Good—Goodness itself—remains undefined, its exact function unclear. Is it, as some passages suggest, different from the Forms in kind as well as degree of power? ("The form of the Good . . . [is] something other than, and even more splendid than knowledge and truth. . . . Although it is the cause of reality, it is not itself that reality, but beyond it, and superior in dignity and power. . . . It must be wonderfully transcendent" [*Republic* 508e, 509b–c].) If so, does the immanence or directive power of the Good generate a Third Good problem, requiring an intermediate Good to connect the transcendent Form of the Good with the immanent goodness of the cosmos? What is the relation between the Good as a metaphysical principle of order and its erotic power to draw inquiry and desire? Is the Good itself Good—systematically ordered—in the same way that the forms exhibit a System? What is the scope of the Good? In what sense—and at what level of particularity—does it explain the behavior and change of particulars? Is it immanent in every individual physical object? If so, at what level of particularity: in each part or in the whole? or does it only apply at a very general level, in the organization of the cosmos? What are the "terms" of goodness; what determines the good of each individual thing or organization? Is "goodness" a primitive property that all good things share? Or does the goodness of things consist in their being internally unified and externally harmonious with the rest of the cosmos? But in what does harmony consist? If the Good is all-pervasive, what explains the apparent failure of proper functioning?

This familiar torrent of questions suggests that Plato's arguments for the *Idea* of the Good set the direction of much of the history of metaphysics and theology as offering competing interpretations of his condensed abstract—and poetic—schema. The questions do not—as they stand—constitute a critique of Platonically inspired arguments. They rather suggest that instead of presenting a demonstration of the existence of the Good or an analysis of its function, Plato offers an abstract schema for a wide range of possible views. Philosophers from Aristotle to Leibniz, perhaps even to Hegel, were content to accept the view that the cosmic order either exemplifies or aims at some good. The questions introduce a "to do" list for metaphysically minded philosophers, who give Plato's Good distinctive aliases and somewhat different functions: the One, the Prime Mover, God, the Totality of the World Sub Specie Aeternitatis. Since the Idea of the Good is just the idea that the cosmos is ordered and intelligible, what—if anything—has been achieved beyond asserting that there is a cosmos?

Not surprisingly, the views that adopt and develop some version of the Platonic conception of the Good vary widely. Ranging from Plotinus to Augustine, from Ficino to Cudworth and Schiller, they present a Platonism so modified, so emasculated, that it probably no longer qualifies as Platonic. Philosophers who undertake the post-Platonic "to do" list find that the Good is indefinable (G. E. Moore) or that it is the name of a placeholder designating the unity of the cosmos, that it is a regulative functional principle of explanation (Platonizing Kantians like Schiller, Cohen, and Natorp) or that it dissolves into a wide variety of distinctive evaluative criteria, each with its own logical structure.[10]

THE GOOD THAT REMAINS OF PLATONISM

Setting aside the fact that Plato's opaque and sketchy views of the *Idea* of the Good generated a vast array of philosophic problems and investigations from Plotinus to Leibniz, from Henry More to G. E. Moore, what remains of Plato's Idea of the Good? Two powerful regulative principles remain to guide the dialectical process of inquiry into truth and value. They are vague, but that is the way of regulative principles.

1. To *understand x*, trace its function in an increasingly larger, increasingly more formal and comprehensive system of explanation. This is the regulative principle that guides dialectical inquiry charted by the Divided Line, moving from confused and contradictory images to the physical objects that explain their appearance, and from conflicting beliefs about the behavior of objects to the laws of mathematics and harmonics that provide a formal, rational account of the phenomena.

2. To *evaluate x*, trace its role in a hierarchical system of increasingly general and encompassing ideals that provide the criteria and rationale of the "goodness" of each level. "The best is the measure of the good." (For example, to evaluate a particular shoe, trace the way it functions as an object designed to protect the human foot . . . and footwear is in turn evaluated for its success in promoting human health . . . and health in turn for how it expresses or maintains human nature . . . and this in turn . . . until we get to the Cosmic Good. Similarly: to evaluate a particular meal, trace its function in promoting human health, thence to human thriving, and so forth.)

Even if there is no guarantee that the system of truth-bound explanation is identical with the system of values, a heuristic method of inquiry that spans them both is a great deal to be getting on with. It is enough to generate the confidence in inquiry that Socrates expresses in the *Meno* (86a–d). Socrates had been led to the border of skepticism by the Paradox of Inquiry: inquiry (into the truths of geometry and the nature of virtue) is impossible because if one does not know what one is looking for, one will not be able to recognize the difference between a true hypothesis and a false hypothesis; but if one does know the answer, there is no inquiry and no point to inquiry. Socrates very briefly introduces the theory of recollection—the myth of the immortal soul's recollection of innate knowledge—as a proposed solution to the paradox. ("If the truth about reality is always in our [immortal] soul, you should always try to seek out and recollect what you do not know at present" [86b].) Although Meno seems to accept this resolution, Socrates surprisingly goes on to say, "I do not insist that my argument [*logos*] is absolutely right." And then he adds, "I [nevertheless] contend at all costs, both in word and deed, that we will be better men, braver and less idle, if we believe that one must search for the things one does not know, rather than if we believe that it is not possible to find out what we do not know and that we must not look for it."

Perhaps Plato's confidence that "we shall be better men" if we continue to inquire into what we do not know—perhaps his trust that believing in the Idea of the Good underwrites rational inquiry—is good enough to justify his "search for goodness." Perhaps the heuristic regulative principles that structure the process of inquiry go some way to justify the search. Nevertheless, it is significant that Plato himself is very careful to have Socrates say that he *believes* we shall be *better* and braver if we continue to inquire. He does not say that he *knows* we shall be better; and he does not say that being better—less idle!—ensures that we will be wiser. And so, ignorant as he claims to be, he does indeed continue to inquire.

HOW TO LEAD A GOOD ENOUGH POST-PLATONIC LIFE

Although Plato's major Hellenistic successors were skeptical about his confidence in the asymptotic ascent to Truth and Goodness, they continued Socrates' commitment to the continuity of inquiry. Each in his own way, Epicurus and Epictetus connected the good human life with a quest for clarity and knowledge. Although Epicurus' radical empiricism has no room for the Idea of the Good, or even for Goodness as such, he held that the counsels for leading a wise, good enough human life included a regimen of intellectual discipline. Like Socrates, he believed that death is not to be feared;

and like Socrates, he held that there is a sharp distinction between desires whose satisfaction is necessary to maintain human life and desires for illusory and evanescent satisfactions. But his understanding of these views — his reasons for holding them — are far from a Platonic faith in the regulative principles of dialectical inquiry. His argument that death is not to be feared is short and succinct: "Get used to believing that death is nothing to us. For all good and bad consists in sense experience, and death is the privation of sense experience. Hence a correct knowledge of the fact that death is nothing to us makes the mortality of life a matter of contentment, not by adding a limitless time [to life] but by removing the longing for immortality. . . . When we exist, death is not yet present; and when death is present, we do not exist. Therefore it is relevant neither to the living nor to the dead, since it does not affect the former, and the latter do not exist."[11]

How should an Epicurean live? What are the skills — the virtues — of an Epicurean? Although Epicurus' counsel that death is not to be feared has a Socratic flavor, his arguments are purely prudential. Rather than expressing an ideal of human nobility that transcends physical pleasure, they rest on calculations about the best ways to avoid the pains of unfulfillable desires for transient and evanescent satisfactions. Instead of a dialectical argument that is meant to lead to the highest Good, he gives a very down-to-earth operational distinction between necessary and unnecessary desires: "The desires which do not bring a feeling of pain when not fulfilled are not necessary; but the desire for them [i.e., necessary goods and pleasures] is easy to satisfy."[12]

A thoroughgoing empiricist, Epicurus argued that knowledge begins with — and is limited to — sensory experience. ("If you quarrel with sense perception, you will have nothing to refer to in judging even those sense perceptions which you claim to be false [or confused].")[13] His counsel goes far beyond abandoning superstitious, unverifiable beliefs about death. It encapsulates an entire way of life. Epicurus argued that most of the things we desire — the desires beyond the satisfaction of the basic necessary needs of human life — are desired in the illusion that they could ensure security and protection from the ills of life. Basic needs — the need for minimal food and shelter — are easily satisfied. The more far-reaching desires for fame, wealth, love, important friends, and worldly achievements cannot, even if satisfied, protect us from illness and death. Fallible as we are, we should hold beliefs about contingent matters lightly, without resting too much confidence in claims beyond our senses. So the motto for a good life is, "Look for the illusion that is at the heart of every belief and desire . . . and free yourself from that illusion." Like the search for perfection, the "search for goodness" is an empty search: the idea of goodness as such is a confused and empty idea. Nevertheless, the goodness of inquiry into what is truly desirable remains central to a well-lived human life. The value of that search is that it brings freedom from illusions and the pains and sorrows that come in their wake. Instead of regulative principles of inquiry that lead to ever more general formal truths, Epicurean regulative principles of inquiry counsel astringent analysis: trace the sources and consequences of beliefs and desires to their sources in the sense experiences that provide the measure of their truth and reliability.

Like Epicurus, Epictetus accepts the Socratic dictum that death is not to be feared, but his reasons have a rationalist rather than an empiricist basis.[14] He follows and expands on Zeno's "To live according to Nature is to live according to virtue" by adding, "It is beneath man's dignity to begin and end where irrational creatures do. . . . [Human nature] ends . . . in understanding a way of life in harmony with nature."[15] Like Epicurus and Plato, Epictetus accepts the role of continued inquiry as central to the search for a good human life. But the regulative principle that guides his liberating inquiry is the converse of Epicurean counsel. The process of casting off illusions cannot be effected by sensory experience: "Make it your study to confront every impression with the words, 'You are but an impression, and not at all what you seem to be.' Then test it by the rules that you possess."[16] We ought to take every passing thought, every passing desire and trace its sources and causes in the vast interconnected system of ideas that constitutes the cosmic Mind. Epictetus' regulative principles of inquiry go beyond reductive Epicurean analysis without being committed to a Platonic dialectic ascent to ever more abstract Forms. As he puts it, "Since it is reason which makes all other things articulate and complete, reason itself must be analyzed and made articulate. What is capable of doing this? Plainly it is reason itself. . . . So if we have not fully grasped and trained to perfection the instrument by which we judge things and understand, how shall we ever be able to arrive at accurate knowledge? . . . It is for this reason that men put the process of logic in the forefront."[17]

The Stoic logic that "make[s] all things articulate and complete" does not move dialectically and teleologically upward toward the True Good. It rather moves outward, placing each thing in an interconnected system, a nexus of necessary conditions. While Epictetus joins the Platonic and Hellenistic chorus in decrying illusions and in treating systematic inquiry as the key to the project of leading a good human life, he understands the goodness of that search in terms distinctively different from theirs. While he argues that the radical empiricism of Epicureans is still enmeshed in the myth of egocentric particularity, he holds that Platonists are committed to a form of explanation that moves to increasingly empty abstractions. The strategies and value of Stoic inquiry lie in seeing every idea and desire as the necessary outcome of all the forces acting on it. The process of tracing the logical connections among particulars overcomes the illusions of egocentric particularity: we recognize ourselves as being caused and constituted by our necessary relations to other particulars. Our "good" consists in seeing ourselves as mere, but necessary, parts of a System. It is in this that knowledge consists, in this that our liberation from superstition and folly consists. As Laszlo Versenyi put it, "[In reflecting on the objects of my desires,] I was led far beyond my individual life and time, to the point where . . . [I] became no more than the accidental point for seeing and ranging over a landscape that has no clear boundaries or direction."[18] "Good" and "evil" have no meaning in such a view: there is only more or less partiality, more or less inclusive understanding and identification. Epictetus' motto is, "Only connect." The search for goodness is now seen as an overreaching, never-ending search for completeness.

The ancient critics of high Platonism about the Idea of the Good—about the search for Goodness Itself—join in thinking that goodness lies in the details. Aristotle's person of practical wisdom (*phronimos*) is a particularist, a contextualist. He has no formula, no criterion or general principle for determining the good that is to be found and realized in every circumstance. Since the "good" of each thing varies with its contextual function, the *phronimos* discerns the right thing to do, at the right time in the right way for the right reasons. Although Epicurus also thinks that the quest for the Idea of the Good is an illusion, he parts company with Aristotle's view that virtue is to be found in the contextualized rational mean. For an Epicurean, the good for man is a minimalist life whose intellectual precision and austere habits save him from the pains and sorrows of unrealizable pursuits. While agreeing that the good for man essentially involves rational inquiry, Stoics hold that the good of inquiry lies in realizing that living according to nature means learning man's place within nature.

For post-Platonic philosophers, the search for goodness lies in the goodness of asking, Good as what? Good for what? Good for whom?

NOTES

1. When I speak of Plato, I shall be referring to the author of the dialogues that are commonly attributed to him. When I speak of Socrates, I shall be referring to a character in *The Republic* and in the *Meno*, who sometimes represents the historical Socrates and sometimes, but not always, also represents the views of Plato.

2. See Judith Thomson, *Goodness and Advice* (Princeton, NJ: Princeton University Press, 2001), and J. O. Urmson, "Grading," *Mind* 59 (1950): 145-69.

3. G. E. Moore, *Principia Ethica* (Cambridge: Cambridge University Press, 1993), chap. 1.6.2.

4. John Keats, *Ode on a Grecian Urn.*

5. Nicholas White, "Plato's Metaphysical Epistemology," in *The Cambridge Companion to Plato*, ed. Richard Kraut (Cambridge: Cambridge University Press, 1992).

6. Joseph Butler, "Everything Is What It Is, and Not Another Thing," in *The Works of Bishop Butler*, ed. J. H. Bernard (London: English Theological Library, 1900), *Fifteen Sermons*, preface.

7. Plato speaks of the *eide* of beds and of mathematical objects, but he typically refers to the *Idea* of the Good. The difference is obviously not a difference between an ontological and a psychological postulate, or between plural *eide* and the singular unique *idea* of the good, or between something that serves as an ideal model and something that does not. I believe—but cannot argue here—that *eide* are constitutive exemplars of the "objects" that imitate them, while the *"Idea"* of the Good is a regulative principle for understanding the functional structure of the relations among the *eide* as well as between them and objects in the world of becoming.

8. See Myles Burnyeat, "Platonism and Mathematics," in *Mathematics and Metaphysics in Aristotle*, ed. A. Graeser (Bern: Haupt, 1987), 213-40, and Burnyeat, "Plato on Why Mathematics Is Good for the Soul," in *Proceedings of the British Academy* 103 (2000): 1-81.

9. See Sarah Broadie, "Why No Platonic Ideas of Artifacts?" in *Maieusis: Essays on Ancient Philosophy in Honor of Myles Burnyeat*, ed. Dominic Scott (Oxford: Oxford University Press, 2007).

10. Friedrich Schiller, *On the Aesthetic Education of Man* (New Haven, CT: Yale University Press, 1954); Hermann Cohen, "Platonic Ideal Theory Psychologically Developed," in *Plato's Theory of Ideas: An Introduction to Idealism*, by Paul Natorp (Sankt Augustin: Academia, 2004).

11. Epicurus, *Letter to Menoeceus*, Diogenes Laertius, 10.123.

12. Epicurus, *The Principal Doctrines*, Diogenes Laertius, 10.XXVI.

13. Ibid., 10.XXIII.

14. We have Epictetus' major writings—his *Discourses* and the *Enchiridion*—in a transcription by Arrian of Nicomedia.

15. Zeno, as reported by Diogenes Laertius, VII.liii; Epictetus, *Discourses*, I.6.

16. Epictetus, *Enchiridion*, I.5.

17. Epictetus, *Discourses*, I.17

18. Laszlo Versenyi, "Going Home," unpublished manuscript.

ROMAND COLES is the Frances B. McAllister Chair and Director of the Program for Community, Culture, and Environment at Northern Arizona University. He is a political theorist exploring democratic possibilities in theory and practice. His recent publications include *Beyond Gated Politics: Reflections for the Possibility of Democracy*, and *Christianity, Democracy, and the Radical Ordinary: Conversations between a Radical Democrat and a Christian* (with Stanley Hauerwas).

PHILIP COSTANZO is Professor of Psychology and Neurosciences and a Senior Fellow at the Kenan Institute for Ethics at Duke University. He bridges the fields of social psychology, developmental psychology, and clinical psychology in his research on children's addictive behaviors and attitude development, persuasion, and moral values. In addition to his many articles, he has recently published *Depression in Adolescent Girls: Science and Prevention*.

J. PETER EUBEN is Research Professor of Political Science and Classical Studies and the Kenan Distinguished Faculty Fellow in Ethics at Duke University. His areas of interest include political thought; literature and politics; political education; democratic culture and politics; and the politics of morality. He is the author of *The Tragedy of Political Theory, Corrupting Youth*, and *Platonic Noise*, and most recently a coeditor of *Debating Moral Education* and author of *When Worlds Elide: Classics, Politics, Culture*.

MICHAEL ALLEN GILLESPIE is Professor of Political Science and Philosophy at Duke University. He works in political theory, with particular emphasis on modern Continental theory and the importance of religion for politics. He is the author of *Hegel, Heidegger, and the Ground of History, Nihilism before Nietzsche*, and most recently, *The Theological Origins of Modernity*.

RUTH W. GRANT is Professor of Political Science and Philosophy and a Senior Fellow at the Kenan Institute for Ethics at Duke University. She specializes in political theory, with particular interest in political ethics. She is the author of *John Locke's Liberalism* and *Hypocrisy and Integrity: Machiavelli, Rousseau, and the Ethics of Politics*. She has recently completed *Strings Attached: Incentives, Ethics, and Power*. She also edited *Naming Evil, Judging Evil*, a companion work to this volume.

STANLEY HAUERWAS is the Gilbert T. Rowe Professor of Theological Ethics at Duke University. His work aims to recover the significance of the virtues for understanding the Christian life, which has led him to emphasize the importance of the church for understanding Christian existence. He was the Gifford Lecturer at the University of St. Andrews, Scotland, in 2001 and was named America's Best Theologian by *Time* in the same year. One of his many books, *A Community of Character: Toward a Constructive Christian Social Ethic*, was selected by *Christianity Today* as one of the hundred most important books on religion of the twentieth century.

AMELIE OKSENBERG RORTY is a visiting professor of philosophy at Boston University and a lecturer in social medicine at Harvard Medical School. She is the author of *Mind in Action* and the editor of *Essays on Aristotle's Ethics*, *Essays on Aristotle's Poetics*, and *Essays on Aristotle's Rhetoric*, as well as of several volumes on personal identity, on the emotions, and on self-deception. She has been a Guggenheim Fellow and a Fellow at the Institute for Advanced Studies in Princeton and at the National Humanities Center.

DAVID B. WONG is Susan Fox Beischer and George D. Beischer Professor of Philosophy at Duke University. He focuses on questions of moral philosophy and has a special interest in comparative and Chinese philosophy. He has written many articles exploring issues of moral conflict, moral motivation, and the role of reason and emotion in morality. His books include *Moral Relativity*, *Natural Moralities*, and a coedited anthology (with Kwong-loi Shun) of comparative essays on Confucianism and Western philosophy: *Confucian Ethics: A Comparative Study of Self, Autonomy, and Community*.